T0330291

The Financialization Response to Economic Disequilibria

NEW DIRECTIONS IN POST-KEYNESIAN ECONOMICS

Series Editors: Louis-Philippe Rochon, *Laurentian University, Sudbury, Canada* and Sergio Rossi, *University of Fribourg, Switzerland*

Post-Keynesian economics is a school of thought inspired by the work of John Maynard Keynes, but also by Michal Kalecki, Joan Robinson, Nicholas Kaldor and other Cambridge economists, for whom money and effective demand are essential to explain economic activity. The aim of this series is to present original research work (single or co-authored volumes as well as edited books) that advances Post-Keynesian economics at both theoretical and policy-oriented levels.

Areas of research include, but are not limited to, monetary and financial economics, macro and microeconomics, international economics, development economics, economic policy, political economy, analyses of income distribution and financial crises, and the history of economic thought.

Titles in the series include:

Post Keynesian Theory and Policy
A Realistic Analysis of the Market Oriented Capitalist Economy
Paul Davidson

Inequality, Growth and 'Hot' Money
Pablo G. Bortz

The Financialization Response to Economic Disequilibria
European and Latin American Experiences
Edited by Noemi Levy and Etelberto Ortiz

The Financialization Response to Economic Disequilibria

European and Latin American Experiences

Edited by

Noemi Levy

Professor, National Autonomous University of Mexico (UNAM), Mexico City

Etelberto Ortiz

Professor, Metropolitan Autonomous University (UAM), Mexico City

NEW DIRECTIONS IN POST-KEYNESIAN ECONOMICS

Cheltenham, UK • Northampton, MA, USA

Published by
Edward Elgar Publishing Limited
The Lypiatts
15 Lansdown Road
Cheltenham
Glos GL50 2JA
UK

Edward Elgar Publishing, Inc.
William Pratt House
9 Dewey Court
Northampton
Massachusetts 01060
USA

A catalogue record for this book
is available from the British Library

Library of Congress Control Number: 2016931783

This book is available electronically in the **Elgar**online
Economics subject collection
DOI 10.4337/9781785364761

ISBN   978 1 78536 475 4 (cased)
ISBN   978 1 78536 476 1 (eBook)

Typeset by Servis Filmsetting Ltd, Stockport, Cheshire
Printed and bound in Great Britain by TJ International Ltd, Padstow

Contents

Contributors

Alejandro Álvarez, Senior Professor, Economic Faculty, Universidad Nacional Autónoma de México, Mexico City.

Eufemia Basilio, Research Assistant, Instituto de Investigaciones Económicas, Universidad Nacional Autónoma de México, Mexico City.

Riccardo Bellofiore, Senior Professor in Political Economy, Economic Department, University of Bergamo, Italy.

Hassan Bougrine, Full Professor and Chair, Economic Department, Laurentian University, Sudbury, Canada.

Alma Chapoy, Retired Researcher, Instituto de Investigaciones Económicas, Universidad Nacional Autónoma de México, Mexico City.

Alan Cibils, Senior Professor, Political Economy Department, Universidad Nacional de General Sarmiento, Buenos Aires, Argentina.

Christian Domínguez, Assistant Professor, Posgraduate Department, Escuela Superior de Economía, Instituto Politécnico Nacional, Mexico City.

Francesco Garibaldo, Director of the 'Claudio Sabattini' Foundation, Bologna, Italy.

Ma. Guadalupe Huerta, Senior Professor–Researcher, Faculty of Administration, Universidad Autónoma Metropolitana – Azcapotzalco, Mexico City.

Luis Kato, Senior Professor–Researcher, Economic Department, Universidad Autónoma Metropolitana – Azcapotzalco, Mexico City.

Noemi Levy, Senior Professor, Economic Faculty, Universidad Nacional Autónoma de México, Mexico City.

Teresa López, Senior Professor, Economic Department, Facultad de Estudios Superiores-Acatlán, Universidad Nacional Autónoma de México, Mexico City.

Juan Marroquín, Senior Professor, Posgraduate Department, Escuela Superior de Economía, Instituto Politécnico Nacional, Mexico City.

Sandra Martínez, Assistant Professor, Economic Faculty, Universidad Nacional Autónoma de México, Mexico City.

Mariana Mortagua, PhD student, School of Oriental and African Studies, London University, UK.

Etelberto Ortiz, Senior Professor, Economic Department, Universidad Autónoma Metropolitana, Xochimilco, Mexico City.

Luis Á. Ortiz, Senior Professor, Economic Department, Facultad de Estudios Superiores-Acatlán, Universidad Nacional Autónoma de Mexico, Mexico City.

Germán Pinazo, Assistant Professor, Political Economy Department, Universidad Nacional de General Sarmiento, Buenos Aires, Argentina.

Louis-Philippe Rochon, Associate Professor, Economic Department, Laurentian University, Sudbury, Canada and coeditor of *Review of Keynesian Economics*.

Carlos A. Rozo, Senior Professor, Economic Department, Universidad Autónoma Metropolitana, Xochimilco, Mexico City.

Domenica Tropeano, Associate Professor, Economic Department, International Monetary Economics, University of Macerata, Italy.

Alessandro Vercelli, Professor (by contract), Department of Economic and Statistics of Siena, Italy and Professorial Research Associate, School of Oriental and African Studies, University of London, UK.

Acknowledgements

This book emerged from the international seminar, 'Economic policy, external imbalances and income inequality' hosted by the Faculty of Economics at the National Autonomous University of Mexico (UNAM) and the research project 'Financialization and economic policies: a theoretical and institutional analysis for developing countries' (IN 303314) supported by the Dirección General de Asuntos del Personal Académico, UNAM, together with the 'Area of Dynamic Macroeconomic and Structural Change' of the Universidad Autónoma Metropolitana, Xochimilco (Mexico City, 24–25 September 2014). We would like to thank these institutions and the contributors to the research project, in particular Roberto Escorcia at the Metropolitan Autonomous University (UAM) and Alma Chapoy from the Institute for Economic Research at the UNAM, as well as the Programa de Apoyo a Proyectos de Investigación e Innovación Tecnológica (PAPIIT) project assistants who supported the seminar and ordered the texts. We would also like to thank Louis-Philippe Rochon and Sergio Rossi for accepting this book in their series, New Directions in Post-Keynesian Economics. Chapter 1, 'A structural and monetary perspective of the euro crisis' is an updated version of a paper published in *Review of Keynesian Economics*, volume 3 (4) and Chapter 8, 'Financialization, crisis and economic policy' is a revised version published by the authors in *Review of Keynesian Economics*, volume 3 (2). Both are published with special permission from the copyright holder.

Introduction: what are the issues now? Controversies about disequilibria, economic growth and economic policies

Noemi Levy and Etelberto Ortiz

Mainstream economic theory and economic policy actions are based on an intellectual approach that establishes economic equilibrium as the central reference point around which economic and social processes are discussed, particularly the mechanisms that generate economic growth and redistribution of profits (Lucas, 1976; Goodfriend, 2002; Woodford, 2003). The major limitation of this theoretical approach is that it cannot account for changes in direction, or indicate how economic conditions change (Hicks, 1946; De Vroey, 1999); the use of comparative statics, in an ideal case, enables analysis of the change from one state of equilibrium to another. However, it does not explain the transition from one position to another over time (Woodford, 2003). Of particular importance to the situation currently facing the international economic system is the dismissal or improper interpretation of financial disequilibria (see Woodford, 2009).

The major changes to the dominant theory, presented today by the New Macroeconomic Consensus (Woodford, 2003), are, first, a greater mathematical formalization and sophistication that does not offer explanations of the dynamic nature of the capitalist economy and, therefore, this perspective still fails to provide consistent arguments about the nature of the phenomena that supposedly established a balanced trajectory. Second, due to institutional changes (movement of capital in the international market) monetarism (which proposed control of monetary aggregates, Friedman, 1968) was displaced by the Austrian School's monetary approach, reformalized in the New Classical Consensus (which rejects the conventional treatment of the quantity theory of money). The latter view is presented on the basis of a model where the money market is replaced by the interest rate, which is determined by a reaction function of the central bank (Hüfner, 2004) that deploys monetary policies aimed at stabilizing prices. This approach retains the postulate of the 'Treasury Perspective' (first raised in the 1930s), which is completely opposite to fiscal deficits and in favor of the reduction of wages (Hawtrey, 1913).

In parallel with the dominant theories, alternative economic visions were developed that incorporate the dynamic condition of the capitalist economy and the trajectories of economic processes, and despite being less mathematized or formalized, have a broader analytical perspective that contains evolutionary processes and essential transformations, which originate in breaks and crises, accompanied by a process of gradual abandonment of equilibrium. From this alternative framework the various visions of effective demand were developed, led by J.M. Keynes (1936), M. Kalecki (1984), H. Minsky (1986), the Circuitists (Lavoie, 1992; Rochon, 1999), among others,[1] and at the present time a large number of economists, under the aegis of financialization, are seeking to understand the genesis of the economic and financial breaks that triggered the Second Great Financial Crisis (2008), which has not yet been able to lay the groundwork of a new organization capable of restoring growth to all capitalist economies.

In the heterodox school of economic thought there is consensus that the dominant capitalist system is eminently monetary, with uncompetitive market structures that generate the accumulation of debts, imbalances between demand and supply and concentration of income, which is governed by the unequal distribution of wealth and income, and which taken together can slow economic growth through economic downturns, financial crises and even deep recessions.

The common denominator of this book is its adoption of the analytical framework of heterodox theory. It assumes that the capitalist system works on the basis of inherent disequilibria, which, it should be emphasized, are not caused by market failures, incomplete information or policy mistakes, and nor by external elements or shocks. On the contrary, the imbalances are structural, and are part of social arrangements with different interest or power groups that have the ability to determine the productive and financial structures, control the size of the surplus and – most significantly of all – influence its distribution between social classes and within subclasses. This is accompanied by the generation of a large debt, which gives rise to an interesting discussion on the impact of the financial system on the size and distribution of the surplus.

It may be added that the imbalances are not just the result of asymmetrical power relations between capital, on the one hand, and labor, on the other. The unequal power between countries should be considered, where some acquire hegemonic power (the USA) that allows them to appropriate the surpluses generated by others, leading to structural imbalances in their external accounts. The conquest of economic hegemony rests with the country's ability to impose its signs of value (the international currency of account, nowadays the US dollar) in international trade transactions and the global payments system; these may be accompanied by regional powers (for example, Germany in the eurozone) that are distinguished by their ability to influence the movement of capital, goods prices, and to determine economic policy (especially monetary policy). Furthermore, the hegemonic countries have the power to impose conditions on the bailout programs for countries in crisis. This further increases the extraction of surpluses, and results in increased inequality between the distribution of surpluses on a global or regional level; more significantly still, it delays finding solutions to the crisis.

In this context, it is argued that economic theory must consider the key features of the development of contemporary capitalism that arise from major imbalances (between hegemonic economies and underdeveloped or peripheral countries) that guide economic processes. The current dominant capitalist mode is organized on the basis of the institutional changes imposed through deregulation and globalization. This process changed the global financial system, endogenizing the provision of money in the form of private debt, expressed under the hegemonic power sign value (US dollars), without institutions capable of functioning as lenders of last resort to governments, or applying regulations that limit the movement of capital between nations. This led to a disproportionate increase in international liquidity, which put the financial markets in a context of asymmetric powers, dominated by financial centers in developed countries (the USA and UK), deepening the imbalances.

Financial capital came to play the leading role in all factors of production, affecting the composition of production, the size of the accumulation and distribution of surpluses among social classes and among countries. As a result of this process, the concept of financialization was coined. There are many definitions of this concept and no clear agreement on its content and the spectrum it dominates. We refer to the frequently cited definition by Epstein (2005, p. 5): '*financialization* means the increasing role of financial motives, financial markets, financial actors and financial institutions in the operation of domestic and international economies'; although it should be noted that agreement is beginning to coalesce around the need to analyze the domination of finance capital from the perspective of the reproduction of the debt and how it affects the income generation and forms of debt (balance sheets) of the major players in modern capitalist societies (financial and especially non-financial corporations), and has increased trade in financial securities and their rotation (Seccareccia, 2012/2013; Toporowski, 2013).

The new international division of labor is another phenomenon particular to this period of economic organization. Its main feature was the decoupling of demand with regard to supply: the hegemonic country (the USA) specialized in financial services, deploying monetary policies that determine interest rates that govern the movement of international capital, which guarantees minimum prices to financial securities by attracting financial flows from around the world. In turn, the USA became the global engine of demand because it distributed manufacturing output among the developed economies of Europe and Asia, with the participation of the least developed economies on the lowest rungs of the production chains. Using global supply chains, real production was transferred to the international market, triggering permanent imbalances in the current and capital accounts.

The hegemonic country is characterized by structural deficits in its current account, accompanied by a permanent surplus in the capital account, especially in periods of instability, first, because it retained the ability to create debts accepted internationally in US dollars, and second, because many of the transactions were made in this currency. For their part, producing economies generated large surpluses in their current accounts and exported capital to developed countries, with the export sector becoming the most dynamic activity in these nations' output. In such an environment, developing and peripheral countries are left with a reduced domestic market that is highly dependent on external demand. Thus, economic crises in the hegemonic or dominant countries at a regional level, or changes to the origin of imports, cause severe economic crises in the least developed countries.

Another key element is that the finance-led model was based on the concentration of income, while competition among countries was generated by reducing wages, which, on the one hand, increased income appropriation by the capitalists (especially in the financial segment), and, on the other, resulted in processes of impoverishment and job insecurity for the workforce. This phenomenon has been widespread, affecting both developed (hegemonic) countries and developing countries, and has been partially neutralized by the debt that households acquire to maintain their level of consumption. The difference between countries lies in the depth and impact of this phenomenon. In the case of peripheral countries, income concentration is more severe because the main competitive element of their manufacturing production and exports (highly dependent on imports) was low wages, without deploying technological advances, or they exported raw materials without achieving robust and lasting surpluses in their current accounts. This forced these economies to import financial flows, which became another source of their high levels of indebtedness. In short, a very unequal income distribution was generated worldwide, accompanied by a growing indebtedness. With respect to higher-income countries with deep financial markets, income became concentrated in the highest strata (the top 1 percent of the population, see Piketty, 2014), while in the less developed countries, the participation of lower-income strata fell drastically.

This structure changed government intervention in the economy. The objectives of economic policy shifted from full employment, based on technological development and deepening of industrialization, to price stability and attracting foreign investment. In this context, public spending contracted and changed its composition, as public expenditure on investments with large multiplier effects fell. Primary surpluses appeared, together with increasing bond issues to stabilize interest and exchange rates, in which commercial banks played an important role that in turn financed governments, depending on the arrangements of the dominant institutions. As a result of this process, public debt increased, and accelerated in times of crisis, as governments had to take over unpaid private debt; this weakened public policies in their counter-cyclical dimension.

The key point arising from the above is that in this new economic policy environment it became harder to emerge from a crisis. Developed (hegemonic) countries used flexible monetary policies (quantitative easing) to restore the activity of financial markets and the profitability of their corporations, but were unable to increase either employment or wages, and also failed to create the conditions for sustained economic growth and leave the crisis behind. The developing and peripheral countries that needed bailouts were forced to deploy primary surpluses with public deficits. This forced them to reduce their level of growth to balance the current account in a context of lower exports, and to increase interest rates higher than the rest of the world and reduce the share of income of wage earners. Economic stagnation and unemployment are accompanied by lower social spending on health, education and so on, thus generating a generalized impoverishment of the lower-income strata, and deepening inequality in income distribution.

On the basis of the above we can assert that the historical period of deregulation and globalization (also known as the neoliberal period) that evolved in the last third of the last century, with domination of finance capital, is built on the basis of large disequilibria that cover all spheres and regions. These reproduce themselves and gradually build up in all nations as a result of the trade and financial imbalances of the hegemonic country, which have reached startling levels. The US prerogative of issuing the international unit of account is, in that context, an essential factor in the design of the international realignment, both for developed and developing capitalist countries. Although this system entered crisis in 2008, new ways of restoring growth and overcoming the widespread stagnation are still to be found.

An additional point to consider is that the financial bailouts supported by the 'Treasury Perspective' and currently applied in Europe have proved to have little effect. These are poised to gain strength in Latin American economies, in light of falling prices of raw materials, the region's main exports. In the 1980s, as a result of the foreign debt crisis, Latin America was subject to harsh experiences. The International Monetary Fund and the main creditors of the region imposed macroeconomic equilibria, reductions in public spending and current account surpluses, which led to a fall in economic growth (those years are known as the 'lost decade'), accompanied by major devaluations and inflationary processes that were resolved only by reducing the amount of debt (Brady Plan). The second foreign debt crisis, which began in 1994, showed the countries in the region that they could not rely on foreign borrowing. Subsequently, the region, in an environment of reduced government intervention in the economy and opening up of capital, has sought to strengthen its export capacity. This process maintained low levels of economic activity, highly influenced by the vagaries of international trade, and from 2014 confronted major challenges with the dramatic fall in the price of raw materials; to this was added the fact that the overvalued currencies serve as an anchor for prices.

Based on the above, we highlight some of the main problems of the current economic system.

First, it is necessary to restructure the financial system in order for it to become an essential factor in the recovery of productive activity in developed countries and developing and peripheral countries alike. In particular, the growing trade in financial securities that generated the financial inflation should be subject to international regulation to ensure liquidity not only to the developed economies, but also to developing and, in particular, peripheral countries.

Second, external imbalances should be limited by economic policies to reduce deficits. The key point is to recognize that growth models based on beggar-thy-neighbor are highly unstable and must be countered.

Third, the development of technological innovations and the expansion of the capital goods sector cannot be left entirely to private initiatives. Government spending has proved to be highly efficient with large multiplier effects, and financing policies aimed at activating the private sector have been successful in other periods.

Fourth, the increase of wages must be a concerted policy in economies and regions in order to strengthen domestic markets. Finally, as a fifth element, the government must deal with income inequality by imposing distributive tax policies, spending on education, health and so on, and in general combating poverty.

I.1 STRUCTURE OF THE BOOK

This book is divided into four parts, with a total of 14 chapters. Part I is titled 'Structural disequilibria in Europe: what to do?' and comprises three chapters. Chapter 1, 'A structural and monetary perspective of the euro crisis' by Riccardo Bellofiore, Francesco Garibaldo and Mariana Mortagua argues that the European crisis cannot be treated as a typical breakdown resulting from balance of payments problems and cumulative price differentials, and nor does it reflect neo-mercantilist strategies. From the authors' perspective, the European crisis should be discussed in light of the structural problems with the productive sector, considering the structural changes generated by the eurozone, which altered the ways of mobilizing capital and promoted accumulation.

Ma. Guadalupe Huerta presents Chapter 2, 'The big financial crisis and the European economic adjustment: a road toward the strengthening of the neoliberal agenda', where it is argued that the institutional design of the eurozone does not allow for the deployment of fiscal and monetary policies to overcome the crisis, which raises the need for a thorough analysis of European integration in terms of macroeconomic and social aspects, accompanied by an assessment of the economic policies necessary to restore growth.

Chapter 3, 'Debt deflation theory and the Great Recession' written by Domenica Tropeano and Alessandro Vercelli. On the basis of the theory of Irving Fisher, the chapter analyzes the accumulation of debt in the USA and Europe, emphasizing that the monetary policy deployed in the former did manage to save the banking system, and this did not happen in Europe due to the European Central Bank being less able to intervene in the economy, and the absence of an authority empowered to coordinate spending.

Part II of the book is titled 'The forces of disequilibria at work: their impact on growth' and comprises five chapters. Alan Cibils and Germán Pinazo present Chapter 4, 'The periphery in the productive globalization: a new dependency?' In this chapter the authors analyze the role of peripheral countries in what has been called the new international division of labor from two perspectives. First discussed is the theoretical debates centered on new growth theory, neostructuralism, and the renewed interest in structuralist and dependency theories. Second, a broad range of statistical aggregates are presented and analyzed. The authors conclude that there is justification for the use of dependency concepts for peripheral countries in today's international division of labor.

Chapter 5, 'Latin America in the new international order: new forms of economic organizations and old forms of surplus appropriation' is by Noemi Levy. It discusses the limits of growth in Latin America based on the disequilibria of the productive sector resulting from the financial and technological dependence of the region's countries, emphasizing that they are subject to a two-fold extraction of profit that hinders recirculation of surpluses to the economic system.

Chapter 6 by Carlos Rozo discusses the theme 'Inequality, technological change and worldwide economic recovery', arguing that the financial system becomes dysfunctional when it is uncoupled from the productive sector, because it promotes non-productive activities that produce large short-term profits, accompanied by technological development that leads to unemployment as a result of digital technology and artificial intelligence. In addition, the combination of these processes slows down economic growth and leads to income concentration, preventing full economic development.

Alma Chapoy in Chapter 7 addresses the issue of 'Global disequilibria and the inequitable distribution of income', focusing on the income inequality generated by the disconnect between the financial and productive sectors, which is reflected in growing current account imbalances and large cross-border transactions, explained by the predominant monetary asymmetries in the current capitalist period, generated by the USA that holds the privilege of being the sole issuer of international money.

The final chapter in Part II is 'Financialization, crises and economic policy' by Hassan Bougrine and Louis-Philippe Rochon, who argue that the financial and economic crisis that began in 2007 is part of a general breakdown in the corporate capitalist order that affects real and financial sectors alike. They identify two practices that have generated profound changes in the capitalist system, which altered the practices of financial and banking institutions, enabling financiers to concentrate their wealth independently of the productive sector. This has combined with austerity-based economic policies that have caused productive activity to stagnate below full employment levels.

Part III of the book is titled 'Disequilibria in the Mexican economy: the export growth model, economic stagnation and labor precarization' and includes three chapters. In Chapter 9, 'The limits of the export-led growth model: the Mexican experience', Etelberto Ortiz analyzes the consequences of the export model that placed manufacturing at the center of international trade in the Mexican economy, without creating linkages between traditional and leading productive sectors, and without establishing economic policies that strengthen the manufacturing sector. In light of a combination of theories, it analyzes the limitations of economic growth and possible alternatives to promote successful economic growth are reviewed.

In Chapter 10, Alejandro Álvarez and Sandra Martínez present 'The Mexican economy in 2014: between crisis, free trade, social devastation and labor precarization', delineating two central arguments. First, the effects of prolonged application of neoliberal formulas in public policies and second, the impact on workers' wages of labor and working conditions of developed and developing economies. These issues are discussed in light of the various trade agreements promoted by the USA and Mexico after the 2008 crisis that served the USA in regaining its hegemony and the links to the Mexican social conditions, highlighting the social devastation that has been taken place in recent years. Particular attention is given to the multi-regional integration that deepens the free trade programs by means of various legal and political instruments: the Trans-Pacific Partnership (TPP), the Trans-Atlantic Trade and Investment Partnership (TTIP) and the Trade in Services Agreement (TISA).

Luis Kato is the author of Chapter 11, 'The accumulation mode of production in Mexico and the economic structure of the manufacturing industry'. He discusses the stagnation of productivity of the workforce in relation to the dominance of large corporations that are connected to global commodity chains and use global competitive advantages to maximize profits; meanwhile, small and medium enterprises compete on the basis of lower costs (wages), which reduces the growth of accumulation and productivity.

The final part of the book, 'Disequilibria in Mexico: the financial and fiscal trap', examines the fiscal and financial traps that have been deployed in the Mexican economy in the period of financialization. There are three chapters. Chapter 12 by Teresa López and Eufemia Basilio is concerned with 'Economic growth and financial development in Mexico: from a virtuous circle of a bidirectional causality to financial subordination'. It develops the theme of bank lending to non-financial activities in the context of the Mexican economy between 1990 and 2013. An empirical and econometric assessment shows that deregulation and globalization, instead of increasing savings, caused the banking system to lose sight of its core activity, which is the financing of production. On this basis, the authors assert the need to establish regulatory mechanisms to ensure financial resources for production.

Christian Domínguez and Juan Marroquín in Chapter 13, 'Private sector finance in the era of deregulation and economic openness: Mexico 2000–2014', analyze the trends in the financing of the non-financial private sector in Mexico following deregulation and economic openness. They argue that these processes shaped monetary and fiscal policies that maintain high interest rates making financing more expensive and reducing access to it for companies operating in the domestic market. The authors find that despite reducing interest rate differentials with the US economy, these nevertheless function as a factor that limits access to financing, particularly for small and medium enterprises in the services and commercial sectors.

Finally, Chapter 14 is 'Pro-cyclical fiscal policy and the fiscal support of the Mexican monetary policy' by Luis Á. Ortiz. He argues that monetary policy based on a system of fiscal and financial targets generates a contraction in capital spending and higher quasi-fiscal and financial costs. This is due to an oversupply of foreign exchange causing sterilized interventions in the foreign exchange market. As a result, it is noted that the behavior of the Bank of Mexico, in exercising its autonomy in pursuit of an inflation target, has an anti-democratic bias, not only due to the fiscal support it receives from the government, but also because it prevents the counter-cyclical exercise of fiscal policy.

NOTE

1.   We are not including the evolution of Marxist theory here.

REFERENCES

De Vroey, M. (1999), 'J.R. Hicks on equilibrium and disequilibrium. Value and capital revisited', *History of Economics Review*, **29**, 31–44.
Epstein, G.A. (2005), 'Introduction', in G. Epstein (ed.), *Financialization and the World Economy*, Cheltenham, UK and Northampton, MA, USA: Edward Elgar, pp. 3–16.
Friedman, M. (1968), 'The role of monetary policy', *American Economic Review*, **LVIII**(1), 1–17.
Goodfriend, M. (2002), 'Monetary policy in the new neoclassical synthesis: a primer', *International Finance*, **5**(2), 165–91.
Hawtrey, R. (1913), *Good and Bad Trade: An Inquiry into the Causes of Trade Fluctuations*, London: Kessinger Publishing.
Hicks, J.R. (1946), *Value and Capital*, 2nd edn, Oxford: Clarendon Press.
Hüfner, F. (2004), *Foreign Exchange Intervention as a Monetary Policy Instrument: Evidence from Inflation Targeting Countries*, Centre for European Economic Research, ZEW Economic Studies 23, Heidelberg: Physica-Verlag.
Kalecki, M. (1984), 'Teoriìa de la dinaìmica econoìmica. Ensayos sobre los movimientos ciìclicos y a largo plazo de la economiìa capitalista' ('Theory of

economic dynamics: an essay of cyclical and long-run changes in capitalist economies'), Fondo de Cultura Econoìmica, Mexico.

Keynes, J.M. (1936), *The General Theory of Employment Interest, and Money*, reprinted in 1964, London: Harvest/Harcourt.

Lavoie, M. (1992), *Foundations of Post-Keynesian Economic Analysis*, Aldershot, UK and Brookfield, VT, USA: Edward Elgar.

Lucas, R. (1976), 'Econometric policy evaluation: a critique', *Carnegie-Rochester Conference Series on Public Policy*, **1**, 19–46.

Minsky, H. (1986), *Stabilizing an Unstable Economy*, New Haven, CT: Yale University Press.

Piketty, T. (2014), *Capital in the Twenty-first Century*, Cambridge, MA: Belknap Press.

Rochon, L.-P. (1999), *Credit, Money, and Production: An Alternative Post-Keynesian Approach*, Cheltenham, UK and Northampton, MA, USA: Edward Elgar.

Seccareccia, M. (2012/2013), 'Financialization and the transformation of commercial banking: understanding the recent Canadian experience before and during the international financial crisis', *Journal of Post Keynesian Economics*, **35**(2), 277–300.

Toporowski, J. (2013), 'International credit, financial integration and the euro', *Cambridge Journal of Economics*, **37**(3), 571–84.

Woodford, M. (2003), *Interest and Prices. Foundation of a Theory of Monetary Policy*, Princeton, NJ: Princeton University Press.

Woodford, M. (2009), 'Convergence in macroeconomics: elements of the new synthesis', *American Economic Journal*, **1**(1), 267–79.

PART I

Structural disequilibria in Europe: what to do

1. A structural and monetary perspective of the euro crisis

Riccardo Bellofiore, Francesco Garibaldo and Mariana Mortagua

1.1 INTRODUCTION

This chapter presents an analysis of the financial crisis by combining a Marxian and financial Keynesian perspective. Both are framed in a long-run, structural perspective of capitalist dynamics. We are experiencing the crisis not of a generic neoliberalism or a empty financialization, but of money manager capitalism, which was built upon centralization without concentration of capital, new forms of corporate governance, aggressive competition, capital market inflation, indebted consumption. A world able to gain from the same old exploitation in new forms, to provide internal demand and present itself as a stable Great Moderation. It can be characterized as financially privatized Keynesianism, based on a new monetary policy and a new autonomous demand driving the process, a configuration that is necessarily unsustainable. The crisis is evolving from a Great Recession to a Lesser Depression.

The chapter is divided into seven sections. Section 1.2 first gives a general scenario of the global and European crises since 2007–2008. Sections 1.3 and 1.4 summarize the main approaches – mainstream and heterodox – on trade imbalances, and Section 1.5 offers a truly credit money view of external imbalances. Section 1.6 complements this analysis by looking into the new geography of the industrial and trade relations within the European Union (EU) and Section 1.7 applies the previous discussions to the concrete reality of the euro crisis. Finally, in Section 1.8 some preliminary conclusions are provided.

Mainstream theory woke up relatively late to the euro crisis, and it is fair to say that it is still in denial regarding many aspects of the current global trend towards very unstable stagnation. The euro crisis was first posed as a fiscal problem, caused by the profligate behaviour of some peripheral countries, and then moved into a current accounts crisis, caused by nominal rigidities, market distortions and lack of discipline in those same nations. The heterodox approaches underline the role of the Economic and Monetary Union's (EMU) design faults more and more, which have allowed Germany and its satellites to pursue a neo-mercantilist strategy, accumulating huge current account surpluses, recycled as capital flows to the periphery to debt-finance their deficits. Using this outlook the euro crisis is mainly a balance-of-payments (BoP) problem, caused by cumulative differences in relative prices that have led to distinct growth strategies: export-led in the core, and debt-led in the periphery, focused on consumption and real estate investment.

As with most heterodox approaches, we accept as a baseline scenario that (1) public debts are the consequence and not the cause of the European problems and (2) the process of asymmetric integration interacted with growing financialization to create different national economic structures and subsequent modes of existing in the EMU. We also agree that the strategy of real deflation through austerity and labour market reforms is a disastrous option that, in the end, might become the ultimate cause of the problem this strategy is trying to avoid in the first place – the collapse of the EMU. However, this is not to say that everything has been said about the euro crisis, not only on the mainstream side but also on the heterodox side.

We argue that the euro crisis is not due mainly to the current account imbalances, nor to fiscal deficits, not even to the euro itself. In order to understand the euro crisis, one needs to focus on the changes in finance and industry in the last 15–20 years. First, how are the so-called trade imbalances dealt with in the Eurozone, and what is its true meaning, origin and connection with the financial imbalances? Second, how has the restructuring of German manufacturing created a transnational value chain in production and a new geography of industrial and trade relations between, roughly, the Centre-North and the South-West of the European continent?

1.2   A QUICK REMINDER OF THE GLOBAL AND EUROPEAN CRISES

Neoliberal capitalism during the so-called Great Moderation decades was a paradoxical kind of 'financial and privatized Keynesianism' (Bellofiore, 2013). To understand why and how it led to the Great Recession we have to look deeper into the features of what Minsky labelled 'money manager capitalism' (Bellofiore, 2014). During the 1990s and early 2000s, in the USA the tendency was for the household sector to become a net borrower.

The non-financial corporate sector ended as a net lender in the years before the crisis and banks lost their best customers. Financial innovations won the day: they reduced risk individually, but increased it globally. In terms of social class relations, these dynamics had devastating consequences. Workers were 'traumatized' in labour markets and within the capitalist labour process, so that the Phillips curve was flattened. Pension and institutional funds fostered a 'capital asset inflation' that, at least for a while, was hedging corporations' balance sheets *ex post*. Instability was hidden under the carpet as savers entered into a 'manic' phase, deceived by assets appreciation, while the propensity to save from income fell dramatically. 'Indebted' consumers internally boosted effective demand, thereby providing outlets to Asian and European neo-mercantilism.

Wage deflation, capital asset inflation and the increasingly leveraged position of households and financial companies were complementary elements of a perverse mechanism where real growth was doped by toxic finance. Growing debt had its ultimate *raison d'être* in the insufficiency of income to support consumption of non-manufacturing goods and services. This caused an escalation in expenditures generating rents for the financial sector. Based on a burgeoning private debt, the process was unsustainable and collapsed the first time with the dot.com crisis. A return to military Keynesianism (after September 11) and then to a revised form of the asset bubble-driven, privatized Keynesianism led to a second bubble phase. The proliferation of subprime mortgages was an attempt to keep the real estate bubble inflating by any means. Commodities price inflation worried the Fed and other central banks; and from 2004, the Fed began to increase interest rates such that by 2005 US house prices softened. The hope that the increase in borrowing costs could be offset by a further rise in asset values, thereby expanding the value of the collateral used in loan applications, faded away. This time the 'depressive' phase was inevitable, and the economy fell into the biggest crisis since the Great Crash.

The subprime crisis broke out in July 2007. European finance was the first to crumble, and with a lag, the large exporting countries were severely hit by the plummeting demand of indebted US consumers. The consequent sharp reduction in China's growth impacted hugely on Europe's main manufacturing nations. After a brief Keynesian interlude between late 2008 and early 2009, the turning of private debt into public debt created pressures to cut public expenditures. The spread of austerity and the domino effects after the Greek crisis beginning in 2010 brought out into the open the fallacies in the institutional design of the euro. Not only the arbitrary ceilings to public deficits and the debt to gross domestic product (GDP) ratio, but also the rules denying the European central bank the possibility to buy government bonds.

In this chapter we want to extend and go deeper into this perspective, taking into account some characters of current global capitalism and the changing European reality that are somehow underestimated in the present debate, which is focused too much on trade imbalances. We therefore have to take into consideration the deep modifications in the structural productive configurations of different European areas, and the transformation in finance and balance sheets. As we detail below, these considerations put the challenging question of the destiny of the single currency under an entirely new perspective.

1.3   TRADE IMBALANCES: THE MAINSTREAM CONSENSUS

Until the development of the 'sovereign debt crisis', the build-up of external trade and financial imbalances within the Eurozone went unnoticed. Such blindness is the result of the prevailing neoliberal consensus supported, first, by the theory of Optimum Currency Areas, according to which complete financial integration and capital mobility would absorb any future external shocks within the EMU, and more recently by the neoclassical growth theories, in particular the inter-temporal approach to current accounts. According to the latter, current account imbalances in low-income countries are the necessary outcome of the convergence process. One way or the other, an attitude of 'benign disregard' towards the external accounts of Eurozone countries seemed justified. According to the above neoclassical models, based on optimizing and forward-looking households and firms, current account balances are always consistent with efficient resource allocation, as long as excessive public deficits or other (nominal) distortions do not prevail (see Blanchard and Giavazzi, 2002).

When, towards the end of 2009, it became increasingly difficult to ignore Europe's own and internally generated difficulties, national and fiscal policies were seen as the main cause of the external imbalances within the EMU. A new consensus emerged around the idea that it is necessary to 'reassess the sustainability of government finances . . . but that the exclusive focus on fiscal sustainability is unwarranted and insufficient to understand the issues facing the euro area' (Holinski et al., 2012, p. 2). Trade imbalances have received renewed attention as they have started to be seen not as a reflection of a successful convergence process, but the result of nominal rigidities and market distortions that led to the accumulation of large stocks of foreign debt (Giavazzi and Spaventa, 2010).[1]

This new consensus represents a *revisionist* approach to the role of current accounts in a monetary area (Collignon, 2012).

The peripheral countries in the Eurozone (Ireland, Greece, Portugal, Spain and Italy) are charged with having allowed excessive nominal wage growth relative to the core countries. Higher nominal unit labour costs caused higher inflation in those economies, deteriorating its competitive power and introducing disruptions in the way the monetary policy operates at the European level (Mongelli and Wyplosz, 2008, p. 15). These distortions led to a real exchange rate appreciation instead of a depreciation, reduced exports and redirected demand from domestic to foreign goods. At the same time, the behaviour of the real exchange rate also favoured non-tradable sectors. The current consensus is that 'the imbalances that matter for the stability of monetary union are the result of either fiscal profligacy – as in Greece and to some extent Portugal – or of an unchecked expansion fuelled by capital flows feeding unsustainable growth of the non traded sector – as in Ireland or Spain' (Giavazzi and Spaventa, 2010, p. 14). When markets became aware of such unsustainable patterns, these countries started facing problems with their BoP (Giavazzi and Spaventa, 2010; Carney, 2012; Sinn, 2012).

This is the argument made by Merler and Pisani-Ferry (2012) who portray the euro crisis as a classic sudden stop, known in the context of emerging markets. Due to reasons other than productivity differentials, foreigners refuse to provide capital or residents are unable to generate enough liquidity by selling domestic assets. They argue that the 'Troika' loans in Ireland, Portugal and Greece, and TARGET loans in all the peripheral countries have covered up the internal BoP crisis in Europe. According to Sinn, TARGET has been the mechanism through which the Euro system and the Bundesbank in particular have been 'lending money to the crisis-stricken Eurozone members' (Sinn and Wollmershäuser, 2011; Sinn, 2012).

The crisis thus changed the official narrative and, after public debt, trade imbalances gained central stage in the process. Current account imbalances led to the accumulation of large stocks of foreign debt and, when sovereign markets collapsed, risk aversion among private investors left large funding gaps unfilled. The sovereign and external debt led to a BoP crisis, which would have been catastrophic if it was not for TARGET flows and Troika loans, which have replaced private capital flows in the peripheral countries of the EMU.

More recently, a second trend has developed, although not applied to the EMU, based on the idea that the focus on current accounts misses 'the spectacular evolution and integration of international financial markets over the past quarter century. Global imbalances are financed by complex multilateral patterns of gross financial flows, flows that are typically much larger than the current account gaps themselves' and 'entail potential stability risks that may be only distantly related, if related at all, to the global configuration of saving-investment discrepancies' (Obstfeld, 2012, pp. 3, 5). The main thesis behind this growing literature is that current accounts exclude changes in the Net International Investment Position (NIIP) resulting from an increase in the volatility of non-flow factors, such as the effect of price shocks on large stocks of foreign assets. The focus is on the economic significance of NIIP, which is still mostly determined by current accounts, but suffers an increasing influence of factors connected with the growth in gross flows (and corresponding stocks).

1.4 TRADE IMBALANCES: THE HETERODOX APPROACH

Heterodox alternatives have always argued that monetary integration and capital market liberalization are unlikely to bring convergence. Such approaches to the euro crisis can be divided into two main groups. The first focuses mostly on the design faults of the EMU and its theoretical foundations. These design faults led to an asymmetric process of integration, fostered by financial flows, which undermined peripheral countries' capacity to compete in the international markets creating current account imbalances. Probably the most important line of criticism concerns the role of the European Central Bank (ECB) in the defective structure of the Eurozone: 'the Eurozone has a central bank without a government, governments without central banks, and banks without an effective lender of last resort' (Toporowski, 2013, p. 572). Arestis and Sawyer (2001, 2011) pay special attention to the differences in terms of national unemployment levels, and to the deflationary bias imposed by the Stability and Growth Pact.

The second group of heterodox critics includes all those analyses that, albeit in different ways, discuss the European crisis in the context of a finance-dominated capitalist regime. These views see the European crisis mostly as a BoP problem originating in the precarious integration of peripheral countries into the Eurozone and exacerbated by the financial and banking crises. The sovereign debt problems are not the cause but the consequence of such dynamics.

Perhaps one of the most stringent criticisms of the mainstream approach included in these analyses arises from the post-Keynesian view of financial balances.[2] Two main implications can be derived from this analysis. First, the explosion in public deficits did not happen because of governments' chronic profligate behaviour but as a consequence of the shift in the balance of the private sectors towards a surplus, as a consequence of the deleveraging process forced by the financial crisis. Second, for the accounting identity to hold, external surpluses in one country must be matched by external deficits in other countries. This is the main reason why it is almost impossible for all the countries in the Eurozone to run current account surpluses in the same way that Germany does.

It is also consensual among the heterodox community that one of the main causes of the European crisis is the German neo-mercantilist strategy that considers net external surpluses as a crucial source of profits. It is a Luxemburg-Kalecki model, or a Kaleckian foreign trade model (Lucarelli, 2011), in which Germany relies on the deficits of peripheral countries to generate demand for its own exports. It is also undisputed that in the face of a process of wage compression and decreasing labour share of income fostered by the process of European asymmetric integration different regimes of 'capitalism under financialization' (Hein, 2012) emerged in the Eurozone. The export-led neo-mercantilist type,[3] matched by domestic-led[4] and debt-led[5] regimes. In general, both regimes are associated with current account, private sector and public deficits, but only in the first case are these deficits related to high levels of debt-financed consumption. Moreover, these 'growth strategies' were based on the expansion of consumption and/or household debt, in the case of countries like Portugal and Greece, or of corporate investment, mostly in the real estate sector, in the case of Spain and Ireland.

1.5   TOWARDS A TRULY CREDIT THEORY OF MONEY PERSPECTIVE ON EXTERNAL IMBALANCES

We argue that both orthodox and heterodox views that put trade imbalances in the centre miss fully integrating the role of money and finance in their analysis. The specificities of a monetary union, in which reserves are endogenously generated by the creation of credit, question the validity of the argument that the euro crisis is just one more BoP crisis. Moreover, the stress on current accounts fails to capture the relevance of financial flows in the EMU, and its relation with saving and investment decisions, which we have argued is a crucial dimension.

From the mainstream point of view, those theories based on the NIIP represent a major evolution when compared with the traditional approaches, but do not break with its main assumptions. NIIP works as a national constraint, meaning simply that the net present value of the future excess of imports over exports has to be equal to net holdings of foreign assets. Furthermore, current accounts are seen as limited by the predetermined size of international assets and liabilities that can be 'recycled', hence the importance of gross flows. In the end what we have is an upgrade of the well-known 'loanable funds theory': gross capital flows might trigger or amplify specific phases of the cycle, but they have a 'real basis', determined by 'real' economic decisions of saving and investment. This analysis seems to fail to understand that the focus on saving/investment relations is not suited to a credit economy where credit takes place and has 'free will' well beyond real consumption decisions. Underlying this analysis rests the idea of money neutrality, so embedded in the neoclassical theory.

This view resembles what the mainstream considers the 'normal' case of bank deposits creation, in which credit is based on existing resources. In fact, this is a 'soft' version of a *commodity theory of money*, what has been named a *monetary theory of credit* (Toporowski, 2013). It is an instance of a *real analysis*, the essence of the neoclassical growth models, crucial to the process of monetary integration in Europe. As argued by Schumpeter (1954), such an analytical framework applies to a world in which investment can only be carried out by transferring real resources from saving units to investment units. We are rather in favour of what Schumpeter called *monetary analysis*, where money is not secondary, but introduced on the very ground floor of the analytic structure. It is better to start from debt/credit relationship – that is, from capital *finance* as a clearing system that cancels debts and credits and carries forward the difference – with money payments as a residual consequence (*credit theory of money*).

In reality, capital flows cannot be addressed as a stock of pre-existing endowments, necessary to carry on production and investment, in high productivity countries. The loanable funds theory does not hold in a world where, as demonstrated by the modern heterodox monetary theories, the circuit of production is a monetary phenomenon: the starting point is the endogenous creation of credit-money, *ex nihilo*, which will be validated by future production/expenditure. It seems obvious, therefore, that we must look at current account determination and imbalances from a monetary perspective.

There is no intention here to go deeply into the heterodox thinking of money. One should take into consideration two very distinctive functions: money as (bank) credit, the result of decisions relative to production and investment; and money as wealth, the result of savers' choices among different assets according to their liquidity preference. These two are not the same, as assumed by mainstream theory, and the source of the confusion is due to the difference between *saving* and *financing*.

The distinction between saving (income not consumed) and financing (access to purchasing power) is crucial to assess the centrality of current accounts in the explanation of today's imbalances. According to Borio and Disyatat (2011), the common association between (global) current account imbalances and the financing of credit booms implicit in the majority of the analysis is misleading. In a closed economy, saving simply captures all the income not consumed, therefore, the only way to increase saving is to produce something that is not consumed (that is, to invest). And to do so, one needs financing. This means that 'in ex post terms, being simply the outcome of various forms of expenditure, saving does not represent the constraint on how much agents are able to spend ex ante' (Borio and Disyatat, 2011, p. 7). This constraint is determined by financing conditions, which are not necessarily related to the levels of saving or the direction and dimension of current accounts.

In an open economy, current accounts register the net capital outflow/ inflow that is, from the accounting point of view, equivalent to the difference between saving and investment. But this accounting equivalence does not mean that: (1) there is a link between global financial intermediation and current accounts or (2) 'real' saving and consumption decisions determine the type or direction of financial flows. In the same way, current accounts do not tell us: (1) the extent of investment that is financed from abroad or (2) the contribution of offsetting gross flows to the existing stocks of debt and sectoral imbalances.

Within this outlook it is important to consider that countries in the Eurozone share the same payment system: 'a cross border payment between banks in two countries in the euro zone automatically generates balancing credit claims between the national central banks and the ECB. This is the mechanism that irrevocably unifies the former national currencies, converting a set of currencies whose exchange rates are merely fixed at par into a single currency' (Garber, 2010, p. 2). Even though a technical feature such as a payment system does not suffice in order to create a new currency, its existence has important implications in terms of the macro monetary structure of the EMU. In the case of a monetary union, as long as the liabilities created by individual national central banks remain equivalent and valued at par, there is no limit to the amount of reserves the Euro system can create.

The first point is, therefore, that in a monetary union such as the EMU, with a common payments and monetary system, where reserves are endogenously generated by the creation of credit that needs not to be backed by any commodity, a BoP problem loses some of its meaning. This is not to say that individual countries might not face payment difficulties, however, and until the central bank has exhausted all the means at its disposal to prevent a collapse in payments, these difficulties will mainly be a matter of liquidity rather than solvency – though, admittedly, in a big crisis and in a debt deflation/balance sheet recession, it becomes harder and harder to delineate a liquidity crisis from a solvency crisis.

Two other factors seem crucial in assessing individual macroeconomic situations within a monetary union. The first refers to liquidity conditions in the markets, which are related, on the one hand, to the institutional design of every monetary area and, on the other, to the circulation of gross flows. The accumulation of foreign reserves through trade surpluses is no precondition for the stability of the system, as long as there is a central bank willing to act as a lender of last resort, replacing the market in case of a liquidity crisis; moreover, imports from other euro countries do not require any holding of foreign currency by local citizens, since they can be financed by credit generated internally. The second has to do with patterns of investment and balance sheet management, that is, the internal capacity to generate cash flows to meet debt obligations, investment and (gross) financing flows are crucial in determining the adjustment dynamics inside the Eurozone. They are connected in multiple ways, most of them bearing no relation to trade and current accounts.

Similarly, the association of current account imbalances with the financing of credit booms in deficit countries ignores the fact that current accounts are not an indicator of how much of the domestic investment is financed from abroad. Indeed, as pointed out by Johnson (2009), any country can show a balanced current account and still have its investment financed from abroad. Net balances reflect offsetting pluses and minuses, which represent assets and liabilities with different characteristics. As a consequence, the excessive focus on current accounts does not prevent future crisis or the emergence of financial fragility.

The mainstream sees the problem as a lack of saving in the periphery, the heterodoxy as excess saving in the core. Behind the view underlying both heterodox and mainstream approaches that trade deficits are the origin of their financial imbalances looms a causal relationship between the trade and capital accounts that seems unlikely in a world where trade transactions capture only a small fraction of transactions across jurisdictions, all of which require financing.

A *monetary analysis* implies looking beyond the transfers of real resources and net capital flows, as registered in current accounts. In order to understand the structure and dynamics of capitalist economies it is necessary to understand the impact of financial flows on the various sectors, and how these condition economic decisions and increase the fragility of the economy.

1.6 THE CHANGING LANDSCAPE OF THE EUROPEAN AND GERMAN INDUSTRY

A key determinant of the process of change in Europe, before the current crisis, was the capital–labour relation. The rollback strategy led to the weakening of the working class: an outcome also achieved through new productive networks, and to the progressive enfeebling of the national trade unions in the EU countries. This was very instrumental in setting up a highly fragmented labour market. The progressive freedom of the circulation of capital and not of workers in the Eastern countries was also a way to realize what Sinn (2006) nicknamed the German Bazaar economy.

The current industrial vision in the EU is that the only competitive possibility for the EU economy is in moving upstream in the value chain. In this view higher investment accelerates the incorporation of new technologies into the production process, thus leading to more efficient and more environmentally sustainable production. Critics have pointed out that in a perspective like this, unemployment is primarily a problem of labour costs and that the way to a more labour-intensive European economy is to pass through a higher proportion of low-paid service jobs in the private sector.

The building of a European industrial structure was based on a process of 'centralization', but there was no 'concentration' process in the classical way, leading to a highly integrated company. This 'centralization without concentration' consists of a double move. On the one hand, the strategic functions of a corporation become more and more centralized; on the other hand, however, production operations results in a strong disarticulation via the imposition of global supply chains. Centralization conceals a very high level of concentration of capitalistic power; as a matter of fact, the firms at the top of each network have the classical prerogatives of the managers: they decide for the other companies how to plan the quantities of outputs in a given period of time, the pace and the speed to deliver the batches of outputs, how to arrange in sequences a mix of different items and so on.

The network/chain-like structure of the European industry and its geographical dispersion implies that the flows of products and services within each network/chain are made up of sequential acts of import and export, arranged in series. It is therefore extremely useful to understand both who exports and what is exported to a chain where the final product is consumed or exported to another country, and who imports intermediate goods essential to complete its chain of production for both domestic final consumption or for export. This is essential to understand where the added value is created. Looking at intra-European trade in this way, the current account balance fails to focus on the actual process of power and value redistribution occurring in the EU and in the euro area.

In Europe, a process of heightened 'destructive' competition, as well as offshoring through the Foreign Direct Investment (FDI) and outsourcing, culminated in record levels of mergers and acquisitions in the two years immediately before the start of the current crisis, 2006–2007. Greater centralization was dictated by the oligopolistic strategy of controlling larger market shares. Yet the merger movement jeopardized the existing oligopolistic structure in many industrial branches, so that some of the big players were themselves increasingly at risk. The opening up of Eastern Europe to Western European capital after the fall of the Berlin Wall in 1989 accelerated the industrial restructuring that had begun in the late 1970s, while an additional powerful stimulus came from China's entrance into the global manufactures market.

This is what brought about the new social division of labour in Europe: an integrated industrial system with an uneven territorial distribution of core competencies and corporate headquarters. These new extended or virtual companies are the new key industrial players in Europe and they consider the EU territory as a strategic resource. They can, indeed, organize their networks by utilizing all kinds of legal, fiscal and social obligations, as well as skills and competencies availability, as a way to fine-tune their internal division of labour.

This struggle among capitals has generated new productive facilities, though the existing ones already carried significant unused capacity. This is why we can argue that the current crisis is also characterized by oversupply in key sectors. This situation has been compounded by huge investment in 'green prairies' to create industrial bridgeheads.

It is in this context that we locate the German export boom. According to some authors (for example, Danninger and Joutz, 2007), the important factors were new ties to fast growing trading partners as a result of a desirable product mix or long-standing trade relationships and the regionalized production patterns through offshoring production to lower cost countries, partly as a result of European economic integration. The offshoring of production to lower cost countries, also within the EU-27 area, to implement a very aggressive export strategy has compounded wage moderation and shrinking social protection. The rationale of this strategy is that high-tech investment can give Germany an edge over the new competitors such as India and China, making the medium-high sector of these mass markets available for its exports, ahead of a never-ending catch up attempt by India and China.

The current account imbalances among the Eurozone countries are the symptoms of an underlying cause: the nature of the economic model briefly outlined above, intertwined with the underlying power relations among nations both in terms of market and political power. We find the considerations put forward by Simonazzi et al. (2013) extremely useful as they once again argue against the (orthodox, but also heterodox) view that we witnessed a standard BoP crisis in Europe. When the crisis erupted, the key factors triggering the 'external' crisis for deficit economies in the Eurozone were not the 'fundamentals' but instead mounting (speculative) self-fulfilling prophecies.

These authors' perspective fit well with our picture about industrial changes in Europe and Germany. They focus on the crucial factors to explain the accumulation of German current account surpluses after the introduction of the euro. 'Since 1999 the growth of the German economy has been driven not only by exports but also by imports, in particular of parts and components linked to the relocation abroad of supply chains'. Moreover, 'the primary reason for the rise of current account surpluses after 2001 was a sharp fall of domestic private investment as a share of GDP, accompanied by a growth of foreign direct investment driven by offshoring activities' (Simonazzi et al., 2013, p. 659).

Wage deflation and rising inequality (courtesy of the Hartz reforms) has been made tolerable by cheaper prices and inferior quality of goods consumed by an increasing number of the population: a dynamic that appears bad for the export of superior quality consumption goods from advanced Southern countries displaced by emerging areas.

The competitive advantage of Germany within the Eurozone is only partially related to the differences in price competition, and rests mainly on the quality of the products and the coherence of the productive matrix with the external trade demand, namely, from China and other countries, with a new emerging middle class.

1.7 WRAPPING UP ABOUT FINANCIAL AND INDUSTRIAL INTEGRATION IN THE EUROZONE

The task now is to understand in which way the critique outlined above can be extended to the existing analysis of the crisis of the Eurozone. Both the approaches summarized in Sections 1.3 and 1.4 focus on the impacts of monetary integration on trade tendencies and, therefore, on current account imbalances. Mainstream economists point to nominal rigidities and fiscal profligacy, which have disrupted the otherwise automatic convergence mechanism between the euro countries.

Heterodox studies maintain that convergence is not the automatic outcome of free capital movements. The euro mechanism reinforced existing fragilities, by allowing for a neo-mercantilist strategy from the centre towards the periphery. The result was the erosion of exporting capacity and the widening of trade imbalances, financed with the savings from surplus countries.

The main difference between these views is that while the first is based on unrealistic assumptions and theoretical anachronisms, such as money neutrality, the second points to (what we think are the) real tendencies: it is undeniable that financialization and monetary integration worked together to increase the fragility of the already weaker economies in the EMU, and that this has had an impact on trade, which has little to do with downward wage rigidities or excessive public deficits. Similarly, there is no doubt that, as argued by the heterodox authors, the strategy of real deflation through austerity and labour market reforms is a disastrous option that, in the end, might become the ultimate cause of the problem this strategy was trying to avoid in the first place – the collapse of the EMU. However, current account imbalances assume centre stage in both approaches. They diverge largely when it comes to explaining the causes of trade imbalances, and even more so in the strategy to reduce them, but in both approaches the euro crisis is seen, mainly, as a BoP crisis.

In fact, these are very distinctive monetary configurations. First and foremost because, as we described above, countries in the Eurozone share the same payment system. From a theoretical viewpoint, we question the possibility of having a normal BoP crisis in a monetary union. It does not make much sense in fact to think so. These economies are subject to liquidity and financial disturbances that are not necessarily related with current account deficits, and will not experience a BoP crisis as long as the monetary union works as a monetary union. One may then dare to question if trade imbalances are not a necessary part of the functioning of credit economies.[6]

As Toporowski (2013) remarks, in current international monetary systems, exchange rates are driven by capital flows and expectations, rather than trade balance: money is nowadays bank credit, whose value derives from convertibility into other forms of bank credit or into financial assets, with convertibility into other fiat currencies playing a minor role. Consequently, international reserves are less and less made by gold, or central bank fiat money, but claims on or deposits in international commercial banks. On the contrary, the euro is built upon a Ricardian theory of money perspective, where fiat money issued by a central bank claims not to be (as it is) a liability, growing out of debt/credit relations, and must be held scarce by the issuer, setting price and quantity. In this fictional world, employment arises out of competitiveness, and exchange rate flexibility (aiming at competitive devaluation) is a substitute for wage flexibility (aiming at competitive deflation). The single currency leaves only the second option as viable. The desired devaluation, however, internally reduces real incomes because of rising import prices; and it achieves decreasing export competitive advantage the higher the import content. And of course devaluation cuts the real consumption of the working class.

The single currency area must be seen as a credit matter, not just a purely monetary matter. In a truly credit theory of money perspective, wage and price reductions give way to a balance sheet deflation and a rise of the real value of debt. Moreover, exchange rate movement, even when managed by sovereign central banks, affects not only the trade balance but also the cost of managing foreign debt (Toporowski, 2013). From this alternative perspective, a strong, overvalued currency, which negatively affects the trade in goods and services, 'reduces the domestic money value into which foreign obligations may be converted. Specifically, it makes it cheaper to convert a government's foreign debt obligations into domestic debt obligations that are then easier to service from tax revenue' (Toporowski, 2013, p. 578).

Another reason to be wary about the conclusions drawn from a simplistic analysis of the Eurozone crisis as a BoP problem due to trade imbalances is the aggregation of very distinctive countries into one 'periphery'. If we consider the sectoral balances of these 'peripheral' countries of the Eurozone, the only characteristic shared by all of them is indeed their current account deficits. All these countries have faced a liquidity problem, and a subsequent difficulty in obtaining cash flows to finance their liabilities in the short and medium term, but the analysis stops there and does not consider the specificities of the hidden structural dynamics in each country.

1.8 CONCLUSIONS

Both mainstream and heterodox analyses assume that the euro was crucial for the growing trade imbalances. Whether you blame it on well-paid laziness in the periphery, as in the mainstream approach, or neo-mercantilist strategies from the centre, as in the heterodoxy approach, the euro has messed up the price system and led to decreasing exporting capacity in the periphery, compensated by imports from the centre. Actually, there is a prevailing view among the heterodoxy, inspired in the postwar centre-periphery theories, which sees the euro as the product of a deliberate exploitation strategy of the periphery by the centre. Our point is that the common 'periphery-core' dichotomy, based on current account positions, hides important aspects of national economies. We rather think that the euro is part of a broader strategy to reorganize individual capitals and compress the rights of the working class through financial liberalization and exposure of national economies to international competition. The monetary union was one more step towards this strategy, but its fundamental pillars are to be found in the previous process of financial and trade liberalization. It has nothing to do with laissez-faire, or a retreat of the State. It is rather a neoliberal policy variant within the world economy as contested terrain.

The widespread view of European imbalances as the result of a German strategy of 'beggar thy neighbour' is partial and inaccurate. The magnitude of changes in trade patterns happened before and beyond the euro. A key argument in our chapter is the role financial flows play in the growing imbalances: instead of amplifiers of trade problems, financial flows are a crucial factor in building the current account imbalances, either because they can have an impact on the way investment and production are structured or because of the growing importance of other sources of change in current accounts. Current account imbalances could rather be a consequence of the way capital has circulated in Europe. Inflation differentials and relative exchange rates are more likely to be symptoms of financial dynamics (motivated of course by growth and returns expectations in specific sectors) than the drivers of such flows.

The mainstream recipe based on more liberalization, combined with labour market reforms and wage cuts to increase competitiveness and force a shift towards the production of tradables, might even balance trade accounts (as it is now) but will not solve the underlying causes of such imbalances or prevent future financial disturbances. On the other hand, asking for more inflation in the core countries might be a very reasonable demand from the viewpoint of the working rights of German workers, but definitely is not the answer to the euro problems.

From an empirical point of view, we question the true responsibilities of the common currency in the current crisis. There is no doubt that the artificial limitations imposed by the euro institutional framework have made things much worse, but it is equally important to analyze what happened before and beyond the euro. The exposure to liberalized financial markets started before the introduction of the common currency and had major impacts on the way these economies are structured. Financial integration was pursued from at least the early 1990s leading to a common capital market and a common market in financial services. On the other hand, the analysis of industrial and trade relations in Europe cannot ignore the growing importance of Central and Eastern European countries (some of them out of the monetary union).

This leads us to question about exiting the euro. Exit strategies are problematic since their gains are uncertain, and it is even more unlikely that they will be followed by an anti-austerity stance. They are also uncertain, due to the scale of financial and industrial integration, and because of the innovative and productive hierarchical/geographical stratification of the European area.

If we look at the trade imbalances through the lenses of industrial restructuring and geography of European trade flows, like Simonazzi et al. do, we reach the same conclusion: exiting the euro, and the same reflationary policies, do not seem to go to the heart of the matter. The former option may likely turn out sour not only because the exchange rate that would help the needs of trade may lead to worsening balance sheets, but because the most important factors in nurturing disequilibria in the deficit countries are structural. They have to do with the way Germany has constructed a transnational value chain of firms network and articulated beyond national borders its matrix of production, how the geography of trade has been changed, the output composition and import content of different countries, the impoverishment of the ties among peripheral nations and so on.

Here and now, the issue is not to resurrect a generic Keynesianism of anti-austerity policies and boosting effective demand – as necessary as these moves are. The problems are also structural, they pertain to industrial, trade and financial policies on the scale of the continent (within and outside the Eurozone). For sure, the rejection of too simplistic explanations produces all the difficulties of building a holistic, but still coherent, narrative of the world we live in. But it might be worth trying.

NOTES

1. In 2010, Giavazzi and Spaventa published a paper claiming that the external payments situation of member states was disregarded in the monetary union. They criticize the view put forward by traditional convergence models, such as Blanchard and Giavazzi (2002).
2. The sum of the difference between income and expenditures of each of the sectors of the economy must be zero: as long as a country can preserve a trade surplus and a balanced (or deficit) fiscal account, its private sector will be accumulating financial assets (or claims on the external and public sectors). See Godley (1999).
3. Finland, Germany, Austria, Netherlands, Belgium.
4. Ireland, Greece, Spain.
5. Italy, Portugal.
6. Minsky (1986) clarified that the international credit system requires imbalances to let the international debt–credit interconnection on which today's international money is built run smoothly. Toporowski (2013) denotes the failure to provide a trade deficit to accommodate foreign debt payments as a kind of credit neo-mercantilism.

REFERENCES

Arestis, P. and M. Sawyer (2001), 'Will the euro bring economic crisis to Europe?', Working Paper No. 322, Levy Economics Institute of Bard College.

Arestis, P. and M. Sawyer (2011), 'The ongoing eurocrisis', *Challenge*, **54**(6), 6–13.

Bellofiore, R. (2013), 'Two or three things I know about her. Europe in the Global Crisis, and heterodox economics', *Cambridge Journal of Economics*, Special issue Prospects for the Eurozone, **3**, 497–512.

Bellofiore, R. (2014), 'The socialization of investment, from Keynes to Minsky and beyond', Working Paper No. 822, Levy Economics Institute of Bard College.

Blanchard, O. and F. Giavazzi (2002), 'Current account deficits in the euro area. The end of Feldstein-Horioka Puzzle?', *Brookings Papers on Economic Activity*, **2**, 147–86.

Borio, C. and P. Disyatat (2011), 'Global imbalances and the financial crisis: link or no link?', BIS Working Papers.

Carney, M. (2012, January), 'Systemic Financial Resilience', World Economic Forum Annual Meeting, Davos-Klosters, Switzerland.

Collignon, S. (2012), *Competitiveness and Excessive Imbalances: A Balance Sheet Approach*, Brussels: European Parliament: Directorate General for Internal Policies.

Danninger, S. and F.L. Joutz (2007), 'What explains Germany's rebounding export market share?', IMF Working Papers.

Garber, P. (2010), *The Mechanics of Intra Euro Capital Flight*, Deutsche Bank Special Report, London.

Giavazzi, F. and L. Spaventa (2010), 'Why the current account may matter in a monetary union: lessons from the financial in the euro area', CEPR Discussion Paper 8008, Centre for Economic Policy Research.

Godley, W. (1999), *Seven Unsustainable Processes, Special Report*, Annandaleon-Hudson, NY: Levy Economics Institute.

Hein, E. (2012), 'The crisis of finance-dominated capitalism in the euro area, deficiencies in the economic policy architecture, and deflationary stagnation policies', Working Paper No. 734, Levy Economics Institute.

Holinski, N., C. Kool and J. Muysken (2012), 'Persistent macroeconomic imbalances in the euro area: causes and consequences', *Federal Reserve Bank of St. Louis Review*, **94**(1), 1–20.

Johnson, K. (2009), 'Gross or net international financial flows understanding the financial crisis', Working Paper, The Council on Foreign Relations.

Lucarelli, B. (2011), 'German neomercantilism and the European sovereign debt crisis', *Journal of Post Keynesian Economics*, **34**(2), 205–24.

Merler, S. and J. Pisani-Ferry (2012), *Sudden Stops in the Euro Area*, Bruegel Policy Contribution, 2012/06.

Minsky, H.P. (1986), *Stabilizing an Unstable Economy*, New Haven, CT: Yale University Press.

Mongelli, F.P. and C. Wyplosz (2008), 'The euro at ten: unfulfilled threats and unexpected challenges', Paper presented at the Fifth ECB Central Banking Conference, Frankfurt, Germany.

Obstfeld, M. (2012), 'Does the current account still matter?', Working Paper No. 18977, NBER.

Schumpeter, J.A. (1954), *History of Economic Analysis*, New York: Oxford University Press.

Simonazzi A., A. Ginzburg and G. Nocella (2013), 'Economic relations between Germany and southern Europe', *Cambridge Journal of Economics*, **37**, 653–75.

Sinn, H.W. (2006), 'The pathological export boom and the bazaar effect: how to solve the German puzzle', *The World Economy*, **9**, September, 1157–75.

Sinn, H.W. (2012), 'The European balance-of-payments crisis: an introduction', in H.-W. Sinn (ed.), *The European Balance-of-payments Crisis*, CESifo, 3–10; Munich, Germany.

Sinn, H.-W. and T. Wollmershäuser (2011), 'Target loans, current account balances and capital flows: the ECB's rescue facility', CESifo Working Paper No. 3500.

Toporowski, J. (2013), 'International credit, financial integration and the euro', *Cambridge Journal of Economics*, **37**(3), 571–84.

2. The big financial crisis and the European economic adjustment: a road toward the strengthening of the neoliberal agenda

Ma. Guadalupe Huerta

2.1 INTRODUCTION

In the aftermath of the great financial crisis of 2008 the governments of the eurozone countries sought to avoid contagion and widespread bankruptcy of financial intermediaries through capital injections and funding programs with government guarantees that enabled them to support their obligations. Faced with the economic asymmetries between the countries of the European economic bloc, the costs of government intervention generated by bank bailouts after 2010 exacerbated the debt problems of countries with strong fiscal and external imbalances, giving rise to sovereign debt. Attempts have been made to overcome this crisis through programs of economic adjustment and a policy of internal devaluation or deflation, resulting in a marked economic and social deterioration, mainly in so-called peripheral countries.

On the basis of these reference points, this chapter is divided into four sections. Section 2.2 presents a brief review of the formation of the European Union (EU) and the strategies established for the management of monetary and fiscal policy. Section 2.3 shows how the dynamics of financial globalization meant that the policies that facilitated the major international financial crisis penetrated the financial system of the eurozone via commercial banks, generating severe financial instability, which was the trigger for the sovereign debt crisis in the region. Section 2.4 describes the main features of the adjustment programs of the eurozone that, with their marked neoliberal emphasis have severely affected growth and employment. Finally, Section 2.5 sets out the conclusions.

2.2   THE CREATION OF THE EUROPEAN UNION AND THE LOSS OF MONETARY AND FISCAL SOVEREIGNTY

The economic lessons of the First World War and the ravages of the 1929 crisis meant that in the period after the Second World War it was recognized that capitalism had a need for direct state intervention to reverse the devastation caused in Europe by armed conflict and to revive national economies (such as the United States). The financial basis of the reconstruction was outlined in the European Recovery Program, known as the Marshall Plan, which included loans of US$13 billion over four years (1948–1952), distributed among the European economies that had participated in the war, depending on their industrial capacity to boost reconstruction. Britain, France and West Germany received 56.7 percent of the resources, which were allocated to rebuilding infrastructure, and to investing in industry and agriculture in order to boost consumer spending and strengthen effective demand.

An additional element of the effects caused by the economic and social damage in Europe was to promote regional integration strategies. The fledgling customs unions of 1947 that included Belgium, the Netherlands and Luxembourg, France and Italy, and the Scandinavian countries, among others, were followed in 1951 by the formation of the European Coal and Steel Community, the organization that defined the seminal moment of the Treaty of Rome (1957). This was the foundation for the creation of the European Economic Community, which later became the EU. The goal was to create a robust and socially stable economic bloc supported by the expansion of the common European market and trade with America. As a result of these actions, as well as greater global dynamism, between 1951 and 1982 the average gross domestic product (GDP) in Europe was 4.1 percent.

However, trade and financial imbalances resulting from the slowdown in global growth and financial deregulation of the early 1980s reduced this average to 2.0 percent, which revived efforts to achieve economic and monetary coordination, in order to create the single European market. In 1992 the Maastricht Treaty (also known as the Treaty on European Union)[1] was signed, whose member countries agreed to make the necessary institutional changes to create the common economic rules that would support the creation of the Economic and Monetary Union (EMU). These were included in the convergence criteria contained in the monetary and fiscal requirements for nominal economic stabilization of the countries of the EU, which established that price stability should converge on a consumer price index (CPI) of 1.5 percent or less; a government deficit no higher than 3 percent of GDP and a public debt of no more than 60 percent; an exchange rate without abrupt changes or devaluations against the euro; and a nominal interest rate of not more than 2 percent.

Integration was not immediate, but took several stages. In 1997 the Stability and Growth Pact (SGP) was signed, which meant accepting rules of economic and fiscal coordination to limit the increase in the deficit and public debt; in 1999 the euro was adopted and became the common currency of the eurozone; and in 2002 banknotes and coins denominated in euros entered circulation and became legal tender.

The consequences of European integration include the transfer of national powers in relation to monetary policy and foreign exchange to a new supranational institution, the European Central Bank (ECB); the subordination of the operation and objectives of the national central banks to the guidelines and policies of the European System of Central Banks (ESCB); and a system of central banks (the Eurosystem) for which the ECB took over control of issuing currency and of monetary policy, whose mechanisms of transmission were principally the channels of interest rates and credit.[2] In the management of the liquidity of the eurozone, and the establishment of benchmark interest rates for the money market it influences, first, the behavior of retail interest rates and rates for bank refinancing, and then, with a delay, interest rates for consumer finance, savings and investment decisions (Scheller, 2006). In this scheme the regular functioning of local banks is critical to the operation of the ECB's monetary policy transmission mechanisms. In its role as an autonomous bank, together with the Eurosystem, the ECB is responsible for ensuring price stability and protecting the value of the euro. Therefore, its monetary policy is designed on the basis of the convergence criteria, and comprises two aspects: a strategy intended to impose an inflation rate no higher than 1.5 percent and a stable exchange rate, that is, to prevent abrupt shifts, and to maintain these within the margins established by the exchange rate mechanism of the European Monetary System.

From the conventional macroeconomic perspective of the European Commission (EC), price stability accompanied by control of public finances should generate a nominal economic convergence, required to sustain an economic bloc of global significance that, with the introduction of the euro as the single currency, should be 'resistant to global turbulence' (European Commission, 2013), while intra-European trade would be protected. In those terms, signing the Maastricht Treaty obliged the countries wishing to join the EMU to meet specific commitments on monetary policy and public finances that involved adopting the quantitative targets set out in the convergence criteria. Significantly, in fiscal terms its objective is to avoid excessive deficits[3] through the obligation to observe strict budgetary discipline governed by the parameters of 3 percent in the ratio of the planned or actual government deficit to gross GDP at market prices, and 60 percent in the ratio of government debt to GDP at market prices (Official Journal of the European Union, 2012).

However, by accepting the euro as the single currency, countries lost monetary sovereignty because their central banks gave up the power to issue their own money, and became unable to make use of public spending and countercyclical fiscal deficits.[4] More serious still, submitting management of exchange rate policy and the management of official reserves to the ECB's objectives implied giving up the use of the exchange rate as a variable for adjustment of external accounts. This would have been useful to address the production, trade and financial imbalances that are characteristic of the heterogeneity that exists among member countries of the EU and the eurozone.

With the loss of monetary sovereignty, coupled with the separation of monetary and fiscal policy, the sources of financing of public spending focused on taxes and/or contracting debt by offering sovereign debt bonds on the financial markets. In such conditions, the expansion of global liquidity and the relaxation of the conditions of access to credit resulting from the international financial deregulation meant that faced with a reduction in tax revenues resulting from the economic slowdowns in the first decade of the twenty-first century, public spending is increasingly financed via increased borrowing on financial markets. This allowed banks – principally European banks – to become the leading holders of government bonds. This, together with the dynamics generated by strategies of fixed exchange rates and low interest rates fueled financial speculation and swelled the trade deficits of countries peripheral to the eurozone, which previously had the highest production and trade gaps (UNCTAD, 2013).

2.3   GLOBALIZATION, FINANCIALIZATION AND THE FINANCIAL PROBLEMS OF THE EUROZONE

The post-Bretton Woods era policies of deregulation and liberalization of globalization favored an unprecedented mobility of resources, which in addition to encouraging the exponential growth of cross-border financial transactions increased the vulnerability of economies insofar as they reduced the safety margins of financial markets against internal or external shocks. In turn, the inequality resulting from the increased concentration of income in the highest social strata and falling share of wages in income, which, according to UNCTAD (2013), fell from 62 percent in 1980 to

54 percent in 2011, did not present a major problem because the buoyant and deregulated credit markets made use of increased borrowing to finance the operations of non-financial corporations, public spending by governments and household consumption (L20, 2014). In the 1990s this process became entrenched, such that the value of transactions in the financial sector began to exceed those in the real sector of the economy, giving rise to what heterodox economists call financialization, a distinguishing feature of present-day capitalist accumulation (Foster and Magdoff, 2009; Lapavitsas and Morera, 2011; Levy, 2013).

The deregulation and subsequent globalization of the financial system explain the foreign debt crisis in Latin America in the 1980s, and the private debt crisis of the 1990s in several regions and countries around the world. These crises were dealt with by financial aid packages comprising resources from international financial organizations, coordinated by the International Monetary Fund (IMF), private banks and governments of developed countries; financial assistance was made dependent on fulfillment of what is known as *ex post* conditionality, which are a set of macroeconomic policies and structural reforms designed both to attempt to reverse the fiscal and current account imbalances to restore the capacity for growth of the countries requesting financial assistance, and therefore to enable them to repay the resources borrowed. The important aspect of these financial aid packages was their pro-cyclical character, which reduced consumption and investment, slowing aggregate demand, which resulted in economic recessions and unemployment.[5]

Prior to the 2008 crisis, the credit boom boosted consumer credit and real estate speculation, which reached their highest levels in developed countries, as in the case of the United States, UK and Canada, and also reaching the peripheral eurozone countries such as Spain and Ireland (Bank of International Settlements, 2009). The factors behind this boom that led to an increase in indebtedness in Europe were the reduction in interest rates, the expansion of global liquidity and the network of credit markets and interbank funding, where structured products were traded and placed on financial markets, generating the liquidity required to support the credit bubble.

However, between 2005 and 2007 the increased interest rates in the United States, Britain, Japan and Germany[6] meant that loans defaulted and became non-performing, reducing the value of bank assets. The inability to place new packages of value on the market to provide additional resources interrupted the refinancing chain supporting the operation of the financial markets and triggered the problems of liquidity and solvency for the intermediaries comprising the network of speculation, which included mortgage lenders, commercial and investment banks, insurers and a set of non-bank financial institutions operating around the capital market. The financial bubble became unsustainable and brought about the collapse of bank refinancing and credit.

As a result of financial globalization, the great recession of 2008 (the most significant crisis since 1929) spread from the financial center of capitalism, with the bankruptcy of the Lehman Brothers investment bank in September 2008, to other regions and financial centers of the world. The initial response of the governments and central banks in the developed world and the EU (Federal Reserve, Bank of England, Bank of Japan, Bank of Canada, Bank of Sweden, Bank of Switzerland and the ECB) was to inject capital, increase lending, buy assets[7] and provide financial assistance packages, in order to deploy financial support to commercial banks to try to restore liquidity and reverse the lack of confidence about their solvency. Subsequently, those same central banks attempted to stabilize the balance sheets of the financial intermediaries and reduce systemic risk by applying programs and stimulus by auctioning dollars in refinancing operations to support the short-term liquidity of banks and thereby maintain credit flows in interbank markets. This was important because the crisis had severely affected credit and the operation of both retail and wholesale deposit markets.

At about the same time, the ECB applied a monetary policy based on the purchase of securities through open market operations to member banks of the Eurosystem, which reduced interest rates to historic lows of 1 percent in 2009 (Trichet, 2010; Van Reit, 2010). This strategy was intended to restore confidence in the financial system by restoring the flow of credit to the real sector, which most likely would have contributed to reducing the depth of the crisis by boosting effective demand and shortening the recovery period.

However, the banks used the financial assistance funds, backed by government guarantees that were negotiable in the money markets, to clear their balance sheets and begin a round of mergers and acquisitions that led to greater bank concentration – there are currently fewer banks, which handle volumes of assets higher than the amount they held before the outbreak of the crisis in 2008 (Vives, 2011; European Central Bank, 2014). Despite the lax monetary policies, credit failed to reactivate, while confidence in financial systems did not rebound either, and it proved impossible to avoid an economic recession. This caused the growth rate of GDP in developed economies to fall from an average of 2.1 percent between 1996 and 2005 to −3.4 percent in 2009, with a modest recovery of 1.8 percent in 2014. US economic activity also fell, from a GDP that averaged 3.4 percent from 1999 to 2005 to −2.8 percent in 2009, climbing again to 2.2 percent in 2014. The eurozone suffered the same fate and over the same period the region's GDP grew on average by 2.1 percent, falling to −4.5 percent in 2009, and barely reaching 0.8 percent in 2014. The economic downturn affected public revenue, increased government debt and triggered the sovereign debt crisis in Europe.

In short, financial globalization facilitated access to debt and the concentration of economic activity, which reduced the effectiveness of bailout programs in Europe; coupled with falling tax revenue due to the crisis, this appreciably complicated the financial problems in the eurozone.

2.3.1 The Banking Crisis in the Eurozone and the Explosion of Sovereign Debt

Insofar as the convergence criteria were designed to standardize the operation of the disparate economies of the Maastricht Treaty, the EU financial systems – immersed as they are in the deregulatory dynamics of financialized capitalism – were left out of quantitative and qualitative restrictions on its financial operations both within and outside the EU and the eurozone. That meant that in the face of lax regulation, low interest rates and expectations of maximizing profits, ever since 2000 European banks had steadily increased credit to households and non-financial companies. This explains why even though credit to the private sector declined after 2008, the indebtedness of households and non-financial companies remains high, to the extent that in 2014 it reached 95 percent of families' gross income, and 130 percent of GDP in the case of non-financial companies.

A particular feature of this debt is that until early 2006, at the height of mortgage speculation and when it seemed that the eurozone economy would grow steadily, the loans granted by the banking system came from both credits contracted with private banks in countries with stronger financial systems, such as Germany and France, and the issuance of long-term guaranteed bonds (asset-backed securities and mortgage-backed securities) in operations of the real estate sector in the construction and sale of housing. However, the contraction of economic activity after 2007 in the eurozone caused a contraction in investment and a gradual increase in unemployment. When borrowers stopped covering their debts the number of non-performing loans soared, exposing the risky lending practices that commercial banks had engaged in.

After 2008, the rapid deterioration in bank assets caused widespread distrust between intermediaries and meant that banks could no longer obtain additional resources in the interbank market to refinance their debts, worsening their financial fragility and forcing them to offer their government securities as collateral.

Between 2007 and 2009, the ECB sought to avoid the risk of widespread insolvency in eurozone financial institutions through various refinancing programs ranging from three to six months, and then a year.[8] Its aim was to improve the liquidity of banks to reduce money market spreads and maintain low interest rates in the short term.[9] The funds initially committed amounted to 442 billion euros in refinancing operations for a total of 360 financial institutions prior to the outbreak of the crisis, which increased to 800 at its height (European Central Bank, 2010). The provision of overnight credit[10] was subject to granting of payment guarantees, however the collapse in 2008 of the private equity market led these to be substituted by government securities in the form of collateral.

It is important to remember that the convergence criteria prevent central banks financing governments, meaning that if tax revenues do not increase their financing can only come from placing public debt on the financial markets, by means of open market operations.[11] In these auctions the leading participants in terms of the size of their purchases were private banks and other financial intermediaries from other eurozone countries to that of the government issuing debt. As a result, governments with larger volumes of liabilities owed large amounts to banks resident in other countries in the eurozone itself (Figure 2.1).

Acceptance of collateral sovereign debt by the ECB and the Eurosystem banks depended on whether they were negotiable on the secondary markets, and depended on the ability to pay of the issuing country. However, the eurozone countries with high public and current account deficits relative to GDP (Portugal, Ireland, Greece and Spain, among others)

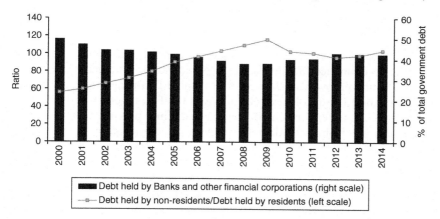

Source: Statistical Data Warehouse, http://sdw.ecb.europa.eu/browse.do?node=bbn192, accessed 8 May 2015.

Figure 2.1   Holders of government debt in the eurozone

raised doubts about their ability to pay their debts. This group was joined by Italy, whose high level of debt was accompanied by a growing current account deficit in relation to GDP, which in 2010 stood at −3.5 percent, the highest since 2000. Doubts about the ability to pay of these countries led to a rise in spreads, particularly for the premiums of credit default swaps, in their debt relative to German debt, a fact that increased the financial costs of the sovereign debt (Vause and von Peter, 2011).

Under these conditions, the downgrading of the debt issued by states meant that from 2010 the public debt collaterals were no longer accepted on secondary markets by the banks of the Eurosystem and/or private banks, which led to the sovereign debt crisis. This coincided with the gradual abandonment of the unorthodox strategies used by the ECB – injections of liquidity and refinancing plans – so that by restoring liquidity to the financial markets and keeping interest rates under control, the tensions in the money markets would diminish and the transmission mechanism of monetary policy directly associated to credit in the eurozone would return to normal operation. Despite these efforts, the financial stress remained, because neither credit nor confidence between intermediaries revived. Thus, financial instability and massive financial support from the European states to the central banks was a key contributor to the evolution of the sovereign debt crisis.

2.4   FROM THE ECONOMIC ADJUSTMENT TO THE STRENGTHENING OF THE NEOLIBERAL AGENDA IN THE EUROZONE

By 2011 and faced with the precarious financial situation of peripheral eurozone countries facing situations of economic emergency, as well as those which enjoyed a relatively more stable financial situation, such as France, the EU authorities, the ECB and the EC, together with the IMF, designed a strategy oriented toward reducing pressures on sovereign debt through voluntary debt swaps with discounts of up to 50 percent of the notional value of the debt in private hands – especially in the case of Greece – as well as partial risk protection to the new sovereign debt issues of between 20 percent and 30 percent by the European Financial Stability Facility (EFSF), and the recapitalization of banks conditioned on the establishment of a public bank debt guarantee system. This was supplemented by the Securities Purchase Program of 207 billion euros for limited purchases of debt by the Eurosystem (Vause and von Peter, 2011). Despite that, and while the problems of bank financing and cuts to growth expectations did not improve, the focus of the analysis of the crisis ceased to be the irresponsible operation and excessive risk taking by banks, and shifted to public debt.[12]

2.4.1 On Austerity, Fiscal Consolidation and Internal Devaluation

Since mid 2010 the economic and financial authorities of the EU decided that the problems of the eurozone countries were the result of policies of irresponsible government spending, and as a result in March 2012 signed the Treaty on Stability, Coordination and Governance in the Economic and Monetary Union. This document contains, under the name of the Fiscal Compact, measures to reinforce the requirement to have balanced or surplus public finances and the actions to be taken to reduce excessive deficit.[13] In addition, revisions to the SGP in 2011 and 2014 introduced new laws to improve economic coordination and oversight, and also included preventive measures to ensure fiscal consolidation.[14]

The excessive deficit procedure enters operation when non-compliance with budgetary discipline is detected, which is defined by the parameters of a government deficit no greater than 3 percent of GDP at market prices, and debt not exceeding 60 percent of GDP at market prices. The next step was the multilateral surveillance of public finances in these countries. This leads to the design of policies for economic correction that are applied in order to restore budgetary discipline within six months. In that sense, the objective of the Fiscal Compact is to attain fiscal consolidation, reduce debt and current account deficits to levels considered safe by the agencies responsible for economic management of the EU and the IMF. But in reality, the goal is to definitively reverse the short-term fiscal imbalances to restore confidence in financial markets (European Central Bank, 2012).

The multilateral surveillance led to the imposition of economic policy measures and structural reforms that, as a result of EU governance, strengthen the ideological and economic program of neoliberalism because the consequence is not only that monetary policy is set at a supranational level, but also policies for management of effective demand. As a result, financial support granted to eurozone countries affected by the crisis has been restricted to the signing of Stand-By Arrangement programs, which establish that the resources loaned are conditional on making adjustments to economic policy and carrying out structural reforms as required by the lender, in this case the ECB, the EC and IMF (which make up the famous Troika). These programs have three main components: institutional reforms to improve the quality of bank assets; tax reforms to achieve the goal of fiscal surplus (1.5 percent of GDP); and structural reforms to promote competition and stimulate growth.

The argument used by the EU authorities to justify these reforms is that the imbalances in public finances and external accounts can only be reversed with tight fiscal policies. Moreover, as the eurozone countries cannot devalue, because they do not have their own currency, they are required to restore their competitiveness through internal devaluation or deflation policies that in the form of budgetary adjustments and structural reforms seek to reduce wages and prices. The budgetary adjustments include increases in indirect taxes, rationalization of subsidies, cuts to education spending and reducing purchases of drugs and coverage of health services. Meanwhile, the structural reforms comprise increased flexibility of labor laws making it easier to fire staff, together with pay cuts, increased retirement age, reducing the number of public administration posts and offices and the privatization of public assets in sectors such as transport, energy and water supply.

It is assumed that this austerity in public spending and increasing revenues will lead primary deficits and debt to begin to decline, in accordance with projections of the ECB. However, the pro-cyclical nature of the measures imposed means that the progress made is minimal vis-à-vis a gross debt that has remained high in a context of economic stagnation (Figure 2.2).

Thus, in 2014 the ratio of gross government debt to GDP in the eurozone was 92 percent, a figure well above the 68 percent of 2000, with

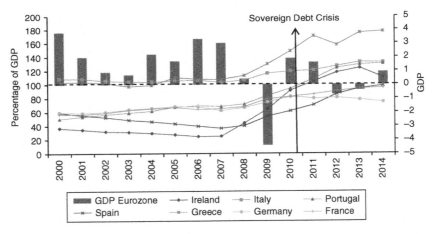

Source: Eurostat. General government gross debt. Annual data available at http://ec.europa.eu/eurostat/tgm/table.do?tab=table&init=1&language=en&pcode=teina225&plugin=1, accessed 18 August 2015.

Figure 2.2   Government debt as a percentage of GDP and GDP growth in the eurozone

an almost identical trend by country; Greece, Ireland, Italy, Portugal and Spain have government debt of up to 177.1 percent, 109.7 percent, 132.1 percent, 130.2 percent and 97.7 percent of GDP, respectively (European Commission, 2015a, 2015b). Meanwhile, the effort to increase productivity and reverse external imbalances has led to a reduction of labor costs, which fell from 4.4 percent in 2009 to 1.1 percent in 2014, savings obtained through wage cuts. To this may be added the loss of employment benefits and the greater flexibility of labor market institutions, favoring individual contracts for the benefit of private companies.

The effect on the overall functioning of the economy of the eurozone due to the internal devaluation policies was to generate a deep recession, fueled by weakening demand caused by the decline in investment, public and private consumption, as well as the persistence of high unemployment levels. As a consequence, between 2010 and 2014 these variables remained stagnant with regard to GDP, at average levels of 56 percent, 21.6 percent and 20.7 percent, respectively. Meanwhile, as a total percentage of the labor force, the unemployment rate of the population under 25 years of age in the eurozone in 2014 stood at 23.8 percent, seven percentage points higher than the rate in 2008 when the financial crisis broke out. The behavior of this variable by country is more critical, since in 2014 it reached 34.7 percent in Portugal, 23.9 percent in Ireland, 52.4 percent in Greece, 53.2 percent in Spain, 42.7 percent in Italy and 24.0 percent in France.

This data demonstrates that the strategies applied first to rescue the European banking system and then to deal with the sovereign debt crisis, using the same pro-cyclical policies as implemented by the IMF in Latin America in the 1980s – and which led to the loss of growth and well-being of the so-called 'lost decade'[15] – once again impacted on key areas of aggregate demand such as consumption and public and private investment, and led to a slowdown in growth and rising unemployment and poverty.

The difference with the case of Latin America is that the eurozone countries, unable to adjust their exchange rates, have borne the economic adjustment in wages, shrinking demand, and without this producing a swift or strong recovery in the European economic bloc.

2.5 CONCLUSIONS

The eurozone crisis is bound up with a number of factors. First, the rigidity of the monetary and fiscal framework that ignores the structural differences of the countries comprising the EU and prevents them from implementing macroeconomic policies commensurate to their needs, which has exacerbated their asymmetries; second, the existence of deregulating financial systems with varying degrees of depth and robustness whose speculative operations were decisive in the sovereign debt crisis experienced by peripheral eurozone countries; and third, the insistence of the EU authorities on the application of economic adjustments and reforms that have already shown themselves to be ineffective, and only serve to strengthen the neoliberal economic and ideological agenda at the cost of economic deterioration and loss of social welfare.

As such, a robust solution to the crisis in the EMU involves reviewing the macroeconomic model of integration in order to delimit its policies and objectives in line with the differences among member countries. In addition, guidelines should be established to create an EU financial system to facilitate the monitoring of banking operations and redirect credit to the real sector of the economy. Finally – and on this point the political component is fundamental – fiscal integration should be promoted that supports public investment in the region and the creation of jobs, especially among young people who have been severely affected by the crisis, and in this way overcome the depression. Otherwise, as well as the persistence of deflationary trends and impoverishment, the challenge to European integration will only grow stronger, and the room for the undemocratic actions of the extreme right across Europe will expand.

NOTES

1. Tratado de la Unión Europea, consolidated text (2007).
2. The other channels for monetary policy concern the exchange rate and the price of assets.
3. Article 126 (previously 104) of the paragraph on Economic and Monetary Policy of the Treaty on the Functioning of the EU.
4. Prior to the crisis, eurozone countries (Italy, Spain and Greece) exceeded the debt criterion of 60 percent in relation to GDP. This situation worsened as the financial costs of the interest rates differentials and spreads for the payment of public debt held by financial intermediaries increased.
5. Corbo and Rojas (1992) analyze why following the financial assistance by the IMF in Latin America in the 1980s middle- and high-income countries in the region fell into recession, and 16 out of 23 experienced negative per capita growth, including Mexico (−0.3 percent), Argentina (−2.3 percent) and Venezuela (−3.4 percent).
6. Since August 2007 spreads began to increase between the Libor Rate and the Overnight Index Swap Rate (OIS), which hindered funding of European banks in other currencies.
7. The collaterals were government guarantees and asset-backed securities (ABS).
8. Long Term Refinancing Operations (LTRO).
9. In 2007 short-term interest rates on the money market began to rise not only in the United States but also on European markets. The first increases were seen on the Euro Over Night Index Average (EONIA), which as a measure of the perception of instability in the financial market sent signals of the insolvency risk between counterparts.
10. One of four major operations.

11. The premiums offered by public debt must be attractive enough to sustain demand at each auction.
12. The work of Reinhart and Rogoff (2010) was used as a reference to explain the effect of high levels of public debt on economic growth. Herndon et al. (2013) reviewed the work and found that in the database used there were coding errors, relevant data had been excluded and an unconventional statistical weighting had been used, all aspects that from their perspective weaken its findings regarding the public debt ratio and economic growth.
13. Protocol No. 12, *Official Journal of the European Union*.
14. Since before the crisis struck some EU countries did not comply with budgetary discipline, the 2011 and 2014 reforms to the SGP improved oversight of the behavior of the public budget and the opening up of procedures in EU countries with severe macroeconomic imbalances and financial instability.
15. In reviewing the effects of the financial assistance programs on the growth of countries requesting IMF support, Przeworski and Vreeland (2000) found that growth declined and that no benefits to offset these losses were reported once the programs had concluded. In contrast, countries that did not request financial assistance grew faster than those that did request it, even though both groups suffered internal deficits and currency crises. Their conclusion is that if restoring growth is the main objective of the IMF, its programs are poorly designed.

REFERENCES

Bank of International Settlements (2009), *79th Annual Report*, 1 April 2008–31 March 2009, Basel, Switzerland.

Corbo, V. and P. Rojas (1992), 'Crecimiento Económico de América Latina', *Cuadernos de Economía*, **29**(87), 265–94.

European Central Bank (2010), 'The ECB's response to the financial crisis', European Central Bank, *Monthly Bulletin*, October, available at http://www.ecb. europa.eu/pub/pdf/mobu/mb201010en.pdf, accessed 26 June 2013.

European Central Bank (2012), 'Un Pacto Presupuestario para una Unión Económica y Monetaria más Fuerte', *Monthly Bulletin*, May, available at http://www.bde.es/f/webbde/SES/Secciones/Publicaciones/PublicacionesBCE/ BoletinMensualBCE/12/Fich/bm1205-3.pdf, accessed 4 March 2013.

European Central Bank (2014), *Banking Structures Report*, available at ecb.europa. eu/pub/pdf/other/bankingstructuresreport201410.en.pdf, accessed 8 November 2014.

European Commission (2013), *Comprender las políticas de la Unión Europea. La unión económica y monetaria y el euro*, Brussels: Dirección General de Comunicación.

European Commission (2015a), *General Government Data. General Government Revenue, Expenditure, Balances and Gross Debt PART I: Tables by Country. Economic and Financial Affairs*, available at ec.europa.eu/economy_finance/db_ indicators/gen_gov_data/documents/2015/spring2015_country_en.pdf, accessed 2 May 2015.

European Commission (2015b), *European Economic Forecast. Winter 2015*, available at ec.europa.eu/economy_finance/publications/european_economy/2015/ pdf/ee1_en.pdf, accessed 2 May 2015.

Foster, J.B. and F. Magdoff (2009), *La gran crisis financiera. Causas y Consecuencias*, Madrid: S.L. FCE de España.

Herndon, T., A. Michael and R. Pollin (2013), *Does High Public Debt Consistently Stifle Economic Growth? A Critic of Reinhart and Rogoff*, Amherst, MA: Political Economy Research Institute, University of Massachusetts.

Lapavitsas, C. and C. Morera (2011), *La crisis de la financiarización*, Mexico City: IIEC-UNAM and CLACSO.

Levy, N. (2013), *Dinero, estructuras financieras y financiarización. Un debate teórico institucional*, Mexico City: UNAM and ITACA.

L20 (2014), Trade Union Statement to the G20 Labour and Employment Ministers' Meeting, Melbourne, Australia, 10–11 September, available at http.://www.labour20.org, accessed 2 May 2015.

Official Journal of the European Union (2012), *Protocolo No. 12. Sobre el Procedimiento Aplicable en Caso de Déficit Excesivo*, C326/279, available at https://www.ecb.europa.eu/ecb/legal/pdf/c_32620121026es_protocol_12.pdf, accessed 4 August 2013.

Przeworski, A. and J.R. Vreeland (2000), 'The effect of IMF programs on economic growth', *Journal of Development Economics*, **62**(2), 385–421.

Reinhart, C. and K. Rogoff (2010), 'Growth in time of debt', NBER Working Paper Series, No. 15639, available at http://www.nber.org/papers/w15639, accessed 27 July 2013.

Scheller, H. (2006), *El Banco Central Europeo, Historia, Misión y Funciones*, 2nd edn, Frankfurt: Eurosistema, European Central Bank.

Tratado de la Unión Europea (2007), *Texto Consolidado con las modificaciones de octubre de 2007*, available at http://www.cooperacionespanola.es/sites/default/files/a-tratado_de_la_union.pdf, accessed 3 March 2013.

Trichet, J.C. (2010), 'State of the Union: the financial crisis and ECB's response between 2007 and 2009', *Journal of Common Market Studies*, **48**, 7–19.

UNCTAD. (2013), *Trade and Development Report. Adjusting to the Changing Dynamics of the World Economy*, New York and Geneva: United Nations.

Van Reit, A. (2010), *Euro Area Fiscal Policies and the Crisis*, Occasional Series No. 109, Frankfurt am Main: Eurosistema, European Central Bank.

Vause, N. and G. von Peter (2011), 'La crisis de la deuda soberana de la zona euro marca el rumbo de financieros internacionales', available at http://www.bis.org/publ/qtrpdf/r_qt1112a_es.pdf, accessed 8 January 2015.

Vives, X. (2011), 'El paradigma de la competencia en el sector bancario después de la crisis', Occasional Paper 196, October, Business School, Universidad de Navarra.

3. Debt deflation theory and the Great Recession

Domenica Tropeano and Alessandro Vercelli*

3.1 INTRODUCTION

Fisher's theory of debt deflation, worked out to explain the Great Depression (Fisher, 1933), has been recently revived by many observers to explain the ongoing crisis and discuss its policy implications (see, for example, Krugman, 2012).

The subprime crisis in the USA materialized in a vicious circle between the over-indebtedness of households and the deflation of housing prices. The subsequent fall in Wall Street stock indexes triggered a vicious circle between the over-indebtedness of many economic units (including bank and non-bank financial institutions) and the progressive deflation of stock prices. The deflation of assets rapidly deteriorated the net worth of most economic units inducing a reduction in their planned expenditures that triggered the so-called Great Recession. The real deflation of consumption and investment, in its turn, further increased the exposure of many private and public units. These vicious circles between over-indebtedness of economic units, asset deflation and recession rapidly propagated to most other countries, in particular, to European countries. In addition, in the Eurozone a further vicious circle was triggered in early 2010 between the sovereign debt of periphery countries and the deflation of their real economy pursued, or imposed, to curb what was believed to be an intolerable debt.

In this chapter we discuss to what extent Fisher's theory, aptly modified and updated, is still useful to shed light on the debt deflation processes observed during the recent crisis in the USA and the Eurozone.

The chapter is divided into five sections. In Section 3.2 we briefly recall a few salient aspects of Fisher's seminal contribution to debt deflation theory (Section 3.2.1); we then discuss some of the suggested modifications and updating of this theory (Section 3.2.2); finally, we consider a few policy implications of his path-breaking analysis (Section 3.2.3). In Sections 3.3 and 3.4 we investigate causes and consequences of debt deflation processes observed during the crisis with reference, respectively, to the USA and the Eurozone. In Section 3.5 we draw a few policy implications from the analysis. Section 3.6 concludes.

3.2 FISHER'S THEORY OF DEBT DEFLATION

The main novelty of Fisher's theory is the 'discovery' of a vicious circle (cumulative feedback) between debt and deflation. He argues 'so far as I know, no one hitherto has pointed out how debt liquidation defeats itself via deflation' (Fisher, 1933, p. 350, n. 4). Within Fisher's argument, however, we detect two other cumulative processes that are part of the main feedback. These are analyzed separately and recombined within a unitary framework. To use a metaphor, we need a classification of the relevant molecules before studying their interaction in a chemical reaction.

3.2.1 The Three Basic Feedbacks

The first and crucial feedback between debt and deflation is triggered by firms' widespread over-indebtedness bringing about a process of forced liquidation of assets. The ensuing generalized deleveraging reduces the amount of deposit currency and the velocity of money circulation, deflating consumer prices and further increasing the real value of debt (Fisher, 1933, p. 342). This chain of events is framed in terms of Fisher's equation of exchange (Fisher, 1911), which is expressed as follows: 'deflation caused by the debt reacts on the debt. Each dollar of debt still unpaid becomes a bigger dollar, and if the over-indebtedness with which we started was great enough, the liquidation of debts cannot keep up with the fall of prices which it causes. In that case, the liquidation defeats itself' (Fisher, 1933, p. 344).

This is explained in terms of what is today called 'herd behaviour':

> the very effect of individuals to lessen their burden of debts increases it, because of the mass effect of the stampede to liquidate . . . Then we have the great paradox which I submit, is the chief secret of most, if not all, great depressions: The more the debtors pay, the more they owe. (Fisher, 1933, p. 344)

Fisher's detailed analysis of this crucial feedback includes seven main factors but he emphasizes that 'in the great booms and depressions, each of them has played a subordinate role as compared with two dominant factors, namely over-indebtedness to start with and deflation following soon after' (Fisher, 1933, p. 341).

Fisher's conviction of the prominence of the debt deflation feedback over the other feedbacks has induced us to examine it in its pure form before recombining it with the other ones.

A second feedback, however, also plays an important role in Fisher's account as it establishes a direct link with the real economy. He emphasizes that during a process of debt deflation the profit rate and the net worth of businesses keep sinking and bring about a growing number of bankruptcies; this leads to a progressive reduction of output, trade and employment that further deteriorates the net worth of businesses and increases further over-indebtedness. This strengthens the debt deflation vicious circle.

The third feedback implicit in Fisher's analysis is based on his influential theory of interest rate: the cumulative processes summarized above produce 'complicated disturbances in the rate of interest, in particular, a fall in the nominal, or money, rates and a rise in the real, or commodity, rates of interest' (Fisher, 1933, p. 341). This increases the real value of debt (Fisher, 1933, p. 343). In addition, there is a flight to safety that has a differential impact on the interest rate of loans according to their perceived risk: money interest on safe loans falls while money interest on unsafe loans rises (Fisher, 1933, p. 343). According to the feedback implicit in this analysis, the rise in the real rate of interest brought about by price deflation worsens the net worth of economic units enhancing their distress sale of assets and thus also the process of deflation that further revaluates the real rate of interest. The reduction in the nominal rate of interest determined from the flight to quality is believed to be insufficient to compensate this positive feedback because there is an obvious downward floor limiting the fall of the nominal rate of interest.

According to Fisher, the second and third cumulative feedbacks are triggered by the first one and reinforce its effects. As we shall see in this chapter, this is not generally true. In the Great Recession the second mechanism has been quite active independently of the first mechanism. This implies a crucial shift of emphasis from the deflation of prices to the deflation of the real economy. In this change of perspective Fisher's theory of debt deflation approaches the Keynesian theory of effective demand.

3.2.2 Updating Fisher's Debt Deflation Theory

Is Fisher's theory of debt deflation still relevant for the ongoing Great Recession? At first sight, it is of very little relevance because there are many significant obstacles to its application to the recent empirical evidence. The first and most macroscopic difference that has often been emphasized (see, for example, Minsky, 1982a, 1982b; Wolfson, 1996) is the almost complete absence of price deflation (in the strict sense of negative growth of price level) in recent financial crises. Although the consumer price index in the USA registered a sizable fall from October 2008 to March 2009, the US gross domestic product (GDP) deflator and all the European indexes of inflation decelerated but never became negative even in the trough of the crisis. The risk of a persistent price deflation was often mentioned, mainly in the USA, as a catastrophic danger to be avoided by any means. We may say with hindsight, however, that this risk was emphasized mainly to advocate and justify a policy of relentless liquidity creation on the part of central banks in favour of distressed financial institutions through techniques of quantitative easing. In our opinion, however, there are many insights in Fisher's theory that are still relevant for the ongoing crisis although they require significant modifications, updating and further development.

In order to work out an operational version of the theory of debt deflation we have to first clarify the meaning of 'over-indebtedness', which has the role of a crucial triggering factor of debt deflation processes. The preliminary step is the choice of a measure of indebtedness. As Fisher observes, (over-)indebtedness has to be measured in relative terms as 'it is always relative to other items, including national wealth and income and the gold supply' (Fisher, 1933, p. 345). In order to remain connected to recent debates we may define indebtedness in terms of a ratio between the debt of a unit and its income. Fisher was unclear about the meaning of over-indebtedness. As Minsky observes, its magnitude has to be understood and measured in terms of the safety margin desired by the unit, as it implies what Keynes identified as a 'system of borrowing and lending based upon margins of safety' (Minsky, 1982b, p. 382). Only when the debt ratio breaches the desired value does the unit tries to deleverage and the sequence of events described by Fisher is triggered (see Vercelli, 2011).

We have now to reinterpret the role of price deflation to adapt the theory to recent events. We may extend the meaning of deflation from the original one of Fisher (negative rate of change of consumer prices) to a much more comprehensive one: rate of change of prices inferior to that expected in extant contracts. As in physics, causality springs from deceleration (in this case relative to the expected rate) rather than from the current rate of change. This is a sufficient condition for a negative real effect of price dynamics (Fazzari and Caskey, 1989). This approach, however, has not so far been systematically pursued since it would require a theory of revision of expectations much more sophisticated than the existing ones. For the same reason, we are not going to elaborate on this approach in this chapter.

A simpler but no less important modification of the theory is the distinction between the price of different categories of goods because their absolute and relative dynamics have different effects on the processes of debt deflation. In particular, we have to distinguish between the price of consumer goods and the price of assets and, within the second category, between the price of stocks and the price of housing. This distinction is not altogether absent in Fisher's analysis although his reliance on the equation of exchange leads him to focus mainly on the general price index.

This example suggests that a thorough development and updating of Fisher's theory has to revise and extend his analysis in a more radical way. First of all, we have to forsake his approach that struggles to study finance instability in terms of a revised version of his famous equation of exchange (Fisher, 1911). To understand the Great Depression, Fisher had to abandon the long-run comparative statics equilibrium approach focusing on the disequilibrium dynamics that characterizes in the short run the transition between two successive long-run equilibria. He had already sketched this sort of analysis in his famous book on monetary theory (1911, chapter 4) but only the unexpected gravity and persistence of the Great Depression made him realize its crucial importance. However, the cumulative process of debt deflation is also likely to affect the long-run equilibrium, and Fisher (1933) seems to get close to admitting it. In addition, he is forced by the events to modify the traditional, strictly monetarist causal interpretation of the equation of exchange. He recognized in particular that deposit currency is endogenous, so that the relation between money supply and the general index of prices is unstable and unreliable. However, the framing of his theory in terms of the exchange equation imposed strict limitations to his analysis. In particular, it prevents an explicit analysis of the interaction between the single units or specific categories of them. Moreover, it clouds the crucial role that the banks are bound to play in the revised conceptual framework in the determination of the monetary variables. In addition, in the real economy the price level crucially depends on the rate of growth of wages that is rather sluggish, being linked to contracts stipulated at given time lags. The agents' attempt to repay their debt curbs aggregate demand in consequence of the increase in their saving and cuts planned expenditures (including investment), triggering a balance sheet recession (Koo, 2011). This in turn feeds back on aggregate demand and so on. Finally, his monetary approach prevented him from including in his analysis the crucial role of the interaction between income and expenditure of units, thereby missing the crucial role of the real channel of interaction and contagion between the balance sheets of economic units. In particular, the multiplier is seen mainly from the point of view of the money multiplier rather than of Kahn's multiplier. Notwithstanding these severe limitations, we believe that Fisher's theory of debt deflation may still be a useful starting point for a systematic study of debt deflation processes, including the very powerful and destructive ones underlying the ongoing crisis.

3.2.3   Policy Implications

Fisher draws clear policy implications from his theory of debt deflation. In his opinion, the vicious spiral between debts and deflation may 'continue, going deeper, . . . for many years' (Fisher, 1933, p. 346). He anticipates Keynes in emphasizing that the market does not succeed in self-regulating itself if not at the end of a dire economic catastrophe: 'There is then no tendency of the boat to stop tilling until it has capsized. Ultimately, of course, but only after almost universal bankruptcy, the indebtedness must cease to grow greater and begin to grow less' (Fisher, 1933, p. 346).

Fisher emphasizes that there is a simple and viable alternative to the traditional, classic policy strategy based on laissez-faire and austerity measures, 'the so-called "natural" way out of a depression' that brings about needless and cruel bankruptcy, unemployment and starvation' (Fisher, 1933, p. 346). In principle, 'it is always economically possible to stop or prevent such a depression simply by reflating the price level' (p. 346). In his opinion, Roosevelt's reflation in 1933 is a case in point:

> Those who imagine that Roosevelt's avowed reflation is not the cause of our recovery but that we had 'reached the bottom anyway' are very much mistaken. At any rate, they have given no evidence, so far as I have seen, that we had reached the bottom . . . Had no 'artificial respiration' been applied, we would soon have seen general bankruptcies of the mortgage guarantee companies, saving banks, life insurance companies, railways, municipalities, and states. (Fisher, 1933, p. 346)

In Fisher's opinion, the Great Depression could have been avoided by preventing deflation. Hoover's policy based on orthodox liberalism and austerity policies is thus responsible for the degeneration of the stock exchange breakdown in 1929 in a great depression. His late attempt to promote recovery was pursued too late in a too timid manner:

> recovery was apparently well started by the Federal Reserve open-market purchases, which revived prices and business from May to September 1932. The efforts were not kept up and recovery was stopped by various circumstances, including the political 'campaign of fear' . . . (Fisher, 1933, p. 346)

Summing up, the policy prescriptions that Fisher draws from his theory of debt deflation are crystal-clear. We can escape from a great depression such as that of the 1930s only by a consistent reflation policy. Owing to his theoretical background, he focuses mainly on monetary measures that would avoid a negative rate of change in consumer prices and would establish a moderate rate of inflation capable of devaluing the burden of debt. This would by itself thwart the first and third mechanisms in their aggregate version. However, we may observe that any policy measure able to improve the net worth of economic units and restore their confidence would improve the situation in light of the second feedback and the disaggregated part of the third mechanism. This includes in principle all the Keynesian policies meant to increase aggregate demand, in particular, real investment. In the second case the words deflation and reflation would refer to the real part of the economy rather than to its monetary part and fiscal policy would come to the front. From Fisher's strictly monetary point of view, these measures could have only been praised as a way to increase the velocity of circulation of money.

Can we still learn something from an updated version of Fisher's theory to escape the ongoing Great Recession? Our answer is positive provided that we focus on the second, real meaning of reflation and on the disaggregated version of the first and third feedbacks. The first, strictly monetary and aggregate, meaning is currently not particularly relevant neither for the analysis nor for its policy implications because the existing trend of cost inflation makes unlikely a persisting negative rate of change of a general index of prices. However, the disaggregate monetary meaning is still inspiring; in particular, its application in the first feedback to asset inflation and in the third feedback to the 'dance of spreads' in the Eurozone. The second meaning, on the contrary, is still illuminating. It helps to understand why, first of all, the monetary policies pursued by the governments during the crisis have been only moderately useful and sometimes counterproductive.

3.3 DEBT DEFLATION PROCESSES IN THE USA

Many observers noticed that Fisher's debt deflation theory is relevant to explain the subprime financial crisis and the subsequent Great Recession (see, for example, Krugman, 2012). In light of the preceding reconstruction of Fisher's theory and its updating, we aim to clarify to what extent this belief is justified.

The unexpected increase in the rate of interest involved in the third mechanism played an important role as the trigger factor of the subprime crisis although for reasons unrelated to Fisher's arguments. The increase in the market interest rates brought about by the sharp increase in the Federal Reserve funds rate in the period 2006–2008 contributed in a crucial way to a sharp increase in delinquencies of subprime and ARM (adjustable rate) mortgage holders in the same period in which the housing bubble had started to deflate. The increase in the market interest rates was induced by the surge of cost inflation determined in the same period, mainly by the spike of oil and food prices. The impact of the rate of interest in triggering the process of debt (at first of the households having an ARM mortgage) and deflation (at first of house prices) did not depend on the impact of inflation on the real value of debt but on the policy-induced increase in the nominal rate of interest on mortgage payments.

For similar reasons, the first mechanism analyzed by Fisher, if taken literally, also did not have a significant role in the recent US crisis. As a matter of fact, in the USA no deflation of the price level, as measured by the GDP deflator, has occurred. This was due in part to the cost inflation mentioned above that continued to run, though at a lower rate, notwithstanding the recession.

It is in fact the second mechanism analyzed by Fisher that is mainly relevant to understand the recent crisis. Variants of this mechanism have been observed first in the housing sector, then in the financial sector and finally in the real sector. The deceleration of housing price increase in late 2006 and the mild decrease in early 2007 occurred at the same time as the increase in the mortgage rates mentioned above. These joint events precipitated a further sharp reduction of house prices, accelerating the deleveraging of households and then also of many construction firms that had built new houses still to be sold. The ensuing fall of mortgage-based assets transmitted the process of debt deflation throughout the financial sector. The generalized attempt at deleveraging further nurtured the vicious circle of debt deflation in the second sense of Fisher.

We may now consider the reaction of policy authorities to the crisis. The US government refused to intervene to bail out the households trapped in the housing process of debt deflation, while immediately acted with unprecedented energy to bail out the financial institutions and a huge insurance firm strictly interconnected with financial firms (AIG). The continued action of the Federal Reserve on money and financial markets with its renewed rounds of quantitative easing contributed to a prompt rebound in the price of assets. However, the ensuing feeble recovery of economic units' net worth was unevenly distributed among classes. As a consequence of the households' deleveraging, the general housing price index rapidly fell, while the price index of shares soon recovered its pre-crisis value.

As a consequence of these different trends, the ratio between the price of shares and the price of housing increased (see Tropeano, 2012). This would by itself amount to an increase in inequality. Wolff (2007) finds that non-home wealth is more concentrated, with the richest 1 per cent (as ranked by non-home wealth) owning 42 per cent of total household non-home wealth in 2004 and the top 20 per cent owning 93 per cent. As a consequence, wealth inequality is positively correlated to the ratio of stock prices to house prices (see Wolff, 2007, p. 13). This view has been confirmed by Weller and

Lynch (2009) who found that total net worth as a percentage of after-tax income was more than 30 per cent lower in March 2001 than in December 2007. They estimate that two-thirds of this loss was due to declines in housing wealth and the rest was caused by financial market losses (see Weller and Lynch, 2009; Weller and Helburn, 2009). The different distribution between net worth and home wealth suggests that the people more damaged by the crisis are those who own only a house and have some debt. While poor households underwent a severe fall in net worth, the richer households managed to avoid significant losses. This in turn did not help demand to grow enough to reabsorb unemployed workers.

Summing up, in the USA the debt deflation mechanism has been successfully counteracted in the case of the financial sector and wealthy households, although not in the case of poor households, especially those directly involved in the housing crisis. As a consequence, the inequality in income distribution has greatly increased, enhancing the severity of debt deflation through a new channel (income distribution) completely ignored by Fisher.

3.4 DEBT DEFLATION PROCESSES IN THE EUROZONE

In the Eurozone there is no evidence of a significant impact of the first mechanism of debt deflation for reasons similar to those already reviewed in the USA. The structural factors underlying the 'Great Moderation' (weak trade unions and flexibility of labour) raised some initial fear about the risk of price deflation in recession. However, also in the Eurozone the process of cost inflation fed by a growing trend in the price of food and oil made it easy to avoid concrete risks of deflation in consumer prices.

As for the second mechanism, its impact has been more complex and devastating than in the USA. In order to compare its working in the USA and in the Eurozone we have to take into account the different patterns of indebtedness in the two areas. In some countries like Ireland and Spain the households sector has become very indebted because of the expansion of the real estate sector. After the burst of the real estate bubble both the indebted home owners and the entrepreneurs who had built the houses had to repay huge debts. While in the USA most deleveraging has taken place by returning the house previously bought, in many European countries this step was more difficult because of different bankruptcy laws. In Spain, for example, even if the owner gives back the house, the debt is not extinguished. The process of deleveraging is thus bound to be slower and more painful than in the USA.

On the other hand, in many European countries the corporate sector has been highly leveraged both for historical and contingent reasons. In most countries bank debt has always been the most important source of finance and recently even big manufacturing firms quoted in the stock exchange have invested a lot of borrowed money in financial activities to boost their profitability. In a period of falling aggregate demand enhanced by austerity policies, the bailing out of the most stressed banks had to rely on the issue of further debt by over-indebted states without any possibility of resorting to a central bank entitled to act as lender of last resort.

Therefore, many states have been compelled to borrow in markets where the risk perception had dramatically increased. Under such conditions the states themselves have been facing borrowing constraints and the yield on their bonds has increased. At this point, most countries have been cut out of financial markets; while the European Financial Stability Fund (EFSF) was raising debt on their behalf, they have been compelled by the new European Union conditionality to cut expenses and to increase taxation in order to repay their debts. This has led to a new variety of debt deflation process in which the states are forced to behave as private agents and thus have to save in order to repay the debt. Since the aggregate income recedes in consequence of falling aggregate demand, the ratio of debt to GDP rises. In addition, the so-called crisis resolution institutions that have been created to borrow on the market to finance the countries that have limited access to the market in fact have further increased the debt of European countries. The debt thus continues to increase while the income that should be used to repay it is forced to fall. This produces a generalized fall in the net worth of private and public economic units.

Therefore, the second mechanism of debt deflation has been particularly significant in the Eurozone as compared to the USA. In fact, while the monetary policy pursued by the Federal Reserve has been effective in restoring the value of financial activities to their pre-crisis level, in the Eurozone the value of shares and bonds has been plunging continuously towards the bottom as available data show.

Comparing various stock exchange indexes, we see that the US Standard and Poor 500 index in 2012 had almost recovered the value lost after the Lehman Brothers bankruptcy in 2008. In the Eurozone only the DAX (the German stock exchange index) had a comparable performance while all the indexes in periphery countries continued to lose value. Even some core countries' indexes such as Austria and France are performing badly. The fall in the value of stock exchange indexes in countries of the European periphery is stunning since the values fell in the range of 50–70 per cent (in the years 2007–2012). This implies a particularly severe fall in the net worth of economic units. This happens also in countries like Italy in which the deleveraging due to excessive debt in the private sector has been limited.

As for Fisher's third mechanism, we find a significant impact in the Eurozone that depends not on price deflation but on the flight to safety that produces larger spreads between different kinds of assets. This has originated a vicious circle between the indebtedness of units issuing unsafe debt, the rate of interest to be paid for its service and its indebtedness ratio. This is what happened to periphery countries in the Eurozone since early 2010 mainly because of a weakening of agents' confidence. For this reason, many residents in Mediterranean countries are taking away their deposits from local banks, bringing them to core countries' banks, fearing a break-up of the common currency and the return to a depreciated national currency.

We have seen that the divergent trend of share prices and housing prices has had distributive consequences in the USA, contributing to a further increase in the already high inequality in the distribution of wealth. In the Eurozone, on the contrary, there has not been such a divergent trend between the two prices of assets. The dividing line is between the group of countries in which both the stock exchange and housing prices have remained stable or have increased, mainly Germany and to a minor extent other core countries, and the majority of countries, in which a significant deflation in both categories of asset price has occurred. In the last group, the countries in which housing prices have fallen more are those, like Ireland and Spain, that had experienced a real estate bubble before the crisis. The two sets of prices have generally moved in the same direction in the Eurozone while in the USA they have moved in opposite directions. Moreover, the composition of wealth is different there with respect to the USA.

Therefore, the consequences of the price changes in the Eurozone on the distribution of wealth after the crisis are different from those prevailing in the USA. In the Eurozone, wealth is held mainly in the form of tangible assets, in a range from 70 per cent to 90 per cent of total assets. The richest core countries have the highest shares of financial assets in the composition of wealth and a higher wealth inequality; the Southern and poorer countries have very low shares of financial assets over the total and lower wealth inequality (see Mueller et al., 2011). Thus, inequality in income and wealth are not strictly correlated. The increase in inequality in some core countries may be due to the increased share of financial assets in the portfolio of richer households and the booming financial markets of the 2000s. In Southern countries, net worth has become negative for the poorest part of the population that had increased its debt before the financial crisis. Moreover, wealth has become more costly for the middle class because of negative income inflows deriving from higher taxes on wealth and in consequence of the austerity policies.

Thus, while the fall in financial assets prices has not hit the richest so much given the low share in their portfolio, lower housing prices have worsened the conditions of poorer households that have bought a house and have borrowed to finance it. This is more relevant for the countries in which a real estate bubble has occurred. In general, however, a channel through which the falling assets prices may have had repercussions on the net worth of agents, particularly microenterprises, is through the effects of falling bonds and share prices on the balance sheets of banks. Banks that suffer losses on their portfolios are compelled either to cut credit or increase interest rates to restore profitability. This means that small entrepreneurs have difficulty refinancing short-term loans and are charged higher interest rates. So the only chance to avoid bankruptcy is to sell assets at a falling price. This of course means also a fall in wealth and in some case produces a negative net worth. Another channel through which lower asset prices may negatively affect small family enterprises is the fall in the value of collaterals. In Italy, for example, banks base their decision on whether to grant a loan on the value of collateral.

Finally, the richest households also have the option of withdrawing their assets from their countries and transferring their wealth abroad given the current arrangements in the European Union. The Target 2 accounts are continually registering outflows from peripheral countries to core ones.

3.5 POLICY IMPLICATIONS OF THE RECENT DEBT DEFLATION PROCESSES

Fisher's confidence in the efficacy of monetary policy in avoiding or aborting a great depression seems to be unjustified for the recent experience. For example, while the narrower monetary aggregate M1 has increased, the wider definition M3 has not in the Eurozone (see *ECB Bulletin*, May 2012) notwithstanding the extraordinary liquidity injection programme started in December 2011 by the European Central Bank (ECB). This in turn implies that the money multiplier in its textbook version does not hold, since the money in circulation is not exogenous and depends on the behaviour of commercial banks. In particular, their credit granting depends on expectations, risk valuation and liquidity preference (see, for example, Wray, 1992). So it is easy to understand why, under the current circumstances, they have resorted to credit rationing. Monetary policy has succeeded in a first moment to increase the narrow money base but has failed to increase the credit available to the real economy and did not succeed in reviving a sufficient degree of reciprocal trust among financial institutions regarding the true state of counterparties' balance sheets (see ECB Statistics, 2012, table 2, p. 24).

The trend in the broad money supply aggregates is divergent in different regions of the Eurozone. In particular, yearly growth rates of loans to non-financial corporations are mildly positive for countries of the European core such as Germany, the Netherlands, France, Finland; they are instead in the negative range for countries of the European periphery like Greece, Italy, Spain, Ireland, Portugal (Figure 3.1).

Even in Italy, where the rate of growth of credit is around zero, different patterns are observable between big and small firms. Recent data released by the Bank of Italy for the last months show that there has been a contraction in loans to so-called 'producing families', which are microenterprises

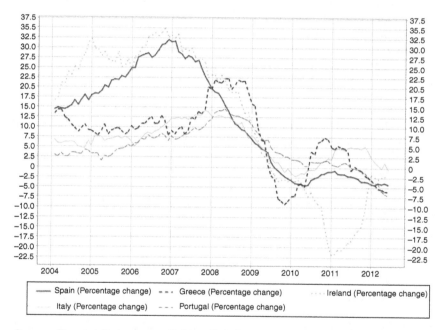

Source: Eurostat, Dataset name: Balance Sheet Items; frequency: monthly; adjustment indicator: neither seasonally nor working date adjusted; balance sheet reference sector breakdown: MFIs excluding ESCB; balance sheet item: loans; original maturity: total; data type: Index of Notional Stocks; counterpart area: euro area (changing composition); balance sheet counterpart sector: non-financial corporations (S.11); currency of transaction: all currencies combined; balance sheet suffix: annual growth rate.

Figure 3.1 Loans to non-financial corporations of southern European countries (rates of change)

consisting mainly of a family unit (see Banca d'Italia, 2012, appendix Tav. A14.5, p. 127).

These divergent measures of decline in credit and money supply are related not only to macroeconomic performance but also structurally different financial systems. Thus, the countries in which the banks, particularly the big ones, were more actively involved in the financial crisis in 2007–2008 survived quite well by reviving, or creating *ex novo* new dangerous financial assets, while the banks in the periphery, traditionally lending to enterprises and having as assets mainly government debt, were charged a much higher capital burden or were compelled to register the day by day losses in government bonds portfolio holdings. The anticipated introduction of new regulatory measures included in the Basel 3 financial architecture did not discourage big banks in continuing their trading in activities that increase systemic instability (such as trading in over-the counter (OTC) derivatives). The new version of the Basel Accord still foresees regulatory discounts on capital for institutions that use the CDS market to buy protection (see, for example, Tropeano, 2011). The big banks in the core countries have continued their business as usual encouraged by the new regulation. The banks in the periphery have been hit by higher capital requirements because they have in their portfolio a much higher proportion of loans (see, for example, Montanaro and Tonveronachi, 2011). While the speculation by big banks is flourishing again (see the revival of synthetic CDS in the market and the recent JP Morgan losses), the credit supply to small businesses has been severely constrained. As the number of bad loans increases, banks are still less eager to grant new loans and are struggling to securitize those bad loans or to buy protection against possible losses only in order to decrease short-term capital requirements.

The fall in value of assets also depends on the resurgence of derivatives trading and the convenience attached to their purchase according to the new Basel III rules (see, for example, Tropeano, 2011). According to a recent study, the 20 biggest banks in the Eurozone have in the last year changed the composition of their portfolio by replacing securities with derivatives (Mediobanca, 2011, 2012). The securities held in their portfolios have been falling by 10 per cent with respect to Eurozone's GDP and the share of derivatives has been increasing by the same amount. Even in countries in which private sector indebtedness was not very high, like Italy, a debt deflation process has started because of a policy mix consisting of fiscal austerity and new financial rules for banks.

On the other hand, budgetary policy in the Eurozone did not succeed in thwarting the vicious circles of debt deflation. On the contrary it nurtured them, becoming an active part of their momentum. This is reminiscent of the President Hoover austerity policies pursued in 1929–1932 that crucially contributed to transform the collapse of Wall Street in 1929 into what came to be called the Great Depression. Analogously, Roosevelt succumbed in late 1936 to the pressures of orthodox circles under the illusion that the depression was over and tried prematurely to reduce the budget deficit through restrictive measures that plunged the economy into a new phase of depression that only the war was eventually able to overcome. This time the austerity policies have been no less devastating as they triggered a new form of policy-induced debt deflation. In order to reduce the ratio between debt and GDP, the 'Troika' (EC, ECB and International Monetary Fund) forced the adoption of policies meant to severely cut public expenditure. The ensuing reduction in the absolute value of debt has been typically accompanied by a larger reduction in GDP that forced a new round of austerity measures.

Summing up, the only way out from the Great Recession, as Fisher knew, is reflation. In this case, however, since the vicious circle involves real deflation and real budgetary austerity policies in a crucial way, reflation has to be understood mainly in real terms by sustaining aggregate demand and, in particular, investment. Reflationary policies should be pursued by surplus countries, although a mild but synchronized reflation by periphery countries could help.

3.6 CONCLUDING REMARKS

As Minsky maintained, 'when Irving Fisher . . . identified the characteristics of a debt deflation process . . . [he] identified essential forces which make for the observed instability of capitalist economies' (1982b, p. 393). This chapter has confirmed this opinion, showing that Fisher's theory, aptly modified and updated, still provides useful insights on the causes, consequences and policy implications of the crisis. Notwithstanding his neoclassical theoretical background, he understood that a theory of great depressions has to focus on the analysis of disequilibrium processes that reveal the intrinsic instability of capitalist economies. He also understood that the explanation and control of these processes requires the abandonment of his former monetarist interpretation of the equation of exchange since the money in circulation (or a crucial part of it, 'deposit currency') has to be conceived as endogenous while the velocity of circulation and the money multiplier become highly volatile (Steindl, 1999).

The conceptual and policy revolution initiated by Fisher remained ambiguous and incomplete because Fisher did not liberate his mind from the conceptual straitjacket of the equation of exchange. The subsequent re-elaboration and updating of Fisher's debt deflation theory tended to embed it within a Keynesian conceptual framework. The most ambitious and successful attempt of this kind has so far been that of Minsky who, however, was fully aware that its updating and fitting to evolving facts have to be conceived as a never-ending story: 'although the processes that make for debt deflations ... are persistent characteristics of economies that are capitalistic the actual result of these processes in observable behavior depends upon the institutional context and the force of policy interventions' (Minsky, 1982b, p. 393). This assertion has been confirmed by this chapter that has shown how different the debt deflation processes were in different countries and periods.

In particular, it has been highlighted that in the USA the monetary policy pursued by the Federal Reserve and the treasury expenses to save the banks have at least brought some order in the financial markets. In the European case instead the monetary intervention strategy by the ECB and the rescue interventions have worsened the situation. The combination of the creation of further debt to be serviced and austerity policy has triggered a debt deflation process based on the fall in the value of the net worth of families, enterprises, states. While the incomes are lowered by austerity policy, the payment obligations increase because of various so-called rescue packages and for some periphery states an increase in interest rates too.

The relevance of the policy considerations by Fisher for the recent policy debate within the Eurozone is striking. The recession triggered by the process of debt deflation reduces fiscal income more than public expenditure increases public debt. The orthodox reaction adopted by President Wilson's administration in the early 1930s and the policy authorities of the Eurozone since late 2009 triggered a further vicious circle. The severe austerity policies adopted by the European governments further slowed down economic activity by reducing income more than public expenditure. The ensuing growing debt/income ratio triggered a new round of stricter austerity policies that deteriorate the debt/income ratio.

In light of Fisher's analysis we may say that, under the present circumstances, the current practice of monetary policy can abort in the short run a debt deflation process in the security markets, but cannot start a process of sustainable recovery in the real economy while the financial distress is likely to re-emerge soon. On the other hand, the misuse of monetary policy and of regulation measures in the Eurozone started, and continues to feed, a debt deflation process even in countries in which over-indebtedness was not present or was only present to a limited extent. The policy strategy characterizing the current austerity fad is ultimately based on a deep faith in the self-regulating virtues of unfettered markets so that it is better to 'let nature take her course'. However, as Fisher efficaciously said, in the real world 'it would be as silly and immoral to "let nature take her course" as for a physician to neglect a case of pneumonia' (Fisher, 1933, p. 347).

NOTE

* The research of Alessandro Vercelli leading to these results was funded by the European Union Seventh Framework Programme (FP7/2007-2013), Grant Agreement No. 266800.

REFERENCES

Banca d'Italia (2012), *Relazione del Governatore per il 2011*, Ufficio Stampa B.d'I., Roma.
ECB Bulletin, various issues, ECB Press, Frankfurt.
ECB Statistics, Historical data, ECB Press, Frankfurt.
Fazzari, S. and J. Caskey (1989), 'Debt commitments and aggregate demand: a critique of the neoclassical synthesis and policy', in W. Semmler (ed.), *Financial Dynamics and Business Cycles: New Perspectives*, Armonk, NY: M.E. Sharpe, pp. 188–202.
Fisher, I. (1911), *The Purchasing Power of Money. Its Determination and Relation to Credit Interest and Crises*, New York: A.M. Kelly.
Fisher, I. (1933), 'Debt-deflation theory of great depressions', *Econometrica*, **1**(3), 337–57.
Koo, R.C. (2011), 'The world in balance sheet recession: causes, cure, and politics', *Real World Economics Review*, **58**, 19–37.
Krugman, P. (2012), *End this Depression Now!*, New York: W.W. Norton & Co.
Mediobanca (2011), *Ricerche e studi*, Milan, available at http://www.mbres.it/sites/default/files/resources/download_it/rs_bancheuropaGiugno11.pdf.
Mediobanca (2012), *Ricerche e Studi* (MBRS), Dati cumulativi delle principali banche internazionali e piani di stabilizzazione finanziaria, available at http://www.mbres.it.
Minsky, H.P. (1982a), *Can 'It' Happen Again? Essays on Instability and Finance*, Armonk, NY: M.E. Sharpe.
Minsky, H.P. (1982b), 'Debt-deflation processes in today's institutional environment', *BNL Quarterly Review*, **143**, 375–93.
Montanaro, E. and M. Tonveronachi (2011), 'A critical assessment of the European approach to financial reforms', *PSL Quarterly Review*, **64**(258), 193–226.
Mueller, N., S. Buchholz and H.-P. Blossfeld (2011), 'Wealth inequality in Europe and the delusive egalitarianism of Scandinavian countries', Working Paper, University of Bamberg.
Steindl, F.G. (1999), 'Irving Fisher, the Quantity Theory, and the Great Depression', in H.E. Loef and H. G. Monissen (eds), *The Economics of Irving Fisher. Reviewing the Scientific Work of a Great Economist*, Cheltenham, UK and Northampton, MA, USA: Edward Elgar, pp. 157–69.
Tropeano, D. (2011), 'Finance regulation after the crisis', *International Journal of Political Economy*, **40**(2), 45–60.
Tropeano, D. (2012), 'Quantitative easing in the United States after the crisis:

conflicting views', in L.-P. Rochon and S.Y. Olawoye (eds), *Monetary Policy and Central Banking*, Cheltenham, UK and Northampton, MA, USA: Edward Elgar, pp. 227–42.

Vercelli, A. (2011), 'A perspective on Minsky moments: revisiting the core of the financial instability hypothesis', *Review of Political Economy*, **23**(1), 49–67.

Weller, C.E. and A. Helburn (2009), 'Public policy options to build wealth for America's middle class', Working Paper, Political Economy Research Institute, University of Massachusetts at Amherst, available at http://EconPapers.repec.org/RePEc:uma:periwp:wp210.

Weller, C.E. and J. Lynch (2009), 'Household wealth in freefall', Center for American Economic Progress, available at http://www.americanprogress.org/wpcontent/uploads/issues/2009/04/pdf/wealth_declines.pdf.

Wolff, E. (2007), 'Recent trends in household wealth in the United States: rising debt and the middle-class squeeze', New York University Working Paper No. 502.

Wolfson, M.H. (1996), 'Irving Fisher's debt-deflation theory: its relevance to current conditions', *Cambridge Journal of Economics*, **20**, 315–33.

Wray, L.R. (1992), 'Commercial banks, the central bank and endogenous money', *Journal of Post Keynesian Economics*, **14**(3), 297–310.

PART II

The forces of disequilibria at work: their impact on growth

4. The periphery in the productive globalization: a new dependency?

Alan Cibils and Germán Pinazo

4.1 INTRODUCTION

The demise of the Bretton Woods system in the early 1970s, the crisis of Keynesian demand-management policies and the growing acceptance and popularity of monetarism in academic and policy circles resulted in a radical shift in macroeconomic and financial policies worldwide. Industrialization and domestic market-oriented protectionist policies were abandoned in favour of 'market friendly' policies aimed at improving international and domestic competitiveness through trade, finance and labour market liberalization, privatization of state enterprises and deregulation of goods and financial markets.

These changes in economic policy orientation had their counterpart in academic circles. Keynesian theory, dominant in centre country universities during the post World War II (WWII) period, was displaced by neoclassical theory with roots in Marshallian marginalist analysis and Ricardian trade theory. The theory of (static) comparative advantage and 'new growth theory' became the theoretical framework of choice to explain economic growth. In periphery countries, the rich theoretical heritage of structuralist and dependency analyses, originally developed at the United Nations' Economic Commission for Latin America and the Caribbean (known for its Spanish acronym, CEPAL) in Santiago, Chile, was abandoned. Instead, neoclassical and Ricardian trade theories were widely adopted. Import substitution industrialization policies, characteristic of the post-war era, were replaced by export-oriented industrialization policies (Cypher, 2007).

As these changes took place, and partly because of them, a profound transformation, global in scope, began to occur in manufacturing. Indeed, enabled by a series of developments in information and telecommunications technologies, numerous segments of production were automated and productive strategies of the main transnational manufacturing corporations were transformed, resulting in a global reconfiguration of manufacturing and trade (Arceo, 2005). The impact of these changes on production and trade patterns of various groups of countries will be analyzed in this chapter.

In this context, an interesting debate has developed in the social sciences more broadly and, more specifically, in Latin American development thinking, about the role assigned to the periphery in what we could call the new international division of labour. Specifically, the debate centres on what are the development possibilities for periphery countries in this new context and on whether the concept of dependency continues to be relevant.[1]

The analysis presented in this chapter is a contribution to this debate from two complementary perspectives. First, we review what we consider to be the central theoretical contributions to this debate, focusing on the main Latin American hypotheses and contributions. Second, we synthesize a broad range of statistical information that we believe backs up some of the main hypotheses reviewed.

This chapter is structured as follows. In Section 4.2, we review what we consider to be the main theoretical contributions on the new international division of labour and the current dependency theory debates in Latin America. In Section 4.3, we present and discuss a broad range of statistical data that we believe gives credence to the hypothesis that a new form of dependency for periphery countries has developed under the current globalization of finance and production. Finally, in Section 4.4, the chapter concludes with a brief summary of our main findings.

4.2   THE NEW INTERNATIONAL DIVISION OF LABOUR AND DEPENDENCY THEORY DEBATES

The structuralist theory developed by CEPAL economists diverged in important ways from the mainstream economic theory of Northern academia. Structuralists, like dependency theorists later, rejected the Rostovian conception of development, according to which all capitalist economies evolved from underdevelopment to development following a linear succession of stages – assuming the implementation of correct policies.[2] One key aspect of this process was to produce and trade internationally those goods for which the underdeveloped country had a comparative advantage, following Ricardian trade theory.

Structuralist economists rejected this view, highlighting instead the need to consider specific historical processes and social and political structures of underdeveloped countries, and the characteristics of the relationship between centre and periphery countries.[3] According to this view, periphery country conditions were radically different from those prevailing in countries that industrialized during the Industrial Revolution. For the latter, technology development was an integral part of their development process, responding to their needs and relative factor availability. For periphery countries, technology was imported from the centre, imposing a series of conditions and constraints on their development process unrelated to factor availability or other conditions prevailing in the periphery.

Additionally, primary product specialization in periphery countries, with their prices set in international markets, resulted in productivity gains being transferred to centre countries. On the other hand, centre countries were able to retain productivity gains of their exports (technology) because a unionized labour force could negotiate real wage increases. The result of centre–periphery exchange resulted in a secular tendency to the decline of the periphery's terms of trade, according to the classic works of Raúl Prebisch and Hans Singer.[4] As a result, structuralist economists promoted the implementation of import substitution industrialization (ISI) policies that would, in the long run, allow countries to overcome chronic foreign exchange shortages through the local production of technology. Industrialization would also generate an important income redistribution process as new, higher real wage jobs were created in industry and manufacturing protected by trade barriers. According to structuralist economists, none of this would happen if, following Ricardian trade theory, periphery countries specialized in primary production.

In CEPAL's view, the state in periphery countries had a fundamental role to play, since it needed to build from scratch political and economic structures. The state's role was to plan productive activity, which would require the implementation of tariffs, making credit available, providing incentives to private investors and creating state enterprises where private investment was lacking. State enterprises were key in periphery countries because, unlike what had occurred in centre countries, the development of capital-intensive production went against existing periphery capitalist rationality (Rodríguez, 2001).

The different strains of dependency theory went beyond structuralism and questioned whether periphery countries could ever leave underdevelopment behind. Reformist dependency theories emphasized the role of transnational corporations (TNCs) in bringing about a new international division of labour and the influence exerted by TNCs on periphery institutions and governments. Along these lines, Furtado (1966, 1971) highlighted the central role of technology and how the adoption of technology developed and produced in centre countries deepened the periphery's dependency on the centre. Technology can also contribute to explain key differences between centre and periphery development processes. For centre countries, technology development and production emerged as a necessity of their own economic development process. In the periphery, technology production did not result from its own economic development. Rather, it was imported from the centre, and with it development and production modalities that were not the result of local development needs. This contributed to generate an international division of labour according to which intellectual or conception labour resided primarily in centre countries while the periphery contributed manual labour, thus reinforcing centre–periphery dependency relations.

The terms of the debate on economic development changed profoundly starting in the early 1970s in both centre and periphery countries. The demise of the Bretton Woods system when the USA unilaterally terminated the dollar-gold convertibility and the period of stagflation that ensued were some of the new phenomena that gave rise to economic liberalism in the centre. In Latin America, military dictatorships, the crisis of national industrialization projects due to cyclical foreign exchange shortages and high inflation, and the restructuring that began to take place in international manufacturing redefined development thinking. Latin American intellectuals turned from developing autochthonous thinking based on critical assessments of local reality characteristic of structuralist and dependency theories, to adapting the theories developed in centre countries.

The new liberal theories were built on neoclassical economics, Ricardian trade theory based on static comparative advantages and on new growth theory. Special emphasis was given to learning by doing effects, best practice transmission through competitive imports and technology transfers though foreign direct investment (FDI) (Cypher, 2007).

New growth theory was key in revitalizing the neoclassical framework, making it possible to move beyond the restrictive assumptions of balanced trade and full employment derived from productive specialization in Ricardian theory.[5] Assuming increasing returns in the traded goods sector, resulting from learning by doing and synergy effects from technology spillovers, and positive externalities from research and development, Ricardian trade effects not only materialize but endure in time (Adelman, 2002). With these modifications to the neoclassical framework, orthodox economists predicted that trade openness and export-oriented industrialization would have positive and lasting effects on a country's economic structure.

Latin American development thinking experienced significant changes in this new economic and political context. CEPAL's structuralists became neostructuralists, substantially transforming many of the structuralist assumptions, approaches and recommendations in a process that was not exempt of controversies. Not only did their approach to industrialization, economic development and policy change, but the interdisciplinary approach and rejection of the North's universalist theories characteristic of structuralist thought were explicitly abandoned.[6]

Officially, CEPAL has acknowledged that these changes were controversial. As Bielschowsky (2009, p. 177) observes, '[f]or some, this meant surrendering to neoliberalism, but for others it was an alternative that would make it possible to continue influencing the region's destinies from ECLAC's [Economic Commission for Latin America and the Caribbean] traditional theoretical and methodological perspective'. On the other hand, according to Guillén-Romo, neostructuralism builds primarily on a critique of the social consequences of neoliberalism rather than on a critique of its theoretical basis. Therefore, rather than constituting an alternative to neoliberalism, neostructuralism shares many of its basic premises. As a result, CEPAL thinking lost much of its originality and relevance (Guillén-Romo, 2007, p. 312).

In sum, development thinking in the Latin American periphery changed its focus from industrialization based on state planning and policies to how to make best use of the opportunities provided by the international division of labour through technological innovation. Changes in the international division of labour, particularly in manufacturing, played a key role in this process and it is still unclear whether these changes are to the periphery's benefit.

4.2.1   The New International Division of Labour

Perhaps the main factor contributing to the changes described above is what has been labelled the globalization of production or new international division of labour, which began to emerge in the mid 1970s (Bresser-Pereira, 2007). Over the past 40 years, there have been a number of technological developments that, applied to the process of production and commercialization, have resulted in what has been alternatively labelled global value chains or internationalization of production (Arrighi, 1997; Kaplinsky, 2000, 2005; Gereffi, 2001; Arceo, 2005, 2009; Minian, 2009). As a result of these developments, it is possible to produce different parts of a given good in different geographic locations based on the latter's economic incentives. It is therefore possible to design a product in one country, produce it in a different country and sell it in yet other countries, responding to specific regional demands, public policies, access to natural resources and labour cost differentials.

In this new context, transnational corporations have experienced important transformations in order to assert control over globalized production, redefining geographic patterns of production and trade (Gereffi and Korzeniewicz, 1994; Gutman, and Gorenstein, 2003). This was not a spontaneous process, nor was it a scientific shock external to the logic of capital accumulation. According to Duménil and Levy (2007), the globalization of production originated during the crisis caused by the fall in the rate of profit in centre capitalist economies in the 1970s. Seeking higher profits, transnational corporations transferred labour-intensive segments of production to the periphery where labour costs were lower. This process was made possible by the technological developments mentioned above, which together with lower freight costs, enabled global or regional corporation headquarters to control global production.

According to Arceo (2005, p. 28), the result of this process was a new type of corporation, the transnational corporation (TNC), which was structurally different from their previous incarnation, the multinational corporation (MNC). In the case of the MNC, its branches engaged locally in autonomous production that frequently used highly specialized technology and were frequently managed by local managers who were supposed to carry out headquarter-defined annual production plans. In the case of the TNC, production objectives are determined on a short-term, often daily, basis, depending on demand variations and branch capacity availability. This new mode of TNC operation is often enabled by the use of programmable means of production that allow units spread around the world to take on a range of different tasks.

Developments in information and communications technologies were key to the emergence of the new international division of labour. According to Arceo, information technology made possible the effective geographic displacement of the different segments of manufacturing and lower freight costs turned it profitable, allowing for the shipping of assembly activities and intermediate inputs as well as finished goods. It is therefore now possible to direct from the historically industrialized centre countries production processes with high technological content that are physically located in what have been historically underdeveloped periphery countries. The products of this process can then be exported to other regions of the world.

During the period of ISI in the mid twentieth century, FDI sought strong internal markets where capital goods could be over-amortized (Marini, 1977). However, starting in the mid 1970s with the advent of export-led industrialization, the opposite is true. In their classic work on the new international division of labour, Froebel et al. (1980, p. 34) point out that this new FDI seeks an abundant labour force with year-round availability, which can achieve high productivity with little training and that is not unionized, from which to select workers with specific characteristics (for example, young women for repetitive tasks and so on).

In other words, one of the main objectives of this new, increasingly transnationalized productive investment is to compete internationally on the basis of securing increasingly lower labour costs. 'Rising costs of production in home economies . . . are a potentially major push factor for developing-country TNCs. Consequently, all else being equal, host countries with low costs of labour or other required resources are more likely to receive inward FDI' (UNCTAD, 2006, p. 155).

In the following section we analyze a series of aggregate indicators that we believe illustrate key aspects of the new international division of labour. Specifically, we track the evolution and characteristics of FDI flows during recent decades, their impact on the productive structures and real wages of different groups of centre and periphery countries.

4.3 THE NEW INTERNATIONAL DIVISION OF LABOUR: INDICATORS

Based on the theories that sustain the export-led industrialization framework,[7] economists proposed policies and made multiple predictions about expected results of their implementation. In this section we focus on a subset of these predictions. The first prediction is that the periphery's incorporation into the new international division of labour through incoming FDI flows will promote technological change and increase productivity. Second, FDI will have spillover effects on the economy resulting in a virtuous cycle of generalized technological and productive modernization. Finally, as a country moves towards Ricardian productive specialization through export-oriented industrialization, per capita income will rise resulting in generalized welfare improvements.

In what follows we analyze aggregate indicators for different countries and groups of countries in order to better understand the process of productive globalization and its impact on national and regional economies. Additionally, we are able to tentatively evaluate whether the predictions enumerated in the previous paragraph have materialized. We examine data on FDI flows, hourly wages, import content of exports and output intermediate import ratios.

The evolution of inward and outward FDI flows for different groups of countries and for the period 1970–2012 in five-year averages is shown in Table 4.1. Three aspects of the data presented are worth noting. First, FDI flows have experienced a sustained and significant growth over the last four decades. Indeed, the first line of Table 4.1 shows a phenomenal growth in total FDI flows over the last 40 years. Measured in current

Table 4.1 *Inward and outward FDI flows to selected regions, 1970–2012 (as percentage of total flows in millions of current dollars, five-year averages)*

	1970–1974	1975–1979	1980–1984	1985–1989	1990–1994	1995–1999	2000–2004	2005–2009	2010–2012
OUTWARD									
Total (millions of current dollars)	17,467	30,472	57,732	128,124	201,304	604,114	842,132	1,501,154	1,470,324
Developed economies	99.39%	98.32%	94.18%	93.73%	88.53%	87.33%	88.13%	79.62%	68.10%
Transition economies	0.00%	0.00%	0.00%	0.00%	0.00%	0.23%	0.98%	2.76%	4.15%
Developing economies	0.61%	1.68%	5.82%	6.27%	11.21%	12.36%	10.90%	17.62%	27.75%
Africa	0.25%	0.55%	1.17%	0.31%	0.61%	0.50%	0.07%	0.47%	0.66%
Latin America and Caribbean	0.26%	0.67%	1.64%	1.04%	1.87%	2.69%	3.63%	4.76%	7.20%
Asia	0.11%	0.46%	3.00%	4.92%	8.71%	9.18%	7.20%	12.36%	19.84%
INWARD									
Total (millions of current dollars)	17,467	30,472	57,732	128,124	201,304	604,114	842,132	1,501,154	1,470,324
Developed economies	77.50%	72.40%	68.07%	81.21%	69.47%	66.73%	69.24%	60.45%	46.87%
Transition economies	0.00%	0.00%	0.02%	0.00%	0.68%	1.35%	2.17%	4.99%	5.88%
Developing economies	22.50%	27.60%	31.92%	18.78%	29.86%	31.92%	28.59%	34.56%	47.26%
Africa	6.55%	3.94%	2.62%	2.49%	2.15%	1.64%	2.16%	3.15%	3.23%
Latin America and Caribbean	10.82%	12.54%	10.74%	6.15%	7.93%	11.43%	9.41%	9.41%	15.54%
Asia	4.52%	10.95%	18.31%	10.02%	19.66%	18.80%	16.98%	21.89%	28.32%

Source: Authors' calculations based on UNCTAD data.

dollars, total incoming FDI flows are 7000 per cent greater in 2005–2010 than they were in 1970–1975 and 2500 per cent greater than in 1980–1985.

A second important observation that emerges from Table 4.1 is that developed countries have a dominant role both as generators (outward) and recipients (inward) of FDI flows. Developed countries are the main generators of FDI flows throughout the entire period. Even if other regions of the world have grown considerably, developed economies still account for almost 70 per cent of outward flows. Until the early 2000s, developed countries also received more than half of FDI flows, although at a declining rate. However, as of the second decade of this century, more than half of FDI flows were going to regions other than developed countries.

Finally, Table 4.1 also shows that developing countries have become increasingly recipients of – and to a lesser extent generators of – FDI flows. Asia plays an increasingly dominant role as a recipient of FDI flows mainly due to the emergence of China. FDI flows to Latin America show considerable variations, ending the period with a moderately higher value than its previous peak in the late 1970s. In Asia, China has become the major recipient of flows. In the early 1980s, China accounted for approximately 3 per cent of flows to developing countries. By the mid 1990s it accounted for 25 per cent of flows to developing countries, decreasing to approximately 18 per cent by 2010.[8] Outward flows from developing countries reflect a strong growth from the year 2000, particularly flows originating in Asia due to the increasingly prominent role of China in the world economy.

The increase in FDI flows has not been a neutral process for developing countries. Global investment dynamics have been characterized by the relocalization in the periphery of a significant number of industrial and manufacturing productive segments that had been previously located in centre countries (Arceo, 2005). According to Arrighi (1997, p.188), 'we are in the presence of a new division of labour where the centre is predominantly the locus of the intellectual activities of corporate capital and the periphery is the locus of muscles and nerves'.[9] As a result of this process, we can highlight three issues for periphery countries that are recipients of FDI. First, there has been an important increase in employment in manufacturing in the periphery. Second, there has been an increase in productivity of labour in the periphery. Finally, there has been an important transformation of the export profile of the periphery.

China plays a special role in the new international division of labour. This is partly due to the size of its internal market, to its low labour costs and also to the assurances that the Chinese Communist Party offers those willing to invest. Based on reforms that began in the 1970s (and accelerated in the 1990s), China has experienced profound transformations that enable us to talk of it as a new locomotive of contemporary capitalism.

Indeed, China's opening up to global capitalism resulted in the incorporation of 20 per cent of the world's population (in 1990) into the capitalist realm with two important effects. First, this incorporation represented an enormous source of low-cost labour for this newly fragmented global industry. As an example, in 2009 China's employment in manufacturing was 99 million strong, that is, more than 50 per cent larger than the combined employment in manufacturing of the USA, France, Germany, Japan, South Korea, Mexico and the UK.[10] In addition, average daily labour cost in China in 2009 was approximately $1.5, that is, 6 per cent of the US labour cost, 4 per cent of the Eurozone and 22 per cent of Brazil. As we shall see below, this has enabled China to become the main world exporter of manufactures of high technological content (exporting three times more than the USA).[11]

A second, related point is that this incorporation also resulted in a huge source of demand for the capitalist centre's production. China's industrialization in the context of the new international division of labour has not only resulted in a substantial growth of its gross domestic product (GDP) per capita, but also in an exponential growth of imports (more than 40 per cent per year since China joined the World Trade Organization in 2001) with a resulting 12 per cent share of total world imports.

In some aspects, the Chinese experience has not been unique. Table 4.2 shows the evolution of total labour productivity relative to US labour productivity for a selected group of countries. Two aspects of these data are worth highlighting. First, total labour productivity has increased significantly in underdeveloped countries over the last four decades. Second, the productivity gap between some underdeveloped and developed countries has also decreased very significantly.

A salient aspect of Table 4.2 is the evolution of productivity in three of the Asian countries we have selected (Singapore, Taiwan and South Korea). These countries have not only been privileged recipients of FDI flows, but have also managed labour productivity growths of 5.4 per cent, 6.2 per cent and 8.6 per cent, respectively. To understand the relative importance of these numbers, we can compare them to those of Germany, Japan and the USA, which were 2.5 per cent, 3.5 per cent and 4.4 per cent, respectively.

Interestingly, in Latin America both Argentina and Brazil experienced relative productivity increases during ISI decades, and with the advent of neoliberalism previous gains were lost. Losses were not across the board, however. In Argentina, hourly labour productivity in manufacturing has grown at about 7 per cent per year between 1990 and 2010.[12] This has

Table 4.2 GDP per employed worker relative to the USA for selected countries and years

	France	Germany	USA	Russia	China	India	Japan	Malaysia	Singapore	South Korea	Argentina	Brazil
1960	56.7	49.9	100.0	0.0	3.7	6.7	26.8	16.7	25.3	14.9	47.2	20.6
1970	73.2	60.1	100.0	0.0	3.3	7.0	50.0	17.6	36.5	19.3	50.5	22.2
1980	85.5	69.8	100.0	0.0	4.0	6.3	64.3	25.0	48.7	27.5	55.3	30.0
1990	90.2	72.5	100.0	31.9	5.3	7.4	75.5	28.0	58.8	43.1	36.1	21.9
2000	83.2	68.2	100.0	20.5	8.0	8.6	67.9	32.9	70.4	56.7	41.5	20.6
2010	77.4	63.5	100.0	27.3	19.4	12.7	66.7	35.3	72.9	65.9	41.5	20.1

Source: Authors' calculations based on data from the Conference Board Total Economy Database, http://www.conference-board.org/data/economydatabase/, accessed 5 January 2016.

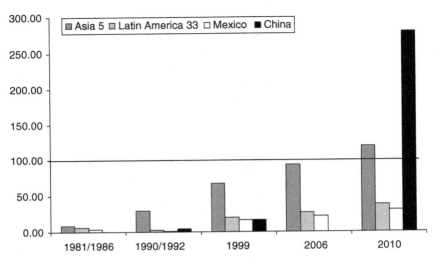

Source: Authors' calculations based on UN Comtrade data.

Figure 4.1   High technology exports for selected countries relative to the USA (USA = 100)

resulted in a sustained reduction of the hourly manufacturing labour productivity gap with the USA of approximately 30 per cent between 1990
and 2010 (measured in constant 2005 dollars).

Figure 4.1 shows high technology content exports for some regions and
countries. We have chosen this specific indicator to illustrate how the new
international division of labour is different from the one prevalent in the
post-WWII era, where centre and periphery exports were predominantly,
respectively, technology and primary goods. Clearly visible in Figure 4.1 is
the place of South-east Asia and China in the production and export of
high technology content manufactures. According to the United Nations'
Comtrade database,[13] China's high technology exports grew 9000 per cent
between 1992 and 2010, while Asian tigers' (Malaysia, Singapore, Taiwan
and South Korea) combined high technology exports for the same period
grew 1000 per cent. Altogether, China and the Asian tigers have moved
from a practically non-existent participation in high technology content
production and exports in the early 1980s, to represent more than two-
thirds of global trade of these products.

It is worth noting that this process has not resulted in a corresponding
increase in these regions' participation in global value added nor in a reduction of the wage gaps (measured in dollars) with centre countries. With the

exception of South Korea, this is partially the result of the periphery's participation in the labour-intensive segments of production processes (with few linkages to domestic economic structures), which are directed and managed from corporate headquarters in centre countries. In the case of the five South-east Asian countries mentioned above, their participation in world value added has remained constant at approximately 2 per cent since the mid 1980s, according to International Monetary Fund (IMF) data. In the case of China, as a result of radical economic reforms, its participation in world value added has grown from 2 per cent to 17 per cent over the last three decades according to the same source. However, China's export product participation in world value added and its labour costs continue to be among the lowest of this globalized production system.

To complete our partial analysis of the new international division of labour, we present data on import content of manufacturing and on wages for selected groups of countries. We use data from the Organisation for Economic Co-operation and Development (OECD) and the US Bureau of Labor Statistics (BLS). For our analysis, and based partially on data availability, we have assembled the following groups of countries: (1) centre (USA, Great Britain, France, Germany and Japan); (2) BRICS (Brazil, Russia, India, China and South Africa); (3) South Korea and Taiwan; (4) Latin America and Turkey (Argentina, Mexico, Chile and Turkey); (5) South-east Asian countries (Indonesia, Singapore, Thailand and Vietnam); and (6) European periphery (Bulgaria, Czech Republic, Lithuania, Latvia, Poland, Romania and Slovakia).

Table 4.3 shows average imported intermediate inputs in manufacturing and the average import content of exports for the groups of countries enumerated. These data allow us to complete the picture on the contribution of local production to each region's production.

Looking first at the average imported intermediate inputs in manufacturing, we note that group 5 (South-east Asia) experienced a strong decrease in imported intermediate inputs from 55 per cent to 38 per cent. Group 3 (South Korea and Taiwan) also experience a drop during the period, although of a smaller magnitude (35 per cent to 32 per cent) and with a lower starting percentage than group 5. In the case of group 4 (Latin America and Turkey) we observe an inverse trend, with intermediate input imports increasing from 27 per cent to 38 per cent, and increasing sharply towards the end of the period. Group 6 (European periphery) also experienced a considerable increase in intermediate input imports, from 44 per cent to 55 per cent, with the sharper increase in the first five years. Groups 1 and 2 (centre countries and BRICS) experience moderate increases throughout, although their overall percentages are significantly lower than the rest of the groups.

Table 4.3   *Average percentage of intermediate inputs and import content of exports for groups of countries, 1995–2005*

Groups of countries	Average imported inputs in mfg			Import content of exports		
	1995	2000	2005	1995	2000	2005
1. Centre	0.23	0.28	0.28	0.19	0.23	0.26
2. BRICS	0.15	0.19	0.19	0.14	0.18	0.24
3. South Korea + Taiwan	0.35	0.31	0.32	0.40	0.42	0.48
4. Latin America + Turkey	0.27	0.29	0.38	0.20	0.23	0.35
5. South-east Asia	0.55	0.55	0.38	0.46	0.48	0.36
6. European periphery	0.44	0.53	0.55	0.41	0.49	0.48

Source: Authors' calculations based on OECD data.

Looking at the import content of exports (the three right-hand columns of Table 4.3), we can observe similar trends as those described above for all groups, but with some differences worth highlighting. Group 4 experiences an important increase in the import content of exports. BRICS countries also exhibit an important increase, although overall levels are significantly lower than those of group 4. The rest of the groups of countries, with the exception of group 5 (as before), experience increases but of lesser magnitude for the period studied.

Worth noting is the relatively lower weight of imports for BRICS countries and South Korea and Taiwan. In the case of BRICS, it is even lower than for centre countries. A possible explanation for this is the role of South Korea, Taiwan and BRICS in the new international division of labour. For reasons related to specificities of regional markets (logistics, consumer characteristics, market structure and size), these countries have taken on the role of regional centres of operation of a new form of manufacturing planned on a global scale in corporate headquarters in the centre, but which still maintains a regional scale in many cases. Specifically, due mostly to the scale of their internal market, these countries serve as a base for many of the corporations that function as suppliers for branches and other industries located in other periphery countries of the region, which essentially become huge assembly platforms.

In sum, regarding manufacturing productive structures, the new international division of labour exhibits three clearly differentiated trends. First, the South-east Asian countries have managed to reduce intermediate input

*Table 4.4   Hourly wage gap between centre and different groups of
periphery countries 1996–2010 (current dollars)*

	Centre–Brazil	Centre–S. Korea + Taiwan	Centre–Latin America	Centre–South-east Asia	Centre–European periphery
1996	14.73	12.43	15.46	10.15	17.28
1997	13.77	11.88	14.26	8.96	16.32
1998	14.09	13.37	14.1	9.43	16.26
1999	16.1	12.98	14.25	9.55	16.58
2000	15.52	11.82	13.48	8.55	16.22
2001	15.75	11.79	12.93	7.96	15.73
2002	16.99	12.21	15.94	8.88	16.2
2003	19.6	14.28	18.46	11.07	18.25
2004	21.22	15.53	20.15	12.61	19.69
2005	20.95	14.75	20.11	12.97	19.67
2006	20.72	14.14	20.00	13.00	19.59
2007	22.06	15.46	21.43	13.51	20.36
2008	22.98	18.15	22.3	12.72	20.7
2009	22.44	18.6	21.77	13.24	20.62
2010	20.88	17.05	20.32	11.72	20.4

Source: Authors' calculations based on BLS data.

imports and the import content of exports. Second, for the rest of the groups with the exception of BRICS, the opposite is true even if differences exist between regions. Worth noting is the performance of Latin America, where the growth of imports for manufacturing is very strong.[14] Third, BRICS countries show consistently low levels of imports, indicating a strategy of becoming regional supply centres of inputs for manufacturing.

Finally, Table 4.4 shows the evolution of the average hourly wage gap between the different groups of countries and the centre between 1996 and 2011. Similar to data presented in Table 4.3, we can observe a considerable difference between the South-east Asian countries and the rest of the groups. Indeed, the wage gap between South-east Asian and centre countries remains relatively unchanged throughout, exhibiting a decreasing trend towards the end of the period. On the other hand, the wage gaps between the rest of the groups or countries and centre countries has an increasing trend throughout. The greatest gap is for the BRICS, even though the gap for Latin American and European periphery countries has similar values.

Table 4.4 clearly shows that the new international division of labour has not resulted in wage convergence for its different regions. To the contrary, an increasing wage gap between the centre and the different periphery regions, with the exception of the South-east Asian countries, is clearly reflected in the data. The obvious conclusion is that in the new international division of labour, periphery countries compete mainly by lowering wages, resulting in a race to the bottom as further evidence of the fallacy of composition pointed out by Blecker and Razmi (2010).

4.4   CLOSING REFLECTIONS: RENEWED DEPENDENCY?

In the preceding sections we have summarized what we consider the main changes in Latin American thinking on development and selected data on the new international division of labour. Latin American theories transitioned from CEPAL thinking, with its original autochthonous elements and focused on specific development problems on Latin America, to using theories imported from Northern (mostly US) academia, characterized by a linear and ahistorical conception of the development process and with no reference to Latin America's specific context.

We also analyzed a series of aggregate indicators of what has come to be called the new international division of labour. Data reflect a different reality than that described by the new development thinking. In spite of changes in productive structure and activities, rather than convergence between periphery and centre countries, we observe the persistence of substantial differences in which the former compete in reducing labour costs and the latter continue to be the locus of intellectual and conception labour. However, we also observe significantly different trajectories within the periphery. South-east Asian and some BRICS countries (especially China and Brazil) have managed to place themselves as suppliers of manufactured goods to manufacturing sectors in other periphery countries.

Based on these stylized observations and the structural characteristics of present day capitalism, we would like to formulate the following hypotheses in the hope of contributing to current debates on development in the periphery.

Our first hypothesis is that the new international division of labour has disarticulated the material foundations upon which much of the Latin American development thinking in the twentieth century was built. The radical redefinition of the scale, design and trade of industrial manufactured goods that characterizes the new international division of labour is antithetical to the developmentalist discourse together inasmuch industrialization is no longer a synonym of development of the internal market.[15] Unlike what happened during ISI, corporations – regardless of their geographic origin – that choose a given country to establish some of their productive activities do not need to develop a supply chain structure nor sell most of their production in that country's market. Indeed, given the possibility of establishing regional and even global supply chains, the development of integrated industrial systems in small periphery countries is economically irrational. From the point of view of this new transnational productive capital, wage costs are today (perhaps more than ever before) a variable to be controlled and minimized rather than a demand factor to be stimulated.

Our second hypothesis is that the capacity of the state to intervene has been significantly eroded inasmuch as the processes that have given rise to this new transnationalized production and the class conflicts it generates are settled in loci far beyond a national state's reach. Thus, the state's ability to set trade policy, fiscal and monetary policies, and labour regulation, to mention a few, have become strongly constrained by the free mobility of capital and the threat by TNCs to move production elsewhere or to take the country to international courts for settlement of investment disputes.

In sum, one can conclude that the new international division of labour has resulted in a substantial erosion of the possibility of intervening at the national level to address problems of production and class alliance. In this way, the capacity to articulate and implement policies aimed at the periphery's modernization and the achievement of a more egalitarian distribution of income has been lost. Developmentalism, for all its shortcomings, was based on the premise that it was possible to build productive structures linked to local consumption capacity in periphery countries.

In some regards, the neodevelopmentalist discourse is a product of these tensions. Taking the new international division of labour as a starting point, neodevelopmentalism promotes a strategy that, at least implicitly, assumes that periphery countries should (and can) compete with each other and with centre countries for a place in global industrial production.[16] However, it is difficult to imagine how this can become a job creation process with high wages in the periphery when the centre-determined logic of the new international division of labour is the rationalization of domestic production structures, the search for low wage locations and the establishment of regional supply chains. In other words, even if one accepted that corporations located in a given periphery country could develop some degree of industrialization through learning and innovation dynamics, this cannot constitute a strategy for *all* periphery countries. This clearly diverges from developmentalist thinking, where ISI was indeed a strategy that all periphery countries could aspire to implement with some degree of success.

In the context of the periphery – and Latin American periphery in particular – today, it is relevant and appropriate once again to analyze centre–periphery relations using dependency concepts and analysis. In this regard, we find useful Cardoso's (1971 [1995]) definition of dependency as a dynamic, 'historically referenced' process. This process requires that social scientists make an effort to understand 'concrete' forms of capitalist expansion that condition (and exist through) specific periphery development situations.

The crisis of neoliberal experiments in the Latin American periphery has resulted in the emergence in the last decade and a half of official discourses that reflect a certain degree of nostalgia for the developmentalism of the mid twentieth century. This discourse clearly reflects the belief that national development can still be achieved, ignoring the profound transformations contained in the new international division of labour. However, as anthropologist Escobar (2007) suggests, what has perhaps been lost is the ability to articulate a discourse on development and income distribution within the specific limits of today's academic discourse. In other words, it will continue to be argued that development must be achieved but without radically discussing the property and dependency structures on which the periphery was built and continues to be sustained. As long as these structures are not fully accounted for and dissected, it will be difficult to leave this new dependency behind.

NOTES

1. For example, Amin (2003), Arceo (2005), Beigel (2006), Hernández López (2005) and Kay and Gwynne (2000).
2. To be fair, the linear conception of development is not exclusively Rostow´s. A linear view of development is also characteristic of many Marxist analyses – the development of the productive forces exacerbates contradictions leading from capitalism to socialism – even if the overall conception of society and capitalism are fundamentally different from Rostow's.
3. See, for example, Prebisch (1962) and Furtado (1966, 1971), among others. Indeed, it was CEPAL's structuralist economists that introduced the centre-periphery terminology into the economic analysis of underdevelopment (Sztulwark, 2005).
4. While generally referred to as the Prebisch-Singer hypothesis, the observation emerges from two separate but concurrent publications by these economists: Prebisch (1962, originally published in 1949) and Singer (1950).
5. See Ackerman and Gallagher (2008) for a critical survey of these issues.
6. See Bielschowsky (2009) for a critical analysis of similarities and differences between structuralist and neostructuralist thinking. For Guillén-Romo (2007, p. 312), neostructuralists discarded fundamental aspects of structuralist analysis, such as social class, inequality or income distribution. For Sztulwark (2005, p. 106), neostructuralism directly tried to adapt centre countries' theoretical developments to the Latin American periphery.
7. These theories are Ricardian comparative advantage trade theory, new growth theory and neostructuralism. See discussion in Section 4.2.

8. Authors' calculations based on UNCTAD data.
9. Authors' translation. This analysis is shared by Arceo (2005, 2009).
10. International Labor Comparisons, US Bureau of Labor Statistics, http://www.bls.gov/fls, accessed 20 November 2013.
11. http://www.bls.gov/fls, accessed 20 November 2013.
12. Centro de Estudios para la Producción (2011). Data available at http://www.industria.gob.ar/wp-content/uploads/2012/12/Fichas-sectoriales-TRIMESTRALES-2014.xlsx, accessed 5 January 2016.
13. http://comtrade.un.org/, accessed 28 December 2015.
14. This is consistent with the economic strategy followed by many Latin American countries, which has resulted in a substantial reprimarization, as described by Pérez-Caldentey and Vernengo (2010).
15. Indeed, as Pinazo (2015) shows for the case of the Argentine automotive industry, the contrary is true.
16. This strategy ignores the fallacy of composition eloquently highlighted by Blecker, Razmi, Palley and others: what may be good for a given country is not necessarily good for every country if all embark on the same strategy, competing with each other. For example, see Blecker and Razmi (2010), Razmi and Blecker (2008) and Palley (2011).

REFERENCES

Ackerman, F. and K. Gallagher (2008), 'The shrinking gains from global trade liberalization in computable general equilibrium models: a critical assessment', *International Journal of Political Economy*, **37**(1), 50–77.
Adelman, I. (2002), 'Falacias de la teoría del desarrollo y sus implicaciones de política', in G. Meier and J. Stiglitz (eds), *Fronteras de la economía del desarrollo: El futuro en perspectiva*, Bogotá: Alfaomega, pp. 91–124.
Amin, S. (2003), *Más allá del capitalismo senil: Por un Siglo XXI no norteamericano*, Buenos Aires: Paidós.
Arceo, E. (2005), 'El impacto de la globalización en la periferia y las nuevas y viejas formas de dependencia', *Cuadernos del CENDES*, **22**(50), 25–61.
Arceo, E. (2009), 'América Latina, Los límites al crecimiento exportador sin cambio estructural', in E. Arceo and E. Basualdo (eds), *Los condicionantes de la crisis en América Latina*, Buenos Aires: CLASO, pp. 61–128.
Arrighi, G. (1997), *A ilusao do desenvolvimiento*, Petrópolis: Editora Voces.
Beigel, F. (2006), 'Vida, muerte y resurrección de las "teorías de la dependencia"', in B. Levy, C. Rodríguez Enríquez, M. Schorr et al. (eds), *Crítica y teoría en el pensamiento social latinoamericano*, Buenos Aires: CLACSO, pp. 287–326.
Bielschowsky, R. (2009), 'Sixty years of ECLAC: structuralism and neostructuralism', *CEPAL Review*, **97**, 171–92.
Blecker, R. and A. Razmi (2010), 'Export-led growth, real exchange rates and the fallacy of composition', in M. Setterfield (ed.), *Handbook of Alternative Theories of Economic Growth*, Cheltenham, UK and Northampton, MA, USA: Edward Elgar, pp. 379–96.
Bresser-Pereira, L. (2007), 'Estado y mercado en el nuevo desarrollismo', *Nueva Sociedad*, **210**, 110–25.
Cardoso, F. (1971), 'Teoria da Dependência ou análises concretas de situações de dependência?', *Revista Estudos Sôbre Teoria e Método em Sociologia*, CEBRAP,

São Paulo, 25–47, reprinted in '"Teoría de la dependencia" o análisis de situaciones concretas de dependencia?' (1995), *Política y Sociedad*, **17**, 107–15.

Cypher, J. (2007), 'Shifting developmental paradigms in Latin America, is neoliberalism history?', in E.P. Caldentey and M. Vernengo (eds), *Ideas, Policies and Economic Development in the Americas*, London: Routledge, pp. 31–61.

Duménil, G. and D. Levy (2007), *Crisis y salida de la crisis, Orden y desorden neoliberales*, Mexico City: Fondo de Cultura Económica.

Escobar, A. (2007), *La invención del tercer mundo, Construcción y deconstrucción del desarrollo*, Caracas: El perro y la rana.

Froebel, F., J. Heinrichs and O. Kreye (1980), *The New Industrial Division of Labour: Structural Unemployment in Industrialized Countries and Industrialization in Developing Countries*, Cambridge: Cambridge University Press.

Furtado, C. (1966), 'Hacia una ideología del desarrollo', *El Trimestre Económico*, **33**(3), 379–91.

Furtado, C. (1971), 'Dependencia externa y teoría económica', *El Trimestre Económico*, **38**(2), 587–603.

Gereffi, G. (2001), 'Las cadenas productivas como marco analítico para la globalización', *Problemas del Desarrollo*, **32**(125), 9–37.

Gereffi, G. and M. Korzeniewicz (eds) (1994), *Commodity Chains and Global Capitalism*, Santa Barbara: Praeger Publishers.

Guillén-Romo, H. (2007), 'De la orden cepalina del desarrollo al neoestructuralismo en América Latina', *Revista Comercio Exterior*, **57**, 295–313.

Gutman, G. and S. Gorenstein (2003), 'Territorio y sistemas agroalimentarios, Enfoques conceptuales y dinámicas recientes en la Argentina', *Desarrollo Económico*, **42**(168), 563–87.

Hernández López, R.C. (2005), 'La dependencia a debate', *Latinoamérica*, **40**, 11–54.

Kaplinsky, R. (2000), 'Globalization, and unequalization; what can be learned from value chain analysis?', *Journal of Development Studies*, **27**(2), 117–46.

Kaplinsky, R. (2005), *Globalization, Poverty and Inequality: Between a Rock and a Hard Place*, Cambridge: Polity.

Kay, C. and R. Gwynne (2000), 'Relevance of structuralist and dependency theories in the neoliberal period: a Latin American perspective', *Journal of Developing Societies*, **16**(1), 49–69.

Marini, R.-M. (1977), 'La acumulación capitalista mundial y el subimperialismo', *Cuadernos Políticos*, **12**, 21–39.

Minian, I. (2009), 'Nuevamente sobre la segmentación internacional de la producción', *Economía UNAM*, **6**(17), 46–68.

Palley, T. (2011), 'The contradictions of export-led growth', Public Policy Brief 119/2011, Levy Institute of Bard College.

Pérez-Caldentey, E. and M. Vernengo (2010), 'Back to the future: Latin America's current development strategy', *Journal of Post Keynesian Economics*, **32**(4), 623–43.

Pinazo, G. (2015), *El desarrollismo argentino: Una mirada crítica desde la industria automotriz*, Buenos Aires: UNGS Ediciones.

Prebisch, R. (1962), 'El desarrollo económico de América Latina y algunos de sus principales problemas', *Boletín Económico para América Latina*, **7**(1), 1–24.

Razmi, A. and R. Blecker (2008), 'Developing country exports of manufactures: moving up the ladder to escape the fallacy of composition?', *Journal of Development Studies*, **44**(1), 21–48.

Rodríguez, O. (2001), 'Prebisch: the continuing validity of his basic ideas', *CEPAL Review*, **75**, 39–50.

Singer, H. (1950), 'The distribution of gains between investing and borrowing countries', *American Economic Review*, **40**(2), 473–85.

Sztulwark, S. (2005), *El estructuralismo latinoamericano, Fundamentos y transformaciones del pensamiento económico de la periferia*, Buenos Aires: UNGS Ediciones and Prometeo Libros.

UNCTAD (2006), *World Investment Report 2006, FDI from Developing and Transition Economies: Implications for Development*, New York and Geneva: United Nations.

5. Latin America in the new international order: new forms of economic organizations and old forms of surplus appropriation

Noemi Levy*

5.1 INTRODUCTION

Throughout its history, Latin America has been unable to generate an economic boom and achieve a balanced development of its productive forces. The region's economies are characterized by their notable technology gaps and a high level of financial dependence that is needed to stabilize their growth. This phenomenon has existed independently of the region's prevailing accumulation models (import-substitution industrialization (ISI) and the neoliberal-financialized model).

There are various explanations for the region's structural dependence. From the heterodox perspective, two groups stand out: one argument suggests that the predominance of foreign capital has prevented the development of a growth strategy that will generate the balanced development of productive forces and expand the domestic market with external balances. The other argues that the absence of financing and underdeveloped financial markets are the elements responsible for the economic gap, because they are unable to convert the economic surpluses into savings that recirculate into production or debt cancellation.

This issue has often been addressed by dependency theory and financialization theory. Both agree that the economic gap is caused by the hegemonic countries' withdrawal of the economic surplus derived from the domination of foreign capital in production and through international trade; this occurs in addition to the lack of liquidity toward production in an environment of deepening capital markets.

Dependency theory prevailed from the end of the nineteenth century to the 1970s. It highlighted the limitations (or impossibility) of the less developed countries achieving the capitalist development of the relations of production due to the disassociation of the export sector from the rest of the productive sectors, growing disequilibria in international trade and, as a result of the region's high concentration of income, reduced technological development with low levels of investment, all of which are explained by the withdrawal of the surplus from the local economies by the hegemonic countries. These assumptions served as the basis for theories describing 'underdevelopment–development', 'center–periphery' and 'developing–developed countries'.

The neoliberal revolution in the 1970s imposed a new explanation for the economic gap, focused on the low levels of savings or excess consumption, without eliminating the issue of reduced domestic markets associated with the intervention of foreign capital in underdeveloped countries upon which the financialization discussion rests. These assumptions analyze the contradictions of the model of accumulation directed by financial capital, expressed in structural imbalances, which prevent balanced economic growth in underdeveloped countries.

This chapter suggests that the economic gap in the Latin American region is a combination of the absence of robust financial institutions that are capable of transforming liquidity into financing for production, and structural productive disequilibria, explained by low levels of investment and reduced internal multipliers.

One serious problem facing the economies of underdeveloped countries is that the partial recirculation of the surpluses in the domestic economy prevents internal markets from developing and leads to constant current account deficits.

The hypothesis presented herein is that Latin American countries have not been able to fully develop their productive forces because they have been unable to overcome domestic structural limitations, as evidenced by low levels of investment and reduced internal markets; these are accompanied by considerable external disequilibria, which are obviously presented in new forms of capitalism that is dominated by foreign capital.

During the neoliberal period, although the liquidity of the economies increased through the high availability of external savings and the activation of the region's export sectors, the conditions for expanding the domestic market were not created. In contrast, the combination based on the empowerment of financial capital and the growing activation of the external sector did not expand the accumulation sector, reversing important achievements from the ISI period. Private flows of external capital, which are fundamental to closing external gaps, eliminated the financing channels toward production and dismantled state intervention in the basic sectors of the economy. The external sector stopped producing raw materials, without taking into account the cyclical nature of the terms of trade, and manufacturing export sectors were developed that lacked technological innovation. Within this context, the old disequilibria reappeared in greater force, although under new forms; they perpetuated one of the typical syndromes of lagging economies – reduced internal markets derived from economic processes that do not guarantee the circulation of surpluses into the economy. This highlights the fact that low salaries continues to be their main competitive advantage, while production is carried out in the international market, accompanied by growing levels of imports. The contradiction between capital and labor expanded, expressed as growing productive and financial disequilibria, especially in less developed countries.

This chapter is divided into three sections. Section 5.2 provides a concise review of the approaches taken by dependency theory with regard to the limitations of growth in less developed countries, followed by a brief analysis of the main contradictions in the neoliberal approach, directed by financial capital (also known as financialization). Section 5.3 analyzes the financial sectors and productive structures in Latin America to determine the limits of economic growth. Finally, the conclusions are presented in Section 5.4.

5.2   EXPLANATORY THEORIES OF LIMITED ECONOMIC GROWTH: FROM DEPENDENCY THEORY TO FINANCIALIZATION

A common denominator among these approaches is that the economic gap and the crisis affecting the region's countries are not the result of a lack of savings or prices that are distorted by government intervention, characterized as structurally inefficient. This approach was presented by neoliberal theorists who suggested that the post-war economic gap in Latin America was due to the weak development of financial markets, which were graded as small, segmented and self-sufficient, with low interest rates in productive financing (Gurley and Shaw, 1960; McKinnon, 1974) with significant discussion on the level of the types of changes, which were administered by governments.

The central argument in dependency theory is based on the withdrawal of surplus from the lagging economies by the developed countries, giving rise to the binomials underdeveloped–developed and periphery–center, followed by the concept of developing countries.

The dependency view that put forward the concept of underdevelopment vis-à-vis development is grounded in the work of R. Luxemburg. This theorist maintained that the expansion of the developed countries toward less developed (colonial) territories was needed for the full realization of their profits. She indicated that the main domination mechanisms used by the developed countries are international financing (credits, bonds), direct foreign investment (in the export sector), infrastructure financing and production in the less developed countries. From Luxemburg's perspective, this set of mechanisms destroys self-sufficient modes of production and causes these economies to become structurally backward, since they are producers of primary goods and foodstuffs for the developed countries, and become financially dependent in order to acquire the intermediate goods and capital that are necessary for producing their exports and the luxury goods for consumption by the oligarch class (Luxemburg, 1913). This prevents the less developed countries from achieving full (capitalist) development from their productive forces.[1]

Following this approach, dependency theorists argued that the local bourgeoisie are dominated by imperialist interests, which perpetuate backward modes of production, placing the industrialization processes in opposition to imperialism. 'Underdevelopment' is a central concept in this approach (Baran, 1957; Frank, 1966, 1967; Marini, 1968, among others), based on which they argue that production becomes subordinate to the needs of the developed countries (exports of primary goods and food-stuffs), whose counterpart is the import of capital goods and intermediate and luxury consumption goods from the developed countries. The pro-duction process (supply) is decoupled from the realization of the surplus (demand) and unequal productive structures are generated. This permits a differentiated appropriation of the surplus, implying an exodus of the sur-pluses from the less developed countries toward the developed countries. In these lagging economies, high profits combine with reduced domestic savings as a result of the exit of the surplus from the export sector and the levels of luxury consumption by the social elites in peripheral countries; the trade-off includes reduced volumes of private investment and public investment with low multiplier effects on income (Kaldor, 1959).

This theoretical overview developed the concept of the super-exploitation of labor, defined as the appropriation of the *absolute*[2] surplus value of agriculture and mining export activities, which led to intensified forms of labor exploitation (longer workdays), with more intensive labor, without recompensing the workers even in part for the increased value that they generated (Marini, 1968, p. 4).

An underlying element in this analysis is the differentiation of the pro-ductive sectors. On the one side are the modern sectors that produce for the external market (raw materials and foodstuffs) and, on the other, the lagging productive sectors that produce for the domestic market, with reduced domestic demand. This causes external disequilibria due to the growing imports of capital and intermediate goods for the export sector, and of final goods to satisfy the luxury consumption of the economic elite.

In political terms, it is notable that local governments are dominated by alliances between transnational capital and national elites, which impose barriers to the development of accumulation and to capitalist relations as progressive forces, limiting the eradication of backward production systems (Asiatic and peasant production systems). International capital controls the dynamic sectors of the less developed countries, the export sector of raw materials and foodstuffs. This leaves the local bourgeoisie responsible for certain secondary export activities and for exploiting the domestic market, the expansion of which is dependent on the investible surplus (the difference between the value of the exports and that of the imports, which is highly dependent on relative prices, that is, the exchange rate).

The structuralist view, developed in the 1950s by the Economic Commission for Latin America and the Caribbean (ECLAC), was the main promoter of the ISI project, on the basis of large-scale and direct government intervention in the economy. From this perspective, foreign trade is the central mechanism used to withdraw surplus from the less developed countries.[3] The center countries produce manufactured goods based on oligopolistic structures, allowing them to control the price of their goods, while the periphery countries produce commodities, whose prices are determined based on market mechanisms (or purchasers). This view assumes the center–periphery binomial.

In this approach, the condition of inequality that characterizes the productive structures between center and periphery countries is perpetuated. In the center countries, the productive structures are homogeneous and diversified, with higher levels of productivity (and salaries), while the peripheral countries have heterogeneous and specialized productive structures. At one extreme, there are sectors devoted to the production of commodities for the foreign market, composed of a few activities, with a productivity that is above the economy's average, relatively sophisticated technologies, low unemployment levels and exiguous internal productive chains; at the other (especially in agriculture), goods are produced for the domestic market, with low levels of productivity and a large concentration of population; consequently, they have high surplus volumes of labor, which reduces salaries in the economy as a whole (see Palma, 1981 [1987], pp. 61–2).

An important contribution to structural theory is found in the theory of unequal exchange (Cepal, 1949 [1998]), which was used to develop the concepts of income elasticities of import demand (higher in the periphery than in the center, and therefore in peripheral economies the drop in

income does not strongly affect imports) and export demand price elasticities (lower in the periphery than in the center – higher supply of primary
goods, lower prices) that, in combination, explain the deterioration of the
terms of trade in the international trade of the less developed countries
(see Cepal, 1949 [1998]). This limits the potential of the export sector of
the periphery countries as a source of stable economic growth and reduces
the potential domestic market, which prevents production profits from
being realized.

The main proposal from structural theorists is industrialization policy
(capitalist development of the forces of production), defined as an unavoid-
able requirement for development (Prebisch, 1980) that must be attained
if these economies are to achieve independence. Unlike the dependency
theorists, they recommend the entrance of foreign capital, although they
warn against the danger of excessive foreign liabilities (Cepal, 1949 [1998]).

Fajnzylber (1987 [1998]) underlined the absence of creativity (technology) in the ISI process; he proposed the creation of an endogenous nucleus
of technical progress, and developed the concept of an 'empty box' and
'incomplete industrialization'. His addition of the variable of income distribution indicates that 'transformation with productive equity' is another
basic missing element in the industrialization process.

Following Gerschenkron, who introduced the concept of 'achieving
the development' of the industrialized countries (Amsden, 2001 [2004],
pp. 284–6), Amsden used the concept of developing countries, placing
great emphasis on the development of a high-tech industry, which is rare in
Latin American economies (Amsden, 2001 [2004]). This theorist specifies
that manufacturing should be deployed within a context of reverse linkages with local productive sectors and transfers of knowledge creation and
scientific innovation toward the lagging economies. She rejects the productive processes sustained by *maquilas* (contract manufacturing), which add
a cheap labor force.

The theoretical revolution generated by the imposition of the neoliberal model rejected the direct government intervention in the economy
proposed by the structural theorists and argued in favor of deregulation,
privatization and economic globalization; in combination, these ceded the
control of economic organization to financial capital, without reducing
public participation in economic decisions. However, public policy objectives were modified; the full employment of productive factors and public
spending on accumulation were replaced by price stability and consumption. Purchasing power stability became the central element of economic
policy.

The decoupling between supply and demand reappears, and as global
markets acquire central importance as spaces for carrying out production,

finances internationalize with the appearance of global debt, money and capital markets. The export sector assumes leadership for the growth of the economies, with low dynamism in productive investment in the countries with higher final consumption, in a context of a new international division of labor: the United States specializes in financial innovations and becomes the global engine of demand. Manufacturing production is deployed from the United States to Europe and Japan, and later is integrated into the economies of Southeast Asia, followed by China and India, who emerged as the global suppliers.

In this model, money is recognized as a debt that is created based on the portfolio flows generated by the exchange of existing or recently created assets, also known as the 'flow of funds' accounts (Minsky, 1964), which are independent of the payments related to pending liabilities and assets and income accounts, and are strongly controlled by financial innovations. The movement of capital changes geographically: the US market became the main recipient of financial flows from the rest of the world, generating new structural disequilibria in foreign accounts. The global hegemonic country acquired a deficit in its current accounts and a surplus in the capital account, while the rest of the economies acquired surplus positions in their current accounts and deficits in their capital accounts. This generated global and regional hegemonies that determined their areas of control through net exports, imposing the phenomenon of neomercantilism, which is characterized by its operation with:

> economic policies and institutional arrangements which see net external surpluses as a crucial source of profits. The solution to the problem of effective demand is seen as lying above all in a positive trade balance. Moreover, the current account surplus is seen as increasing the private sector's ability to operate on international capital markets. (Bellofiore et al., 2011, p. 120)

In these new structures, routes of surplus appropriation were modified between hegemonic and peripheral countries, perpetuating the structural condition of unequal distribution of the surpluses. The high liquidity deployed by the global hegemonic country (the United States) and regional powers determined the rhythm of the economic expansion of the rest of the economies through the construction of the surplus; this generated a transfer of resources toward developed economies (De Cecco, 2012, p. 30), which appropriated 'growing yields based on the foreign assets in comparison with their foreign liabilities' (Gourinchas et al., 2010, cited in De Cecco, 2012, p. 30). These bases allowed the United States to appropriate most of the global surplus, notwithstanding its technological strength, and it was able to deploy trade deficits over long periods, which, in turn, allowed it to determine the surplus for the rest of the world. Thus, it influenced the distribution of financial profits, mobilizing financial assets denominated in US dollars.

We note that an unequal surplus appropriation also exists in the group of countries that are producers of goods and services. At the top are the countries that supply (and design) technological know-how, whose geographic axis is located in Germany and Japan. The second tier is occupied by export economies with trade surpluses, whose comparative advantages are based on simpler productive processes, and who compete based on the low cost of wages, without making a significant contribution to technological creativity (Southeast Asia).

Latin American countries occupy a special place in this new international order: they achieve temporary and relatively reduced trade balances and their main export categories are raw materials and foodstuffs, which are subject to cyclical trade conditions that deploy periods of growth and positive terms of trade, followed by a downturn, and even crisis, when the terms of trade are reversed. Although manufacturing exports have been revitalized in certain regional countries such as Mexico, the process has occurred within the region's typical context, that is, without an increase in productivity or productive investment and, therefore, its competitiveness is based on reduced salaries. The disadvantage of lagging economies is repeated: they export merchandise whose prices are determined in the global marketplace, with higher price-demand export elasticities than the rest of the world, and lower income-demand elasticities.

Even economies that specialized in manufacturing maintained their weakness in accumulation sectors. In addition, they must offer attractive conditions for optimizing financial capital, which implies not only offering attractive financial margins (interest rates) and stable exchange rates, but also deploying friendly economic policies for financial capital (privatizing the strategic productive sectors in the lagging economies), offering financial securities with high yields and stable exchange rates, cheapening the labor force and maintaining monetary policies designed to stabilize the value of financial wealth (controlling inflation), with fiscal surpluses, especially primary fiscal surpluses. Within this context, the double withdrawal of the surplus from less developed countries toward developed economies reappears: exports are produced with cheap labor and their prices are determined by global supply and demand, and the structural deficits of the current accounts require external financing. This obligated the region's countries to open their capital accounts and offer profitable conditions for the foreign financial capital yield, losing their freedom through the application of anticyclical economic policies; they were obliged to maintain a surplus in the primary account, keep their debts low and accumulate high reserves in the international currency of the hegemonic country.

The capitalist model dominated by financial capital breaks the financing-investment-savings sequence; and speculation in the financial system prevents debt cancellation. The growth of the financial sector, based on highly complex financial instruments and profit generation through financial channels (Krippner, 2005), deepened structural disequilibria and accelerated the contagion processes among financial markets, both in the boom phases as well as in the downturns and crises, initiating a stage of financial inflation (deflation), based on which an appropriation (losses) of profits was deployed in the sphere of circulation.

The financing, investment and savings ratio is broken, as long as the non-financial corporations provide liquidity to the rest of the economy, strengthening their treasury departments, based on which the financial sector appears as an important source of capturing profits (Seccareccia, 2012–2013). Banks transfer their fundamental activity to the trade of financial contracts, whose purpose is to ensure (or speculate on) specific conditions of the underlying assets (derivatives) and deploy securitization practices; families become the main debtors in the financial system. Under these conditions, financial capital yield becomes a key indicator of the evolution of the economy, affecting all agents, subjugating monetary policies to financial price stability and guaranteeing minimum levels of financial prices (Bernanke, 2005); and above all, the capital markets do not assume their role of providing liquidity to illiquid assets; their refinancing activity is replaced by financial innovations that tend to generate profits through price variations; that is, they are focused on speculation.

5.3　LATIN AMERICA: HIGH LIQUIDITY, REDUCED FINANCING AND STRUCTURAL IMBALANCES

Although Latin America is composed of a group of countries of varying sizes, productive profiles and specializations, as well as different institutional organizations, there are certain common denominators. Most of the countries moved toward the neoliberal model during the 1970s, and the region as a whole was affected by the foreign debt crisis during the 1980s. The general openness of capital markets began during the early 1990s and, in the first few years of the new century, financialization became embedded in the region. The counterpart to this process was the strengthening of the export sector with foreign surpluses, dominated by the primary sector, with manufacturing increases in certain countries, and expansive growth cycles linked to upward movement in the terms of trade.

In order to cover the main disequilibria of the model dominated by financial capital in Latin America and its inherent imbalances, the discussion shall present an analysis of the financial account in the region and the productive structure, placing special emphasis on their composition and foreign trade balances.

5.3.1 The Financial Account of Latin America

The most notable characteristics of the evolution of the financial account for the region was the decoupling between the evolution of the current account and the financial account. The financial account, the current account and the liabilities moved in a coordinated manner during the 1980s; very few assets were in the possession of the inhabitants, where 'other investments' dominated (which contain the credits originating from banks).

During the 1990s and the early 2000s, the financial account experienced deep transformation. It maintained its surplus condition due to the deficit condition of the current account, which, however, suffered a deep reduction (on average, −1.1 percent in terms of the gross domestic product (GDP) in 2000–2012), separating itself from the financial account: liabilities increased (they reached a 4.7 percent average in relation to the product during the period from 2000 to 2012) while foreign capital needs were reduced to balance the capital account. A second element that should be noted is that the composition of inflows of foreign capital was modified based on the openness of the capital market: initially foreign portfolio investment predominated and afterward, foreign direct investment; this reflected the privatization process in strategic sectors of Latin American economies. Finally, we note the increase of foreign assets held by residents, which reflected the possibility of accessing financing abroad or of investing outside national borders (*translatinas*); however, this did not represent even 1 percent of the region's GDP. We also note that the loans (included in other investments) cede their place to direct foreign investment and, to a lesser extent, foreign portfolio investment (Figure 5.1).

The impact of the growing entrance of capital increased financial deepening in relation to GDP, creating an abundance of foreign currency resources. Based on statistics from the World Bank and the Bank for International Settlements (BIS)[4] it is calculated that in 1989 financial deepening was 73.4 percent, and in 1999 it was equated with the level of GDP (105.7 percent), continuing to increase during the financialization period until it reached nearly 180 percent in 2013. By decade, we find that financial deepening, from 1989–1999, represented an average of 88 percent of GDP, surpassing 113 percent in 2000–2009, and grew to 127 percent when the post-crisis years (2000–2013) are included (Table 5.1).

The composition of the financial deepening was very revealing: during

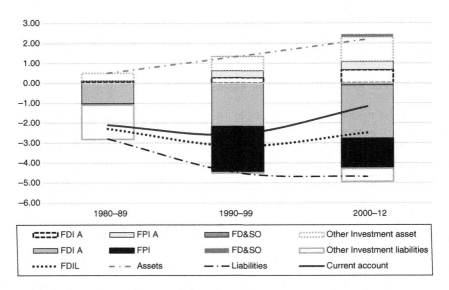

Note: FDI: foreign direct investment; FPI: foreign portfolio investment; A: assets; FD&SOA: financial derivatives and stock options, assets; FD&SOL: financial derivatives and stock options liabilities. Latin America includes: Argentina, Belize, Bolivia, Brazil, Chile, Colombia, Costa Rica, Ecuador, El Salvador, Guatemala, Honduras, Mexico, Panama, Paraguay, Peru, Dominican Republic, Uruguay and Venezuela.

Source: Author's elaboration based on International Monetary Fund, Balance of Payments Statistics data, updated February 2015.

Figure 5.1   Latin American current and financial account structure (average ratio in terms of GDP), in percentages

the 1990s, bank credits dominated (with an average of 35 percent in relation to GDP), followed by the securities market (with an average of 26.1 percent in relation to GDP), so that the bond market reached an average of 10 percent in relation to GDP. In contrast, during the first decade of the 2000s, the three market segments were nearly identical: 30 percent bank credits, 29 percent bond market (led by public bonds with 10 percent participation) and 25 percent stock market. The inclusion of the post-crisis years does not modify that composition (based on Table 5.1).

Based on the foregoing, in general terms, we may state that the external sector presented the old disequilibria characterizing Latin American countries: the current account was unable to reach positive amounts and the financial account was the source of transformation of the financial system, which explains the truncated deepening of the financial system, without increasing production financing; meanwhile, the bond market

Table 5.1   *Latin American financial market deepness (percentages)*
              (average values in terms of GDP)

	1989–2013	1989–1999	2000–2009	2000–2013
Bank credits/GDP	33.6	35.3	30.4	32.3
Total bonds/GDP	24.4	13.4	28.9	33.0
Government bonds	15.3	10.6	16.1	19.0
Financial institutions bonds	7.2	1.7	10.6	11.4
Corporate bonds	1.9	1.1	2.2	2.6
Stock market/GDP	28.1	26.1	25.0	29.7
Financial market size/GDP	110.4	88.2	113.2	127.9

Source: Author's elaboration based on World Bank and Bank for International Settlements data, http://datos.banco mundial.org/ and http://bis/org/statistics, accessed March 2015. Latin America includes: Argentina, Brazil, Chile, Colombia, Mexico and Peru.

grew stronger, especially in terms of public bonds, with low participation in the capital market and generally reduced levels of financing.

5.3.2   The Productive Structure

As a result of globalization, the productive structure experienced a great transformation in the external sector, leaving the internal market relatively unchanged. During the period between 1990 and 2013, private consumption remained practically the same, with an average of 77 percent with small variations in the composition of public and private consumption. The gross fixed capital formation did not show any significant variations, with an average of 17 percent (Figure 5.2).

The major variations occurred in the export sector: exports reached an average of 18 percent, higher than the investment ratio (although not very significant). During the 1990s, the export coefficient reached an average of 15.3 percent (against 17 percent of the gross fixed capital formation (GFCF) in relation to GDP), reaching 20 percent in relation to GDP in the following decade, without any radical changes during the post-crisis period, while the GFCF coefficient remained almost unchanged (17 percent); that is, sales in the international market were the most dynamic element in the region's economies. The import coefficient reached an average of 15 percent (11 percent during the 1990s and 16 percent during the first decade of this century, and 18 percent from 2000 to 2013). This implies a surplus in the trade account of approximately 3 percent (3.4 percent from 1990 to 1999, 4 percent from 2000 to 2009 and 2.6 percent from 2000 to 2013) (Figure 5.2).

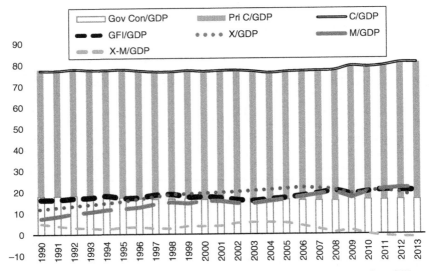

Note: GDP: gross domestic product; Pri C: private consumption; C: consumption; GFI: gross fixed investment; X: exports; M: imports; Gov Con: government consumption.
Latin America includes: Argentina, Belize, Bolivia, Brazil, Chile, Colombia, Costa Rica, Ecuador, El Salvador, Guatemala, Honduras, Mexico, Panama, Paraguay, Peru, Dominican Republic, Uruguay and Venezuela.

Source: Author's elaboration based on Economic Commission for Latin America and the Caribbean data, http://estadisticas.cepal.org/cepalstat/WEB_CEPALSTAT, accessed June 2015.

Figure 5.2   *Latin American gross domestic product by its main spending components*

In general, although all of the countries invigorated their export sector, Chile took the lead in this activity with an average that is much higher than that for the region (36 percent of GDP), followed by Peru (26 percent), Mexico (24 percent), Colombia and Argentina (15 percent); Brazil had very low levels: 9 percent in relation to its GDP. In terms of the regional balance of trade, there was a surplus of 2.6 percent in relation to GDP, explained by the positive trade balance shown by Chile (11.6 percent), Peru (6.4 percent), Argentina (3 percent), Brazil (0.3 percent) and non-significant deficits in Mexico and Colombia.

The composition of the imports was peculiar. According to the statistics issued by ECLACstat,[5] between 1995 and 2012, imports of intermediate inputs dominated (63 percent) without changes during the different five-year periods (1995–1999: 62 percent; 2000–2005: 65 percent; 2006–2012: 63 percent) with the proportion of capital goods remaining at a low level, with an average of 21.4 percent (1995–1999: 21.5 percent; 2000–2005: 20.2 percent; 2006–2012: 22 percent). This composition is a reflection of weak technological development in the region, where not even capital goods are imported to provide higher added value to internal production or to exports. This reflects the fact that *maquila* factories dominate the region, which implies that the companies that are linked into global chains lie at the end of the production process, or export raw materials of limited added value. Latin America did not take advantage of the manufacturing transfer to developing countries; this generated a production model with growing structural disequilibria, which increased external dependence.

Based on the foregoing, it is possible to deduce that the region's internal market did not expand and the decoupling between supply and demand increased, while productive organization based on *maquilas* and the sale of primary goods with low added value continued to predominate.

5.3.3   External Balances

The region's trade balances were positive, which did not imply a replication of the neomercantilist presence of the Southeast Asian countries, since their surpluses were relatively low and, perhaps more importantly, there was no radical change in export composition. Following Lall's methodology (2000), we find that the categories that explain the surplus from the trade account balance during the financialization period were essentially from the primary goods sector, whose surplus during the financialization period (2000–2013) was comparatively higher than in the 1980s (when the highest surplus for the trade account for the entire period was reached). The other category that showed a surplus for the most part was the industrial manufacturing goods sector, which is based on natural resources (Figure 5.3).

The reduced investment coefficient (with low import levels for capital goods) translated into high deficits for the medium and high-tech manufacturing sectors, including the low-tech manufacturing sector during the financialization period (Figure 5.3).

The composition of the balance of trade based on technological intensity indicates that Latin America returned to the primary export period, concentrating its efforts on the extraction sector, whose prices are set by the global marketplace; these prices grew during the financialization period. Specifically, from 2000 to 2013 the Free on Board (FOB) terms of trade increased by nearly 20 points, and between 1990 and 2000, rose by a further 20 points,[6] and the purchasing power of the exports of goods increased by more than double between 2000 and 2012,[7] only beginning to decline in 2014. During the neoliberal period (starting in the 1980s)

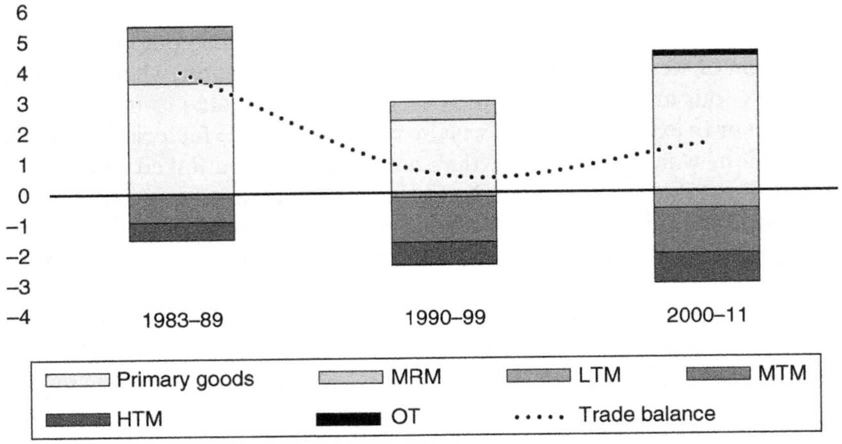

Note: MRM: manufacture balance based on raw materials; LTM: manufacture balance based on low technological composition; HTM: manufacture balance based on high technology goods; MTM: manufacture balance based on medium technological composition; OT: other transactions. Foreign trade grouped by technology intensiveness, methodology based on Lall (2000). Latin America includes: Antigua, Antilles, Argentina, Bahamas, Barbados, Belize, Bolivia, Brazil, Chile, Colombia, Costa Rica, Cuba, Dominica, Ecuador, El Salvador, Granada, Guatemala, Guyana, Haiti, Honduras, Jamaica, Mexico, Monserrat, Nicaragua, Panama, Paraguay, Peru, Dominican Republic, Saint Vincent, Saint Lucia, Suriname, Trinidad, Uruguay and Venezuela.

Source: Author's elaboration based on data from the Economic Commission for Latin America and the Caribbean and the Foreign Trade Statistics Database (BADECEL), http://interwp.cepal.org/badecel/basededatos.asp, accessed June 2015.

Figure 5.3 Latin American trade balance according to technological composition in terms of GDP (average percentage)

that was dominated by financial capital, when the developing countries in other regions of the world began a period of industrialization, becoming the main manufacturing producers, Latin America experienced a de-industrialization process, deploying a growth process that was weak and dependent on external markets, without boosters of domestic growth, increasing the structural disequilibria of the economies in the region with high financial dependence.

5.4 CONCLUSIONS

The region of Latin America has not managed to generate economic models with structural balances that reduce its dependency on the global market. Historically, it has operated with a deficit in its current account and has required inflows of external capital to close the external gaps. This has produced the domination of external hegemonies that have limited technological development in Latin America, preventing the expansion of its internal markets, with differentiated productive structures and a decoupling between supply and demand. A basic element of the structural disequilibria in Latin America has been the partial recirculation of profits toward production, due to the withdrawal of surpluses initiated by the developed economies.

From the perspective of dependency theory, this is caused by the withdrawal of surpluses from their economies by the hegemonic countries, without implying the cancellation of capitalist development in peripheral countries. Dependency theorists explain the underdevelopment and the appropriation of surpluses by the developed countries based on the alliances between the local bourgeoisie and international elites, which limited domestic accumulation in strategic productive sectors and prevented profits from recirculation into production, due to the exit of profits through the transfer of profits and imports. The structuralist view linked the withdrawal of surpluses with international trade and unequal terms of trade, and assumed an industrialization process, the ISI, which should be accompanied by technological innovation, a failed element in the region.

The transformation of the capitalist system, with the imposition of the neoliberal model, moved the discussion toward the lack of savings and the reduced development of the capital market, and highlighted the limitations of the process of production within the context of the new international order. The generation of internal liquidity (and even external flows) may be resolved through appropriate policies and, although this is a necessary component of economic growth, it cannot fully explain the gap suffered by the peripheral countries. The survey of the evolution of the financial sector has shown that the structure of spending and external disequilibria have a long history in Latin America, where the principal limitation is the extraction of surpluses toward the hegemonic countries.

The new financial and global order that dominates in the finance-led economic model recreated old disequilibria under new forms. First, Latin America moved toward the primary exports model and specialized in providing raw materials and foodstuffs, leading to a process of de-industrialization, or manufacturing production based on *maquilas*, which limited internal markets and led to wages becoming the main competitive advantage. Second, the opening of external accounts empowers financial capital and increases external liabilities, which became the second route for extracting surpluses. In the financialized neoliberal model, the two major disequilibria combined within a framework of indiscriminate economic openness, with no regulation whatsoever, and were the source of a large-scale transfer of profits toward the developed countries, limiting the peripheral countries from deploying policies that would counteract the economic crisis. This process became especially relevant during the phase of decline in the prices of raw materials, submerging the region in economic lethargy, a discussion of which falls outside the scope of this chapter.

NOTES

*   This chapter is part of the research project IN 303313, sponsored by the DGAPA-UNAM.
1. Luxemburg's view of the relationship between developed and developing countries is one of the first versions of the theory of imperialism. This explanation is subject to multiple criticisms, because it underestimates the potential for real wage increases in developed countries and endogenous incentives to investment resulting from technological progress. It is also argued that it overestimates the role of developing countries in the capital accumulation process in the developed countries (see Palma, 1981 [1987], p. 30). Other authors note the importance of the financing factor in the theory of financing that is present in the author's discussion (see Toporowski, 2005).
2. This is at odds with the development of the concept of relative gains that dominates in developed countries.
3. One of the main themes of structuralist theory was to question the Hecksher-Ohlin model and Samuelson's proposal on the Ricardian trade theory (absolute and comparative advantages).
4. Calculations performed based on statistics from the World Bank and BIS. See http://datos.bancomundial.org and http://www.bis.org/statistics/, accessed March 2015.
5. See Cepalstat, Statistics and Economic Indicators, External sector, imports of goods by economic category, http://estadisticas.cepal.org/cepalstat/WEB_CEPALSTAT/Portada.asp?idioma=i, accessed 22 June 2015.
6. Based on the ECLAC statistics for Latin America and the Caribbean, the FOB terms of trade for goods in 1980 was 77.78; in 1990: 63.04; in 2000: 80.15; and in 2012: 104.18. See Indexes of the terms of trade and purchasing power of exports, Index 2010 = 100, Cepalstat, http://estadisticas.cepal.org/cepalstat/WEB_CEPALSTAT/Portada.asp?idioma=i, accessed 22 June 2015.
7. The purchasing power of exports in 1980 was 13.25; in 1990: 18.82; in 2000: 55.40; in 2012: 113.73. See Indexes of the terms of trade and purchasing power of exports, Index 2010 = 100, Cepalstat, http://estadisticas.cepal.org/cepalstat/WEB_CEPALSTAT/Portada.asp?idioma=i, accessed 22 June 2015.

REFERENCES

Amsden, A. (2001), *The Rise of 'the Rest': Challenges to the West from Late-industrializing Economies*, New York: Oxford University Press, reprinted in 2004.
Amsden, A. (2004), 'La sustitución de importaciones en las industria de alta tecnología', *Revista CEPAL*, **82**, April, 75–90.
Baran, P. (1957), *The Political Economy of Growth*, New York: Monthly Review Press.
Bellofiore, R., F. Garibaldo and J. Halevi (2011), 'The global crisis and the crisis of European neomercantilism', *Socialist Register*, **47**, 120–46.

Bernanke, B. (2005), 'The global saving glut and the U.S. current account deficit', Paper presented at the Homer Jones Lecture, St Louis, Missouri, 10 March.

Cepal (1949), 'Estudio Económico de América Latina', reprinted in R. Bielschovski (ed.) (1998), *Cincuenta Años de Pensamiento en la Cepal. Textos Seleccionados*, Vol. I, Santiago: Fondo de Cultura Economica-Cepal.

De Cecco, M. (2012), 'Global imbalances: past, present, and future', *Contributions to Political Economy*, **31**(1), 29–50.

Fajnzylber, F. (1987), 'La industrialización de América Latina: de la "caja negra" al "casillero vacío"', reprinted in R. Bielschovski (ed.) (1998), *Cincuenta Años de Pensamiento en la Cepal. Textos Seleccionados*, Vol. II, Santiago: Fondo de Cultura Economica-Cepal.

Frank, A.G. (1966), 'The development of underdevelopment', *Monthly Review*, **18**(4), 17–31.

Frank, A.G. (1967), *Capitalism and Underdevelopment in Latin America: Historical Studies of Chile and Brazil*, New York: Monthly Review Press.

Gurley, J. and E.S. Shaw (1960), *Money in a Theory of Finance*, Washington, DC: The Brookings Institution.

Kaldor, N. (1959), 'Problemas económicos de Chile', *Trimestre Económico*, **26**(102), 170–221.

Krippner, G. (2005), 'The financialization of the American economy', *Socio-Economic Review*, **3**(2), 173–208.

Lall, S. (2000), 'The technological structure and performance of developing country manufactured exports, 1965–98', *Oxford Development Studies*, **28**(3), 337–69.

Luxemburg, R. (1913), *The Accumulation of Capital*, London: Routledge and Kegan Paul.

McKinnon, R. (1974), *Dinero y capital en el desarrollo económico*, Mexico City: Editorial Centro de Estudios Monetarios Latinoamericanos.

Marini, R.M. (1968), 'Subdesarrollo y revolución en América Latina', *Tricontinental*, November.

Minsky, H. (1964), 'Financial crisis, financial systems, and the performance of the economy', in *Private Capital Markets*, Englewood Cliffs, NJ and New York: Prentice Hall, pp. 173–380.

Palma, G. (1981), 'Dependencia y desarrollo una visión crítica', reprinted in D. Seers (ed.) (1987), *Teoría de la dependencia una revaluación critica*, Mexico City: Fondo de Cultura Económica, pp. 21–89.

Prebisch, R. (1980), 'Prólogo', in O. Rodríguez (ed.), *La teoría del subdesarrollo de la CEPAL*, Mexico City: Editorial Siglo XXI, pp. vii–xiv.

Seccareccia, M. (2012–2013), 'Financialization and the transformation of commercial banking: understanding the recent Canadian experience before and during the international financial crisis', *Journal of Post Keynesian Economics*, **35**(2), 277–300.

Toporowski, J. (2005), 'Rosa Luxemburg and the Marxist subordination of finance', in *Theories of Financial Disturbance*, Cheltenham, UK and Northampton, MA, USA: Edward Elgar, pp. 52–61.

6. Inequality, technological change and worldwide economic recovery

Carlos A. Rozo*

6.1 INTRODUCTION

The great recession caused by the collapse of the mortgage sector in the United States officially ended in 2009. However, it is difficult to state that the recession has disappeared given that at the time of writing, in 2015, the average income of most of the world's population remains below 2008 levels and there is still widespread unemployment in many countries. Levels of economic growth and employment figures continue to be below their potential but, most significantly, these weaknesses existed even before the first symptoms of the crisis in 2007. The underlying dilemma involves ascertaining whether the difficulty in putting the economy back on a more vigorous path of recovery is due to one of the two following possibilities. A prolonged financial crisis that will end up being resolved insofar as the excessive leverage that caused it has been eliminated, or conversely whether it is a consequence of shortcomings in the capitalist economy, pointing to the existence of structural imbalances that slow down growth, prevent job creation and are worsened by the fallout from the crisis, making for a weak and unstable recovery.

This chapter focuses on the latter explanation: structural imbalances whose interconnectivity weakens recovery. This weakness is caused by two factors, which act simultaneously and feed back into each other, producing significant effects on aggregate demand due to the combined impact on income distribution. The first factor derives from the symbolic aspect of the economy, which takes place when financial activity is decoupled from the productive sector, and investment is directed toward profitable yet unproductive activities through financialization (Lapavitsas, 2009; Stockhammer, 2012). The other factor derives from the digital revolution's tendency toward artificial intelligence, thus increasing the effect of 'technological unemployment'. The direct effects of these two factors, in the same way as their interconnectedness, provoke extreme polarization between the productive and financial sectors and a high-income concentration; the combination of these two factors affects the capacity of aggregate demand required by the macro economy for a strong recovery to be possible.

The hypothesis proposed to explain the relation between these two factors is that the dynamic of innovation, in both the productive and financial sectors and driven by digital technology, has brought about a very high concentration of income, which weakens the thrust of aggregate demand required for economic growth and job creation. The argument is that these two forces, which operate in parallel, are mutually reinforcing and weaken the aggregate demand that is necessary for a robust recovery.

This introduction is followed by six sections. Section 6.2 looks at the tendencies of economic growth and employment creation between 1980 and 2014 and at some of the explanations for the causes of the crisis and the slow recovery. Section 6.3 analyzes the logic of financial decoupling, followed by Section 6.4 that examines the issue of technological unemployment and the recovery's strength. In Section 6.5, an alternative hypothesis is given for technological unemployment, and Section 6.6 shows how both technological and financial factors are combined and contribute to the slowing recovery. The conclusions are given in the final section.

6.2   GROWTH AND EMPLOYMENT

In 2014, after seven years of crisis, it is not possible to talk about a return to prosperity, or even an imminent recovery. Industrialized, emerging and developing countries have levels of gross domestic product (GDP) growth below those reached prior to the crisis. Global GDP grew between 2007 and 2013 at a lower annual average rate than between 2000 and 2006 because of the asymmetries in the growth of the different groups of countries. Industrialized countries saw a sharp fall in growth, dropping from an average rate of 2.6 percent in the pre-crisis period to 0.97 percent afterward. Meanwhile, growth in emerging economies and developing economies decreased from an average rate of 6.27 percent to 5.81 percent.[1] Growth rates for developed countries stand at approximately one-third of pre-crisis levels, while in emerging and developing economies they have fallen by 7 percent. From the mid 1990s, these latter countries had higher growth rates than industrialized economies, which at the start of the century became stronger, but this was disrupted by the great recession.

The rate of GDP growth in industrial countries experienced a downward trend from the beginning of the twenty-first century because of the 2001 dot.com crisis. At a country level, growth has varied widely: compared to 2007, the US economy is 5 percent larger and the German economy 2 percent, but in the United Kingdom, the economy has shrunk by 3 percent, and in Italy by 9 percent. These results respond to very different types of growth dynamic: whereas between 2007 and 2013 the United States grew at an annual average rate of 1.06 percent and Germany at a rate of 1.11 percent, the United Kingdom barely grew at all, at 0.26 percent, while Italy saw a negative growth rate of −1.01 percent. The stark contrasts in development since 2009 must also be taken into account. In the United States, the financial sector has been stabilized with low levels of debt and price corrections in the real estate sector, and the country now enjoys relative price stability, but in Europe, credit remains expensive, with high levels of vulnerability in banks and large-scale unemployment.

Even more troubling is that the outlook for global growth is uncertain due to the downward revisions by international and domestic organizations that have become normal since the US Federal Reserve (the Fed) announced the end of the quantitative easing strategy in its monetary policy in the summer of 2013. For the 2015 to 2016 period, the International Monetary Fund (2015) predicts that economic growth will be greater in industrial countries than in emerging and developing economies, but forecasts suggest persistently low growth levels for the rest of the decade. The message is clear: the recovery will be weak.

Unemployment in developed countries increased during the great recession to reach an annual average rate of 7.4 percent between 2007 and 2013, compared to the annual average between 2000 and 2006 of 6.3 percent. Levels of unemployment in industrial countries rose after 2007 at different speeds. Eurozone countries are seeing the highest levels of joblessness, reaching an annual average of 10.6 percent in 2014. It should be noted that this is a problem that has affected the region at least since the 1990s when the average unemployment level was 11 percent. Most serious of all is that the widespread trend toward greater unemployment since 2007 will continue for the rest of this decade, according to the IMF's estimates. France will be one of the countries with the highest levels of unemployment, while Germany and the United Kingdom seem to be moving toward greater employment. These trends mean that eurozone countries may experience average annual unemployment rates of 12 percent, and industrial countries will see a rate of 7.5 percent.

The employment panorama in the United States is more promising, given a significant reduction in the highest levels of unemployment, from 10.2 percent in 2010 to 5.6 percent in mid 2015.[2] Nevertheless, millions of people are still seeking full-time and well-paid jobs, which are proving elusive despite the more positive outlook for the US economy compared to other industrial countries; also, in 2013, real per capita income in the United States reached 2007 levels.

These high levels of unemployment undoubtedly have a repercussion on

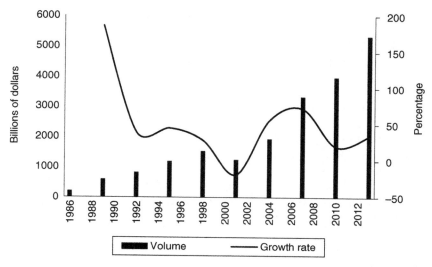

Source: Bank for International Settlements (2013).

Figure 6.1   Trends in the global exchange rate market

aggregate demand and are a drag on economic recovery, as we shall see in the next section.

6.3   FINANCIAL DECOUPLING

One of the most paradoxical events in the current productive anemia is the extraordinary growth seen in the global foreign exchange market. Since the dot.com crisis in 2001, this market has shown unprecedented dynamism (Figure 6.1). A recent survey carried out by the Bank for International Settlements (BIS, 2013) indicates that the average daily value of transactions in the FX market were worth US$5.3 trillion, implying a 35 percent growth compared to the levels reached in the previous survey in 2010, after having grown 72 percent in the 2007 survey and 20 percent in the one carried out in 2010. These growth levels have no correlation to the dynamic of international trade or global productivity.

Simultaneously, the foreign exchange activity is highly concentrated geographically, in just two markets: in the City in London, with 41 percent of the total global transactions, and on Wall Street in New York, with 19 percent. Furthermore, in 2010–2013 the composition of this market changed significantly, due to the growing share of currencies from emerging economies, with the Mexican peso and the Chinese renminbi joining the list of most traded currencies (BIS, 2013, p. 3).

This frenzied increase in the foreign exchange market is combined with the strength of the dollar, despite the collapse in 2008 of the US financial system and the high levels of government debt issued in order to tackle the crisis. These events, which should have weakened the dollar, have had the opposite effect because of the demand for 60 percent of the debt issued by the US federal government by residents of other countries since 2008. Prasad (2014) argues that this situation is the result of US government policies and the dysfunctionality of the international monetary system. According to Tett (2014), the key factor for the dollar's strength is based on investors' fear that creates a 'flight-to-liquidity' due to the lack of safe assets around the world, including US government-issued debt. Under these conditions, the liquid capital market of the United States provides more security.

This development pattern in the foreign exchange market exemplifies what Drucker (1986) termed the decoupling between the productive sector and the monetary-financial sector. He argues that a 'major change that has occurred in the world economy is the emergence of the "symbol" economy – capital movements, exchange rates and credit flows – as the flywheel of the world economy, in place of the real economy – the flow of goods and services. The two economies seem to be operating increasingly independently' (Drucker, 1986, p. 781). Financial activity has acquired its own dynamic that is independent from the productive sector, leading Menkhoff and Tolksdorf (2001, p. 1) to posit that 'events on the financial markets correspondingly follow their own logic, and the real economy has to adapt itself to the consequences of this'. The resulting regime of accumulation dominated by finance has complicated implications for the workings of the system. This decoupling is manifest in the fact that activity in financial markets is far more dynamic than in the real economy, which counters the neoclassical argument that money is an instrument for the efficient operation of the productive sector and for commercial exchange.

The financial sector has transformed its role as an intermediary for savings in order for the real economy to carry out its task of producing goods and services. Its new objective is to guide and strengthen the dynamic of accumulating financial and speculative profits, shifting away from a system of accumulation led by the prices of financial assets and real estate to one of debt and services in which consumption takes preference over investment, leading to so-called financialization (Epstein, 2005; Lapavitsas, 2009; Stockhammer, 2012). In this system of accumulation, the functional relationship between the financial system and the productive structure becomes watered down into a search for short-term financial gain with negative effects on the availability and use of credit and liquidity for long-term productive activities.

The decoupling between these two sectors has meant that the financing structure of a bank-based system has changed to one based on capital markets, which boosts financial activity that is consolidated on the basis of complementary alternatives: 'one is based on traditional financial intermediaries (commercial banks) and the other is related to stock exchanges and financial instruments' (Rozo, 2003, p. 224). The latter system, by taking over from the former, enables and encourages short-term economic activities, thus increasing the fragility and volatility of the financial system.

This decoupling, whereby the symbolic economy acts independently from the productive economy, essentially limits the resources available for the productive sector with negative effects on growth. When financial flows become an autonomous space of profitability, earnings do not come from the production and sale of goods and services, but instead from the profitability of investing in short-term financial assets. This creates unstable conditions, due to the financial sector's asymmetric growth at the expense of the productive sector, giving priority to investments in short-term financial assets and consumer credit that encourages debt at the expense of long-term productive investment.

This regime of accumulation around the world has a far-reaching and complex impact. The main effect is the shifting power balance in the relationship between labor and capital, which now favors capital income, which in turn modifies forms of consumption in a world where, generally speaking, demand is determined by wages. The stagnation of wages, both in Europe and the United States, has led to an increase in the level of debt, which has become the main driving force for demand – as shown conclusively by the real estate bubble. The trouble is the increasing debt-to-income coefficient, which is growing faster among the lower deciles, who have a higher propensity for consumption. Kumhof et al. (2013) state that the highest-earning agents tend to consume less, allowing them to accumulate financial wealth that is backed up by loans taken out by the lowest-earning agents. This in turn leads to a greater financial fragility due to the continuing increase in the debt-to-income coefficient among the lowest-earning sectors of society. The fact that the highest earners tend to speculate rather than consume further exacerbates income inequality and therefore restricts aggregate demand. For the poor and the middle classes, debt is only a way of maintaining consumption levels at times when their real income is tending to stagnate (Rajan, 2010; Reich, 2010). Therefore, debt among the lowest-earning sectors and the preference for financial wealth among the highest earners increases inequality in income distribution.

Financial deregulation has caused cross-border capital flows that have fed the growth of the currency market, allowing many countries to maintain deficits in their trade balances while at the same time exerting pressure on the appreciation of local currencies. In some economies, this dynamic is shown in economic cycles that end up as financial crises with negative effects on global demand, although in other parts of the world this is found in surplus current accounts that encourage financial speculation. The great recession strengthened the financial-productive dichotomy through 'carry trade' by large fund managers by demanding both public and private bonds in emerging economies in order to benefit from the interest rate differential between the north and the south. The determining factor of this 'carry trade' has been the loosening monetary policy of the main central banks, especially the Fed. The appreciation-depreciation trend in currency trading contributes to the slowing growth, as well as the feeble global recovery.

The profit-making logic of financial market operations permeates this stage of financialized capitalism and has been the main reason for the great recession and the weak recovery. The pattern of risks and imbalances caused by consumption based on debt and speculative profits ends up causing global financial imbalances that contribute to the interconnectivity between financial liberalization and polarization in the distribution of income, limiting global aggregate demand and making global economic recovery even weaker still.

6.4   TECHNOLOGICAL UNEMPLOYMENT AND RECOVERY

The additional determining factor in the slow down of the recovery is found in the sphere of technological change. Contemporary technological progress has brought back the age-old controversy about automation and its effects on employment. Some suggest that technological change is pushing down employment at a faster rate than new jobs are being created, while others defend technological change by continuing to argue that it leads to greater levels of production and income, hence increasing demand and generating jobs. Any disagreement with the latter is a form of Ludditism.

The incontrovertible fact is that technological progress has a significant impact on the labor–capital relation, which can be observed through different channels. One channel is the change made in the use of the capital factor, oriented toward savings in labor costs, making it a channel that reduces employment. Another channel works by increasing the demand for a workforce that is highly qualified in the use of new technologies, consequently becoming a channel that creates employment. The net result depends on the strength of each one of these channels. In a traditional production function, where the product depends on labor and capital, these are complementary factors. Therefore, increases in capital are accompanied by a rise in labor and worker productivity. As a result, greater capital will tend to increase wages, as implicitly represented by the traditional production function:

$$Y = F (K, L) \qquad (6.1)$$

This relationship is modified by capital's different potential uses: one is that usually found in the production function that is contained in equation (6.1). With this production function, an alternative result can be produced when capital tends to replace workers, as proposed by Summers (2013, p. 4) in equation (6.2):

$$Y = F (\beta K, L + \lambda (1 - \beta) K) \qquad (6.2)$$

This function is based on the capital (βK) used to increase output while the other part of the capital $(1 - \beta) K$ is used to substitute labor. One unit of capital is equivalent to λ units of labor. Capital is used in these two ways to the point where its marginal productivity is the same in both activities, which determines the proportion that is regularly used and that used to substitute for labor. Summers proposes three possible outcomes: (1) the availability of capital that substitutes labor increases the production opportunities, thus the level of output also increases; (2) by allocating capital to substitute labor, the stock of effective labor rises and the stock of conventional capital is reduced, and therefore the wage rates fall; and (3) the capital share, which includes the total return to capital of both varieties, increases as a corollary of output rising and wages falling. This latter result represents the current situation with capitalism, by reflecting the nature of technological change that increasingly takes the form of capital that effectively substitutes for labor.

The consequences of this new mechanism can be summed up in two effects. First, the asymmetric increases in labor productivity due to the power of digitalization to substitute labor by capital. Insofar as productive capacity grows due to a technically more sophisticated capital, the wages of less-qualified workers tend to fall, which puts pressure on the distribution of income in favor of capital and the more highly skilled workers. Second, the success of increasing productivity in the capital-intensive sector causes this sector to lose relative economic importance in value terms as well as in the creation of jobs. This effect of de-industrialization is what alters the share of different sectors in total output, just as happened initially with agriculture and is now happening with manufacturing.

With this development, the system shifts toward a concentration of property and a worsening income distribution. The process becomes more perilous proportional to the increase in the potential of digital technology to achieve this substitution on a large scale. Success in improving productivity plus the existence of inelastic demands translates into fewer jobs that in turn is reflected in the share of labor in the added value produced by national economies (Jorgenson and Timmer, 2011). In the 1980–2005 period, a tendency toward substituting labor with capital in the United States led to a decline in the share of labor from 67 to 63 percent in the manufacturing sectors and communications industries. In the European Union, there was an even greater reduction in this proportion, from 72 percent in 1980 to 66 percent in 2005, across all sectors; in Japan, this share dropped from 63 percent to 54 percent.

The substitution of labor by capital has been beneficial for the owners of capital because they receive the lion's share of profits from productivity. This logic explains why in the United States manufacturing jobs have fallen from 31 percent to 8.7 percent of total employment between 1950 and 2014, and that in the service sector employment has risen from 47.9 to 70.5 percent.[3] The result of these changes is that since 1980 the share of workers in the global output has contracted from 64 percent to 59 percent (*The Economist*, 2014, p. 9). In the United States, the level of employment has fallen since the year 2000 when 65 percent of US citizens of working age were in employment, whereas only 59 percent had jobs in 2012. However, employment in the financial sector has risen from 3.85 percent in 1952 to 6.15 percent in 2003, and later falling to 5.7 percent in 2014. These changes in employment and remuneration necessarily led to a new redistribution of wealth, benefiting the owners of capital, specialized and highly qualified workers.

An additional aspect of the digital revolution is that the number of companies in this sector has grown at an accelerated and exponential pace that has had significant impacts on employment since these are organizations that operate with fewer workers. Instagram is a clear example: when it was sold to Facebook for US$1 billion in 2012 it had 13 employees. Alternatively, take Kodak, which employed 145,000 people at the time of its bankruptcy, whereas Google only had 33,000 employees in 2013.

Effects that are even more dramatic can be created from another basic contemporary technological development, namely, the Nano technological revolution enabling manipulation at an atomic and molecular level in order to improve productive processes through the use of Nano materials, which can also have a significant effect on the composition and level of employment (Corley et al., 2002; Fabrice and Harris, 2007). Invernizzi and Foladori, after examining the characteristics of products derived from nanotechnology, concluded, 'The impacts of nanotechnology will add to global unemployment and underemployment. There is no technological solution, nor is there a market solution for this problem. Like other social problems, this one requires a political solution' (2010, p. 78).

6.5 AN ALTERNATIVE HYPOTHESIS ON TECHNOLOGICAL UNEMPLOYMENT

The logic of technological innovation requires a new hypothesis on technological unemployment because of a fundamental change over time in the type of technical change. In the past, manual, mechanical and repetitive work were automated, freeing up the workforce to engage in more creative activities that help create new jobs for the workers who had been left unemployed by technology. Textile, food production and assembly line work are such activities affected by this substitution.

Since the late twentieth century, automation of repetitive manual work has given way to the automation of cognitive work that depends on intellectual ability to process information in order to solve problems by ordering mental models and rational priorities (Kitcher, 2001, p. 91; Morales and Amaro, 2014). This qualitative turnaround in the logic of technological change gives meaning to the concept of 'the knowledge economy' where the basic productive supply is information that becomes knowledge once it is processed. Our key question today is this: Who processes this information – human beings or machines?

The cognitive division of labor is essential for us to understand the innovative drive given that cognitive abilities are the main input for technological companies, although the complexity of innovation permeates every sector. As a result, if information constitutes the basic input to push back the border of knowledge, the success of innovation depends on the capacity for assimilating and processing information.

The progress of the digital revolution is exceeding the predictions of Moore's Law, which postulated that computing capacity by unit of cost would double each year, thus bringing down the cost of production. In reality, the exponential increase in microprocessors' processing power doubles not every 18 months, as Moore argued, but every 12 months. This implies that the digital revolution may have a greater impact, one related to the power of processing information and transforming it into knowledge; in other words, artificial intelligence (AI). The crucial factor is that digitalization brings computers into fields that used to be only within the realm of human intelligence. Two factors are key here. One is that the complexity of the activities performed by the computers depends on the information processing capacity that these machines have and which is growing exponentially and seemingly has no limits. One of the reasons for this is the exponential growth in the capacity of microchips to store information and to process it at speeds unimaginable just a few years ago. The other factor is the accumulation and ordering of information, which has led to the processing of colossal amounts of information, a development known as Big Data. These storage and information processing capacities are bringing machines closer to being 'intelligent'.

The problem is that these new technological capacities have significant knock-on effects for employment and income distribution by creating a dynamic whereby jobs involving mid- to high-level cognitive skills are being displaced, as opposed to previously when only manual skills with a lower cognitive content were affected. Around the world, this had the specific consequence of creating a profound dichotomy between the high- and low-skilled workforces. The former are well remunerated while the latter experience wage stagnation, leading to a regressive income redistribution that contributes to the stagnation in aggregate demand.

It seems reasonable to conclude that feedback between the decoupling of the productive and financial sectors in relation to technological progress through the digitalization of cognitive skills is altering the employment structure due to the greater demand of qualified workers at the expense of low-skilled labor (McAffe, 2014). The widening income gap between those with or without good jobs will have negative consequences, exacerbating social and economic inequality.

6.6   FINANCIAL DECOUPLING AND TECHNOLOGICAL CHANGE IN THE RECOVERY

Inequality of income and social mobility are being discussed as two of the most important challenges facing contemporary society due to their economic and social ramifications. According to economic theory, inequality behaves like an inverted U: it initially grows because of technological progress, first benefiting the most highly skilled workers and the owners of capital before stabilizing, bringing greater benefits for the middle and lower classes, which necessarily reduces the inequality. Moreover, as long as the gap between the highest and lowest earners does not widen, there is no cause for concern. Three such processes have been documented in history since the Industrial Revolution. The first appears as a result of the first Industrial Revolution favoring the owners of the means of production at the expense of the working class. This situation is repeated when the United States took over leadership in the concentration of income, with the emergence of the 'robber barons' in the United States. This concentration later triggered the Great Depression that began in 1929, as shown by Piketty (2014), with inequality growing at an accelerated rate in the 1920s, leading to the top decile receiving 50 percent of the income. Subsequently, inequality fell in the two decades after the 1929 crash, stabilizing and becoming less concentrated in the 1940s and 1980s when the top-earning 1 percent were receiving around 30 percent of the income.

A third process of concentration emerged in the 1980s at the same time as the development of a globalized economic process. This concentration has continued into the twenty-first century, exacerbated by the great recession, without any signs yet of slowing down (Galbraith and Hale, 2014; Hellebrandt, 2014; Piketty, 2014). According to Oxfam International (2014), the world's 85 richest millionaires have the equivalent resources to those owned by half the population of the planet. In addition, the richest 1 percent owns US$110 trillion, equivalent to 65 times the total resources owned by the poorest half. In 2013, there were 1426 people on the super-rich list (210 more than in 2012) who own a combined fortune of US$5.4 trillion (Oxfam, 2014, pp. 2–3). The Bloomberg Index of the richest 300 individuals shows that their wealth increased by US$524 billion to US$3.7 trillion at 31 December 2013. According to the McKinsey Institute (2013), millionaires' wealth grew annually by 8.3 percent between 2009 and 2012 reaching US$69 trillion. This income redistribution has led to 90 percent of those with the lowest incomes seeing a reduction in their share of global income from 54.7 percent to 50.4 percent between 2000 and 2012. Wealth-X, in its first report in 2011 on the world's super-rich[4] counted 185,795 individuals with a combined fortune of US$25 trillion (Wealth-X, 2011, p. 8), 1235 of whom had a net value above US$1 billion (Wealth-X, 2011, p. 10). It is forecasted that 37 percent of the super-rich will be in developing countries by 2016. We can see this trend in the following examples: in India, the numbers of super-rich increased from 6 to 61 between 2000 and 2012 with up to US$250 million, while Mexico has five super-rich individuals and 27 of the richest 2325 individuals in the world in 2014. The Latin American region has the highest growth rate of ultra-high net worth individuals (Wealth-X, 2014).

In some emerging economies, this dynamic of inequality has a similar pattern of behavior found in industrial countries although with differences, the main one being that the concentration of the top decile is far lower in emerging economies compared to industrialized countries. In the 1940s, the highest level of concentration reached 26 percent in the country with the least equality, which at that time was Argentina. Also in these countries, concentration fell after the Second World War, until levels lower than 10 percent were reached at the beginning of the 1980s, far below what happened in industrialized countries. Since the beginning of this decade, a tendency toward concentration has been underway, though nowhere near the levels reached in the United States and in Europe. In Colombia, the country currently with the lowest level of equality, the top decile barely reaches 20 percent of the total income.

In this redistribution trend, the most notable aspect, as Piketty clearly shows, is the different behavior found in capital gains and high wages in these cycles of concentration. Capital gains determined the concentration of income in the early twentieth century, whereas high wages play a lesser and secondary role, with this correlation weakening since 1970. Therefore, the remuneration of highly qualified workers shows a pattern of behavior that highlights the importance of technological change (Jorgenson and Timmer, 2011) and this pattern can be related to the fact that technology-based knowledge industries produced the highest earnings with an average of 28 percent a year (Bloomberg, 2014).

This trend varies across the productive spectrum: 'finance and business' ranks as the most intensive area in terms of skill and hence remunerations, while manufacturing is the least intensive. In fact, since the 1929 crash, improved income distribution in the United States has been fundamentally connected to the reduction in capital gains, but in the new tendency of concentration in the late twentieth century, it has been the well-paid, highly skilled work that has had the strongest effect on the unprecedented levels of concentration. Independently of the upturn in capital gains, as a result of the financialization brought about by the decoupling of the financial sector from the real sector, it is important to note that in the last two cycles of concentration, a different class has benefited: in the early twentieth century, the beneficiaries were capitalists and business owners, while at the end of the century the most highly paid workers profited most. Nevertheless, the result has been the same in the sense that a greater concentration in the top decile ends up translating into a significant slowing down of global aggregate demand. The explanation is that global aggregate demand will contract depending on whether there is a rise or fall in profits.

6.7 CONCLUSIONS

The financial-productive decoupling and the new direction taken by technological change appear as factors severely eroding a recovery in the global economy due to the negative effect on income distribution and, therefore, on aggregate demand. This dilemma is illustrated by the low levels of growth expected in the next five years.

These tendencies in income distribution point toward how financial decoupling in addition to the qualitative shift in technological innovation have an impact on the capacity of aggregate demand, and therefore on the possibilities of a stronger economic recovery. These levels of inequality not only constitute a challenge for social equality but also create a significant obstacle in the path of economic growth. In fact, income inequality can be considered not only a factor that is partially responsible for the great recession but also a determining factor in the feeble recovery. More decoupling and inequality lead to less credit and investment, thus contracting aggregate demand.

The stability and the global economic recovery are being threatened by the vulnerability caused by the interconnectedness between national economies under the circumstances of financial-productive decoupling and by the new direction of technological change. The risks caused by the interaction of these phenomena mean that the economy and public policies are unaffected by apolitical and asocial forces, and that in fact political and social factors control the behavior of all types of physical and financial assets. At the heart of the debate, therefore, lies the question about why and how asset prices are having a global impact. Carry trades and exchange rate imbalances show that the international monetary system is dysfunctional due to the lack of balance between the needs of the productive sector and the actions of the financial sector.

Experience with the recovery's strength clearly shows that growth will not come from freedom given to the markets. What society needs is a rethinking of public policies in order to find solutions to improve the demand capacity of the majority of the population through income redistribution policies. If income continues to be concentrated in the hands of 1 percent of the population, it will prove very difficult to find a new balance that may promote investment and credit. It is undeniable that the anticrisis policies have contributed to exacerbate inequality: fiscal austerity and monetary expansion benefit owners of assets, and the obsession with reducing the deficit may be positive for fiscal discipline but does nothing to reduce inequality gaps. In terms of political economy, the failures of public policies before and after the crisis were undoubtedly worsened by the inequality and greater political power of the aforesaid 1 percent of the population.

The most important question is whether inequality will improve with a recovery, or if, on the contrary, it will continue to worsen. The global economic system requires a move toward productive investment, rather than financial engineering, in order to improve stability and growth. Currently, investment in infrastructure is needed in order to contribute to long-term growth. At this time of low interest rates and high levels of unemployment, public investment in bridges, highways, electricity networks and mass transport systems can prove very inexpensive. This work does not necessarily have to be carried out by the state, for it can also be placed in the hands of the private sector. Economies with a capacity for fiscal maneuvers, such as in the case of Germany, require a boost in demand so that Europe's peripheral countries can grow more.

Distribution must also be improved through a progressive taxation on net worth so that those who own millions of dollars in assets pay more in taxes rather than those who are simply trying to earn enough to have dignified living conditions. This implies redistributing profits on a global scale.

This option requires greater responsibility among governments to tackle the imbalances generated by new technological shifts and the real-financial decoupling, with the combined effects that this has on the concentration of income and wealth. A body of evidence shows that imbalances are not resolved by unfettered markets. The opposite is true: markets left to their own devices will end up creating more imbalances and therefore eroding the possibility of greater dynamism in order to counteract the lethargic global economic recovery.

NOTES

*   My thanks to Hilda Dávila Ibáñez for her comments on an early draft of this chapter.
1.   The data from this section comes from the International Monetary Fund, World Economic Outlook Database, April 2015.
2.   This reduction in the level of open employment was strongly influenced by those who chose to retire instead of remaining unemployed.
3.   Author's estimates on the basis of data from Bureau of Labor Statistics (2015).
4.   Individuals with an ultra-high net worth of US\$30 million.

REFERENCES

Bank for International Settlements (2013), *Triennial Central Bank Survey: Foreign Exchange Turnover in April 2013: Preliminary Global Results*, Basel, September.
Bloomberg (2014), 'Crece riqueza de multimillonarios en 2013', *El Financiero*, 3 January, Mexico City, p. 17.
Bureau of Labor Statistics (2015), *Employment, Hours, and Earnings from the Current Employment Statistics Survey (National)*, available at http://data.bls.gov/pdq/SurveyOutputServlet, accessed 30 April 2015.
Corley, M., J. Michie and C. Oughton (2002), 'Technology, growth and employment', *International Review of Applied Economics*, **16**(3), 265–76.
Drucker, P. (1986), 'The changed world economy', *Foreign Affairs*, Spring, 781–2.

Epstein, G. (ed.) (2005), *Financialization and the World Economy*, Cheltenham, UK and Northampton, MA, USA: Edward Elgar.

Fabrice, C. and D. Harris (2007), 'Technology shocks and employment', *The Economic Journal*, **117**(523), 1436–59.

Galbraith, J.K. and J.T. Hale (2014), 'The evolution of economic inequality in the United States, 1969–2012: evidence from data on inter-industrial earnings and inter-regional incomes', *World Economic Review*, **3**, 1–19.

Hellebrandt, T. (2014), 'Income inequality developments in the great recession', Peterson Institute for International Economics Policy Brief No. PB 14-3, January, Washington, DC.

International Monetary Fund (2015), *World Economic Outlook*, April, Washington, DC.

Invernizzi, N. and G. Foladori (2010), 'Nanotechnology implications for labor', *Nanotechnology Law & Business*, Spring, 68–78.

Jorgenson, D.W. and P. Timmer (2011), 'Structural change in advanced nations: a new set of stylised facts', *Scandinavian Journal of Economics*, **113**(1), 1–29.

Kitcher, P. (2001), *El Avance de la Ciencia*, México City: UNAM, Instituto de Investigaciones Filosóficas.

Kumhof, M., R. Ranciere and P. Winant (2013), 'Inequality, leverage and crisis: the case of endogenous default', IMF Working Paper/13/249, November, Research Department, Washington, DC.

Lapavitsas, C. (2009), *El Capital Financiarizado. Expansión y Crisis*, Madrid: Maia Editores.

McAffe, A. (2014), *The Second Machine Age*, New York: W.W. Norton & Co.

McKinsey Institute (2013), *Global Private Banking Survey 2013*, Boston, MA.

Menkhoff, L. and N. Tolksdorf (2001), *Financial Market Drift. Decoupling of the Financial Sector from the Real Economy?*, Germany: Springer-Verlag.

Morales, M.A. and M. Amaro (2014), 'División cognitiva del trabajo, estructura organizacional e innovación: el caso de la empresa biotecnológica Mexicana', *Economía: Teoría y Práctica*, **40**, January–June, 137–64.

Oxfam (2014), 'Working for the few, political capture and economic inequality', Oxfam Briefing Paper 178, 20 January, available at http://www.oxfam.org, accessed October 2014.

Piketty, T. (2014), *Capital in the Twenty-first Century*, Cambridge, MA: The Belknap Press.

Prasad, E.S. (2014), *The Dollar Trap*, Princeton, NJ: Princeton University Press.

Rajan, R.G. (2010), *Fault Lines: How Hidden Fractures Still Threaten the World Economy*, Princeton, NJ: Princeton University Press.

Reich, R. (2010), *Aftershock: The Next Economy and America's Future*, New York: Random House.

Rozo, C.A. (2003), 'Apertura, crecimiento y estructura financiera. El desacoplamiento financiero a la mexicana', in de A.G. Mántey and N.O. Levy (eds), *Financiamiento del desarrollo con mercados de dinero y capital globalizados*, UNAM-Porrúa: Mexico, pp. 207–52.

Stockhammer, E. (2012), 'Financialization, income distribution and the crisis', *Investigación Económica*, **71**(279), January–March, 39–70.

Summers, L.H. (2013), 'Economic possibilities for our children', *NBER Reporter*, No. 4, 1–6.

Tett, G. (2014), 'Por qué el dólar se mantiene estable?', *El Financiero*, 7 February (syndicated article from the *Financial Times*).

The Economist (2014), 'The future of jobs. The onrushing wave', 17 January.

Wealth-X (2011), *World Ultra Wealth Report 2011, Uncovering Pockets of Opportunity*, Wealth-X Pte Ltd and its affiliates, Singapore, available at http://www.wealth.com, accessed November 2015.

Wealth-X (2014), *Wealth-X and UBS Billionaire Census 2014–2015*, Wealth-X Pte Ltd and its affiliates, Singapore, available at http://www.wealth.com, accessed November 2014.

7. Global disequilibria and the inequitable distribution of income

Alma Chapoy

7.1 INTRODUCTION

The monetary and financial problems that erupted in 2008 aggravated existing disequilibria: between the financial and real economies, between capital and work and between the rich and the poor. This is because, since the early 1980s, the financial market has increasingly led the economy. One of the most damaging consequences of this situation is the disproportionate earnings from financial speculation, even in mid-crisis. This led to a further disequilibrium in the balance of power between business owners and workers, which results in a growing inequality in the distribution of income.

The deregulation of the financial system and the liberalization of the capital account, which was made possible by the reduction of the state's role in the economy, led to the financial sector having a growing share of gross domestic product (GDP). The financial system became less concerned with the needs of the productive economy, real investment or the international trade in goods, choosing to do business with – considerably more lucrative – financial assets. The above have led to numerous, persistent and growing global disequilibria in trade and in transnational flows of capital, which have increased since the crisis that began in 2007–2008. Without actually predicting the crisis, many economists had been warning over a number of years of the risks entailed in the large macroeconomic global disequilibria, which helped to inflate the asset bubble until it burst.

The disequilibrium of most interest for the purposes of this research is the asymmetry in the international monetary and financial system (IM&FS). The massive monetary expansion of the US Federal Reserve System (the Fed) and the Bank of Japan led to a great flow of capital to the emerging countries, which saw a rise in their currencies, stock markets and commodity prices. The opposite phenomena have been observed since the Fed began to indicate that it would withdraw its monetary incentives. In other words, the growth prospects of emerging countries seem to be affected to a large extent by the exaggerated magnitude and volatility of the global capital flows.

Since the 1997–1999 Asian crisis, emerging countries began to increase foreign currency reserves to protect themselves from the abrupt stoppages and reverses in the entry of capital. By accumulating reserves these countries transfer financial resources to the developed world, in other words, the poor nations lend, above all to the United States, at interest rates that are close to zero. As a result, instead of being used to boost their own development, the reserves of emerging countries are largely being given to the US financial system, strengthening the role of the dollar as the principal international reserve currency.

For these reasons. it is argued in this research that global disequilibria largely respond to the IM&FS based on the US dollar. The disequilibria of the world economy are perpetuated by governmental debt and the massive creation of money that is not backed up. In this context, it is notable that inequality intensifies as financial innovation increases.

This chapter is divided into five sections. Section 7.2 analyzes the growing inequality of income distribution, Section 7.3 complements this by tackling questions such as austerity, vulnerability and unemployment. Section 7.4 focuses on commodity and farmland speculation, which have a high impact on economic inequality. This speculation is on the whole possible thanks to financial innovation. Section 7.5 brings all these together under the heading of global disequilibria, looking at six aspects in their own subsections: the preeminence of the financial sector; the accumulation of foreign currency reserves; the United States and China: the world's greatest bilateral disequilibrium; exchange rates; the currents of international capital; and lastly, credit expansion and the international monetary system (IMS). The chapter closes with a few final thoughts.

7.2   THE INCREASE OF INEQUALITY

The slow, unequal and volatile recovery of the world economy and the consequent global uncertainty continue to put a break on employment and hence on the possibility of increasing people's wellbeing. The growth of inequality in the distribution of income, and in access to goods, services and opportunities, reveal the obvious need to achieve economic growth capable of creating greater social inclusion and worthwhile jobs.

In the years that preceded the global financial crisis, there had been a slight reduction in inequality in most countries, but the crisis and the world economic recession that followed accentuated the unequal distribution of wealth within and between countries: 842 million people or around

12 percent of the world's population suffer from chronic hunger and over 1.5 billion people or nearly half the workforce have informal or precarious jobs; 80 percent of the world's adult population do not have a pension and have to work or depend on the family (UNDP, 2014).

In contrast, between mid 2013 and mid 2014 the wealth of the world grew by 20.1 trillion dollars, or 8.3 percent, the fastest rate yet recorded, reaching 263 trillion dollars, compared to 117 trillion dollars in 2000. (The US definition of a trillion is used here.) The wealth of the United States grew by 11.4 percent to 91 trillion dollars, representing 34.6 percent of total world wealth. In Europe it grew by 10.6 percent, rising to 85.2 trillion dollars. In both regions capital markets were key to the growth in wealth. In the US stock market capital grew by 22.6 percent while the comparable figure for Canada, France and Germany was nearly 30 percent (Credit Suisse, 2014).

The number of so-called ultra-high net worth individuals (UHNWIs) with fortunes of over 50 million dollars is growing faster than average wealth, which presages another recession. By mid 2014 there were 53,000 UHNWIs in the United States or 41 percent of the worldwide total of 128,000 (Credit Suisse, 2014).

The 2014 Credit Suisse report indicates that it is normal for personal wealth to grow four or five times faster than incomes, not 6.5 times as it did in 2014. This only happened on three occasions over the last hundred years: in the Great Depression of 1929, when the technology bubble burst in 2000–2001 and with the crash of the mortgage market in 2007–2008. This report attributes two-thirds of the increase in wealth to the recovery of Wall Street, which has tripled its value since 2009. In contrast, average incomes in the United States fell to the level of 1995, while assets were 19 percent higher than the 2006 record.

7.3   AUSTERITY, VULNERABILITY AND UNEMPLOYMENT

Full employment was an explicit government policy in the three decades following the Second World War, and at this time productivity, employment and salaries generally grew at a constant pace without suffering significant inflationary pressures. However, labor market 'flexibility' policies were introduced in the 1980s to reduce costs, which among other things implied lowering wages, cuts in severance costs and increases in pensionable age, with heightened conflict between business owners and the unions. Events in Europe are an example of such policies.

An insistence that fiscal austerity is going to increase productive activities is as false as claiming that workers should accept lower salaries to make unemployment disappear and for the economy to get back to dull strength, or that union and government intervention sparked the unemployment problem. It is well known that the austerity policies of US President Herbert Hoover from March 1929 to 1933 helped convert the 1929 stock market crash into the Great Depression. Likewise, the measures applied by the International Monetary Fund (IMF) in East Asia and Latin America in the 1990s converted declines into recessions and these into depressions (Stiglitz, 2014a). Policies based on the dominant economic theories of the past 30 years have been important factors in the increase in inequality (Stiglitz, 2012).

Thus, it is vital that the macroeconomic policies that led to the crisis should be abandoned. According to these policies, the priority of monetary policy is to control inflation while fiscal policy should reduce the deficit. At this point it is evident that these measures limit and actually hinder economic growth. Instead of these, the creation of unemployment and the relief of poverty should be at the core of national and global economic strategies. Similarly, future development programs should focus on reducing vulnerability to financial hardship, which is such a contributor to inequality.

> At its basic level, vulnerability is defined as an exposure to a marked decrease in the standard of living. It is of special concern when it is prolonged, and when standards of living fall below critical thresholds, to a point of deprivation. Economists' traditional single-minded focus on GDP has led them to lose sight of vulnerability. Individuals are risk-averse. The realization that they are vulnerable thus leads to large welfare losses – even before they face the consequences of a shock itself. The failure of our systems of metrics to adequately capture the importance of security to individual and societal well-being was a key criticism of GDP by the International Commission on the Measurement of Economic Performance and Social Progress. (Stiglitz, 2014b, p. 84)

Growing inequality in the distribution of income is an inevitable effect of capitalism, and if it continues to increase it will ruin democracy and economic stability. Inequality is worsened when the capital return rates are higher than the rate of economic growth (Piketty, 2014, p. 1). In turn, an unequal distribution of income undermines growth by establishing an exclusive economy when the requirement is for an inclusive one. Growth for its own sake does not ensure that inequalities are reduced, well-designed government policies are also needed. To begin with, countries need to carry out a profound review of their fiscal systems so that governments can make resources available to achieve change. Nevertheless, this raises challenges since it affects the richest and most powerful sectors, which exert pressure to eliminate fiscal deficits by cutting support for the poor or middle class, or for vital public investment projects.

In a similar vein, Stiglitz argues that recovery cannot rely on monetary policy. To give a strong boost to the economy other government policies need to be put into action, which are coherent and whose values support social justice, responsibility and democracy (Stiglitz, 2012). It is obvious that social justice should not be the sole consideration for the distribution of income. It is also important from a perspective concerned purely with economic performance, particularly if there is a significant difference in the marginal propensity to consume between the upper and lower echelons of society.

Goda and Lysandrou (2014) have noted that in the period immediately before the financial crisis, the extent of market collateralized debt obligations (CDOs) reached such proportions that it caused a general disaster when it collapsed. These authors focus on the global concentration of wealth and present evidence on the specific contribution of high net worth individuals (HNWIs) to this negative effect. After contributing to the problem with yields in the main US debt markets, the HNWIs used risk funds to maintain pressure on the US banks to resolve this yield problem, creating massive CDOs. The aforementioned authors note that the majority of the mainstream economists who shape government policy still believe that the financial crisis was due to a combination of deregulation, mistaken incentives and lax monetary policy rather than to increased inequality in the distribution of income and wealth.

Goda and Lysandrou conclude that priority should also be given to the redistribution of income and wealth because the crisis was caused by financial inequality as well as by regulatory failure. Without the large number of citizens on a low income, US banks would not have had the abundance of raw material necessary to create CDOs on a massive scale. On the other hand, removing the influence of the HNWIs would take away the pressure on the US banks to create major proportions of CDOs.

Another global problem, despite the radical monetary policies of the main central banks, is the growing threat of deflation, and deflation is as much an enemy of stability and growth as inflation. Nearly 7 trillion dollars were injected by three of the world's most important central banks: 4 trillion by the Fed, 2 trillion by the Bank of Japan and 1 trillion by the European Central Bank. This raised share prices instead of the costs of goods and wages, which have remained very steady for years. In the twenty-first century a large part of the US economy has been based on financial engineering and not on investment in productive activities and technological innovation (Reuters, 2014).

None of the aforementioned central banks have been able to stabilize their economies or ensure that inflation sticks to their target of close to 2 percent. In September 2014 the personal consumer price index measured by inflation, which the Fed uses, stood at less than 2 percent for the 29th consecutive month. Such a minimal price rise for a long period may be a sign of economic weakness. The chances of deflation in the eurozone and Japan are sharper. 'The real economy needs spending, which should come from the fiscal side where deficits are anathema and balanced budgets are sought' (Reuters, 2014).

7.4   COMMODITY AND FARMLAND SPECULATION

Even in mid-crisis big investors are receiving increased windfalls as a result of tactics that threaten the most vulnerable. Financial investors treat commodities as just another asset with which to optimize the risk/yield profile of their portfolios without considering that they can cause starvation in the poorest sectors of underdeveloped countries and even in advanced ones.

The commodity price boom from 2002 to mid 2008 was the most pronounced for various decades, and to a large extent it was due to the growing presence of financial investors in the commodity futures markets, which caused much harm, particularly in developing countries dependent on the import of food and energy. The number of commodity futures and options contracts tripled in this period, and the hypothetical value of contracts related to commodities not registered in the stock exchange increased 14-fold, reaching 13 trillion dollars (Mayer, 2010). The subsequent decline in commodity prices in the second half of 2008 was one of the main means by which the economic recession of the advanced countries was transmitted to the developing world. In 2010 the prices began to rise again, once again to a large extent because of the speculation of financial investors.

The situation is compounded by the speculation mania that affects all types of crops, which have also become financial assets for capital risk funds, pension funds and prestigious universities such as Harvard. Between 2000 and 2001 around 500 million acres, or eight times the area of the United Kingdom, were bought or rented in developing countries at the expense of local food security and the rights to the land of local people. When food prices rose significantly in 2008, investors also took interest, and in 2009 land transactions in developing countries rose by 200 percent. In addition to pushing up food prices and the growing demand for biofuels, the financial sector has a growing interest in agricultural land (The Oakland Institute, 2014).

The subsidies given under the European Union's Common Agricultural Policy (CAP) give incentives to rich farmers, agribusiness and speculative land accumulation. In the European Union half the land under cultivation is managed by 3 percent of the farms, which are larger than 250 acres. In a worrying trend, corporately controlled property is increasing, though it still only accounted for 12 percent in 2014.

In the United States investors are increasingly interested in profiting from the hike in the value of private stock-controlled assets and are preparing to buy 400 million acres over the next two decades. This is the equivalent to half the agricultural land in the United States. This land, worth approximately 1.8 trillion dollars, could be exploited for industrial use such as fracking or fossil fuel production. Land prices are rising as a result of the search for quick profits, endangering the future viability of farming and the countryside, and placing the health of the land at long-term risk. The 2014 Oakland Institute report describes irresponsible and environmentally harmful practices carried out on behalf of absentee investor owners.

In relation to the above, the Bolivian President, Evo Morales, who hosted the G77+China[1] summit in June 2014 in Santa Cruz, Bolivia, asserted that the development paradigm dictated by transnational capital through compliant governments is destroying ecosystems by pillaging the natural resources of the less developed countries to drive economic growth, producing ever more disposable products for the consumers of the advanced countries, increasing per capita and collective energy consumption and permanently devaluing the cost of labor, which in turn leads to the creation of enormous industrial reserve armies to lower the end price of products and push large-scale production. All this brings in its wake social unrest, growing political disquiet and natural disasters.

7.5   GLOBAL DISEQUILIBRIA

7.5.1   The Preeminence of the Financial Sector

One of the factors that has accentuated the great global disequilibria is the asymmetrical nature of the present international monetary system (IMS), in which few currencies are used as international reserves, while the rest of the currencies remain unused. This asymmetry is in turn translated into inadequate fiscal, monetary and financial policies in the advanced countries, particularly in the United States where they harm economic growth, employment and global trade.

The mobility of international capital has facilitated the financing of unprecedented deficits in the United States, also with an unprecedented surplus in the emerging nations of Asia and oil exporting countries (Lane and Milesi-Ferretti, 2005). In the United States, the enormous influx of capital in 2007 provided 15 percent of the country's credit (Duncan, 2012).

7.5.2   The Accumulation of Foreign Currency Reserves

The root cause of the 1997–1998 Asian crisis was the accumulation of large-scale foreign currency reserves, coupled with the attitude of the IMF at the time. By doing this, the emerging and developing countries were transferring funds to the industrialized countries, particularly the United States. The value of this transfer exceeded 826 billion dollars in 2011. Obviously, the United States does not have the slightest intention of making adjustments to its economy, which is why the diversification of the reserves is an urgent matter. This continues and the large-scale export of capital to advanced countries runs counter to the economic development of the emerging nations because it involves a loss of investment for development and an increasingly inefficient allocation of resources.

When international liquidity is abundant and the influx of foreign capital exceeds the financing needs of the balance of payments, international monetary reserves will increase. It should be stressed that this is a financial loss for the country that accumulates the reserve, because of the difference in interest rates and the increase in gross public debt. For this reason, the makers of economic policy face a quandary over whether to buy their reserves to avoid a large real overvaluation of their currency or to absorb this extra charge in the gross public debt, sterilizing the monetary effects of this policy. A higher gross public debt to GDP relationship increases a country's risk premium and the expectations for an exchange rate depreciation, which in turn put pressure on internal interest rates (Nassif et al., 2011).

Foreign capital is attracted to developing countries by the growing interest rate differentials between the advanced and the emerging countries, privatization and an increased global appetite for risk and neoliberal strategies in general. A wide exchange rate differential must be maintained in order to continue attracting foreign capital. The effect that this has on growth varies depending on whether it is direct foreign investment or portfolio investment. According to Salama (1999), financialization depresses investment in the productive sector. This also affects the international division of labor with everything that is implied in terms of workforce flexibility, job insecurity and the loss of employment. This increases the danger of dependency on foreign capital and accentuates the unfair distribution of income.

7.5.3 The United States and China: The World's Greatest Bilateral Disequilibrium

The United States has had a balance of trade deficit since the early 1970s, reaching 840 billion dollars in 2006, or 2 percent of world GDP and 6.2 percent of US net domestic product. US net foreign liabilities are equivalent to 8 percent of global production. In 1997 the current account deficit was just 141 billion dollars, but it rose to 415 billion dollars in 2000 and then to 806.2 billion dollars in 2006. When the crisis broke this deficit was partially reduced by fiscal and monetary stimuli, and by liquidity injections, falling to 378 billion dollars in 2009, but it rose again in 2010 reaching 470 billion dollars or 3.2 percent of gross national product (GNP), becoming yet another obstacle to global economic and financial stability (IMF, 2011, table A11).

In contrast to the US deficit, between 2004 and 2007 the Chinese trade surplus quintupled and between 2004 and 2008 its stock of foreign currency reserves rose by 1.5 trillion dollars (Blanchard and Milesi-Ferretti, 2009). The Chinese current account surplus fell from 412 billion dollars in 2008 (representing 9.1 percent of GDP), to 261 billion dollars in 2009 (5.2 percent of GDP), recovering to 305 billion dollars in 2010 (5.1 percent of GDP). The only other countries recording surpluses over 100 billion dollars were Japan and Germany (The World Bank, 2011, table 4).

No country has had a sustained deficit of the size of the US deficit, whether in absolute terms or as a percentage of the global economy. As Alan Greenspan noted in 2005, 'International finance presents us with a number of intriguing anomalies, but the one that seems to bedevil monetary policy makers the most as they seek stability and growth (the topic of this conference) is the seemingly endless ability of the United States to finance its current account deficit'.

The US deficit is due to the country's reduced savings and growing consumption. Between September 2003 and September 2004 the rate of US national savings fluctuated between 1 percent and 2 percent, marking the country's lowest net national savings in history, since it was equivalent to half the figure recorded in the late 1980s and early 1990s. Since the financial crisis broke the savings rate has practically fallen to zero.

The Palais Royal Initiative (Boorman and Icard, 2012) attributes global disequilibria to the lack of an effective discipline that makes adjustment compulsory. Despite its global membership and its mandate to prevent and resolve crises, the IMF has not fulfilled its duty of overseeing global financial stability, since its mandate is not strong enough to confront powerful countries, which among other things do not need to borrow from the institution. Emerging and developing countries are underrepresented in the institution.[2]

Despite the fact that disequilibria in global trade, in capital flows and in the global foreign exchange system were an important cause of the crisis, the subject did not appear on the G20 agenda until the June 2010 meeting in Toronto, when the group committed itself to adjusting its foreign exchange to reduce the global disequilibria by at least half by 2013. This did not take place. It was also agreed to reduce the burden of debt by 2016 (G20, 2011).

The meeting of G20 finance ministers and central bankers focused on establishing shared criteria for the measurement of global disequilibria. In principle, five indicators were established: the current account balance, the real exchange rate, international monetary reserves, public debt and the public deficit and private savings. There was agreement on the internal debt and public deficit indicators, and on the levels of savings and private debt, but not on external indicators. China and other countries opposed the US proposal to set a limit on current account disequilibria of 4 percent of GDP (G20, 2011).

7.5.4   Exchange Rates

The proper operation of the IMS depends on countries carrying out their economic and financial policies in keeping with fundamental economic variables and the global equilibrium. Thus, the setting of exchange rates cannot be left to the market. As exchange rates play a crucial role in the process of rebalancing, it is necessary for them to be subjected to a series of principles and rules, which can be agreed collectively and work hand in hand with the macroeconomic policy of the most advanced countries.

The rate of exchange is the value of one currency in terms of another, and it fluctuates continually, which is why it is the focus of concerns about who should be responsible for studying the problems derived from economic interaction between countries. The exchange rate should be at a level that enables equality between the current account balance and the capital account balance, so that it can move in both directions to achieve a balance. The exchange rate is determined by the interaction of governments, individuals, companies and financial institutions that buy and sell foreign currency in the exchange market for the purposes of making international payments and increasingly for speculation. Important and unforeseeable news from an economic and political standpoint spreads almost instantly across the whole world, often having a decisive effect on the decisions of economic agents to move their capital in the foreign exchange market, thus determining the short-term variations in exchange rates.

The IMS should be modified to allow orderly adjustments in the exchange rates that help the real economy; and without this the solutions to disequilibria are chaotic[3] and could regress to protectionism, which would weaken the global recovery and sow the seeds for the next financial crisis. World economic activity could collapse with devastating effects for all countries, just as it did in the 1930s.

In the first US–China Strategic and Economic Dialogue, held on 27–28 July 2009, a statement was made on what both countries should do: China should consume more, save less and export less while the United States should consume less, save more, export more, import less and be more competitive to convince the world that it will not continue to be the consumer of last resort. Maybe in this way other countries would stop depending on trade surpluses and would generate internal demand (US Department of State, 2009).

In this regard, Stiglitz (2010) has warned that a revaluation of the yuan would not reduce the large trade and current account deficits with the United States considerably. In order to reduce the deficits, basic changes to US public and private savings would be required. China and other countries running a surplus, like Germany, maintain that the threat to the world economy does not come from them, but instead from the lax monetary policy of the United States. On the other hand, the United States accuses them of basing their growth on the rest of the world and not on their internal demand.

7.5.5 Flows of International Capital

Put simply, the IMS is asymmetrical because it is based on the US dollar and this meant that as the crisis unfolded, it spread through different channels to countries that had nothing to do with the institutions that sparked the crisis, and finally it became a global economic recession (Magalhaes and Macedo, 2010).

With the monetary flexibility of the United States, known as quantitative easing, much of the additional liquidity was directed at the emerging countries, pushing exchange rates even higher and increasing the danger of bubbles forming. The same is true of the Long Term Restructuring Operations (LTRO) of the European Central Bank and the monetary policy adopted by Japan in early 2013.

The capital flows, in general, have grown to the point of dominating international transactions in the advanced countries, and they are increasingly dominating those of the emerging countries as well. The global currents of capital tripled from 1995 to 2010, reaching 6.4 trillion dollars, which represents 14.5 percent of world GDP. This proportion had kept between 2 percent and 6 percent between 1980 and 1995 (IMF, 2011). In this sense, they have become a fixture of the IMS, which makes it necessary to control their harmful effects with guidelines agreed at the international level (Boorman and Icard, 2012). UNCTAD (2012) proposed an international agreement on the scale, speed and temporary nature of quantitative expansion policies within a broad framework of objectives to reduce global disequilibria. It also indicated that it would require increased bilateral and multilateral supervision that should not be under the control of the IMF, since it had displayed a lack of willingness to do so.

The problems of the advanced countries, and the measures that are applied to resolve them, make the inflows of capital to other countries volatile, cyclical and short term. On repeated occasions, the emerging countries have indicated that the United States, Europe and Japan should avoid increased volatility in the flows of capital, which of course they will not do.

Although the eurozone crisis will not be addressed here because of lack of space, an important cause, which also makes the solution difficult, should at least be noted: the disequilibrium between Germany and the countries on the European periphery:

> Strikingly, Europe's internal monetary system developed similar imbalances, though for different reasons. Northern capital flowed south in search of higher returns, rather than as part of a drive to build a precautionary savings hoard. That difference helps explain why, though both systems experienced problems after 2008, only the European system sank into serious financial crisis: demand for safe dollar assets when trouble struck while demand for riskier peripheral bonds tumbled (until the European Central Bank intervened decisively). (Avent, 2014)

7.5.6 The Expansion of Credit in the International Monetary System

The economic and financial crisis that broke in 2008 was inevitable given the failings of the IMS after 1971. In 1968, 1.3 billion dollars in credit were backed up by 10 billion dollars in gold. So long as gold was money, the creation of credit was limited by the supply of this metal. When the United States broke the link between the dollar and gold, it took away all limitations on the amount of credit that could be created. Over four decades no more gold was added to the reserve, but 50 trillion dollars of credit were created (Duncan, 2012).

In spite of the enormous costs of the Second World War, in 1945, the total debt of companies, individuals and government in the United States was equivalent to 159 percent of national GDP. In 1981, 36 years later, this relationship had risen slightly to 168 percent. Total debt has risen 214 percent in real terms since 1945, while the economy has grown by

197 percent, therefore the debt to GDP relationship remained stable over this long period, despite disturbances such as the two great oil crises. But between 1981 and 2009 US debt increased by 390 percent in real terms while the economy only grew by 120 percent. Therefore, the debt to GDP relationship in 2009 was 381 percent, an all-time high worldwide. Even in 1930 when GDP collapsed, this relationship was not above 300 percent and it fell rapidly afterwards (Duncan, 2012).

Credit expansion in the United States brought wealth, profits, jobs and abundant tax income, and unprecedented prosperity to the economy. The massive expansion of credit led to a very long economic boom. Above all, it generated a great quantity of finance capital that transformed the structure of economic activity since it went from producing goods to providing services, and finally to speculation (Duncan, 2012).

Corporate executives and holders of debt have prospered alike, while the great majority have seen their salaries decline in real terms and their debts increase. Reducing production, increasing consumption and contracting rising amounts of debt to fill the gap is not sustainable behavior.

The great recession began in 2008 when credit could no longer expand and thereafter the whole debt superstructure began to collapse. Asset and commodity prices fell, spending dropped and payment defaults followed. When the shortage of liquidity was converted into massive insolvency rapidly spreading at a global level, the Fed created 1.7 trillion dollars of liquidity in what became the first of three rounds of monetary flexibility. The financial system would not have survived without it.

Government debt and the mass printing of unbacked-up money have perpetuated the disequilibria. The crisis exacerbated the asymmetry of the IMS, because, among other things, the authorities of the countries whose currencies are used as international reserves injected great quantities of liquidity into their economies, without this affecting the value of their respective currencies. However, as the currencies of the emerging countries are weak they could not increase their supply because if they did the value of these currencies would have fallen drastically. Thus, to tackle capital outflows these countries had to depend on previous accumulations of international currencies and/or multilateral loans.

It has already been seen how instead of being used to boost their own development, the reserves of the emerging countries have been largely given to the US financial system, helping to diminish dollar fluctuations and maintain a system whose break-up could occur and which calls for a response. In their attempts to tackle the situation the emerging countries have again and again questioned the basis of the present international monetary and financial system; they have also made integrationist efforts aimed at monetary and financial stability and the harmonization of macroeconomic policies. To date, these efforts have been mainly expressed through regional monetary agreements with a view to creating alternative reserve currencies since the countries whose currencies perform this role have not acted with the discipline necessary to maintain the integrity of the system (Gilman, 2012).

The most promising agreements include common reserve funds that are hoped will serve as financial protection mechanisms and which in time will modify the global reserve system. As the dollar and the euro ceased to be reliable some time ago, the IMS needs a new benchmark. Nor can the Special Drawing Rights fulfill this role as their basket of currencies is primarily based on the aforementioned currencies, unless of course different currencies are used.

The fear of the collapse of the dollar is because of the failure of credible economic policies in the United States, but this still remains the key currency, not because its value is stable but because the United States does not borrow in other currencies. Thus, despite being an unlimited global debtor it can provide an asset that is free of risk of failure, although this is not completely true, since the United States could print dollars in response to any obligation, eroding the value of the dollar, which would be the same as a partial failure. In reality, it is the power to exercise political, economic and military pressure on other countries that determines the monetary hegemony of the United States (Fields and Vernengo, 2011, p. 3). What is more, the dollar has no rival since it is precisely the creation of a dominant country, resting on its geopolitical power (Cohen, 2009).

7.6   CONCLUSIONS

It is deduced from the above that the financial system has relegated the economic needs of production in favor of financial assets that are very much more profitable.

In the years prior to the crisis, there were substantial flows of capital to the United States and Europe where ever riskier assets were created in the search for higher yields in developing and emerging markets, causing an excessive expansion of credit. These currents of global capital above all benefited the owners of financial assets, with the majority of the losses being borne by wage earners and by people working in the real economy.

Large countries, particularly the United States, adopted lax monetary policies in response to the crisis. When worldwide monetary supply was increased, the banks preferred to capitalize instead of lending these funds;[4] in this manner the liquidity went nearly straight to the financial market, to invest in stocks and to speculate on foreign currency and commodities.

This clearly demonstrates that the world economy is increasingly based on financial innovation and not on productive investment.

It is financial innovation, with its application of new technologies to accelerate the creation of new financial instruments and payment systems, which enables market participants to earn disproportionate profits, as well as to transfer risks. Needless to say, financial innovation had a dominant role in the 2008 financial crash and its influence is on the rise. Maybe the most painful example of all is the speculation on commodities and farmland, which leads to greater inequality.

The prevailing economic thinking since the 1980s has led to an inefficient growth model that is creating ever increasing inequality because of its limited ability to create quality jobs and because the said model marginalizes social and employment policies. There is a link between a high level of income inequality, social discontent and political instability, which put a brake on economic growth. The events of the Middle East and North Africa are a demonstration of this.

The concentration of wealth shrinks this demand and increasing this on the basis of debt will not lead to the path of growth. So long as workers' incomes do not recover, global disequilibria will remain. Rebalancing global demand is key to a sustained recovery and to the efforts in pursuit of global equity.

Contrary to the claims that were made when the floating exchange was established, the level of international monetary reserves has increased considerably, which goes to show that the IMS is not capable of providing a global financial safety net.

The IMS absolutely favors the expansion of financial capital, at the expense of pillaging the resources of the developing world, resources that are transferred to the United States and to a lesser extent to other industrial nations.

Financial regulation with a global reach is required to stop the financial system from serving its own ends, to put a brake on the excesses and ensure that credit reaches those who need it most. Likewise, there is a need for a new economic theory whose objective will be the development of the common good and not the development of individualism. If the primacy of the markets continues, new crises will unfold.

The financial crisis exposed the long-standing weaknesses of the international monetary agreements. It was also evident just how related the economies and financial markets had become. For this reason, the central banks of these countries should move toward increased collaboration in monetary policy, with the aim of limiting the transfer of disequilibria in the international monetary and financial system.

If this is not attended to, the increasingly interrelated world economy will become ever more vulnerable. The form that the IM&FS adopts is very important, as has been noted it has direct implications for developing countries with regard to the growing exchange rate volatility, the acceleration of capital inflows and outflows, increasing macroeconomic instability and the risk of currency war. There is also an urgent need to regulate the commodity markets to end speculation. The reform of the IM&FS is too important for it to remain in the hands of a few countries, the most powerful of which, the United States, is the least interested in this reform.

Even in full crisis the earnings and bonuses of executives are higher than pre-crisis levels of remuneration. In contrast, austerity is affecting the living conditions of millions of people who try to survive in the real economy. This reinforces a quote from the International Labour Organization that 'some financial institutions are "too big to fail", while you have the feeling that "many people are simply too small to matter"' (International Labour Organization, 2011).

NOTES

1. In 1964, 77 developing countries set up this group that now has 133 members. The G77 seeks to make the international system fairer through a better north–south balance. This is strengthened by the increase in the participation of countries that have no hegemony over international decision making. China joined the summit in connection with its policy of trade expansion in Latin America.
2. Fifty years ago emerging markets and developing countries represented around 25 percent of the world's production. Today it is 50 percent and it is very probable that in the next decade the figure will reach 67 percent. Nevertheless, despite the recent changes, the voting power of these countries in the IMF and the World Bank does not reflect their growing share in the global economy.
3. Although it is not very likely, the investors who have financed the US deficit for years could suddenly reverse the huge flow of capital, which would precipitate a chaotic adjustment.
4. Furthermore, because of the prevailing uncertainty neither individuals nor companies are very inclined to request credit.

REFERENCES

Avent, R. (2014), 'The global monetary system, "injured reserve"', *The Economist*, available at http://www.economist.com/blogs/freeexchange/2014/07/global-monetary-system#8Rgqi4W6sxVHUwGc.99, accessed 25 July 2014.

Blanchard, O. and G.M. Milesi-Ferretti (2009), 'Global imbalances: in midstream', IMF Staff Position Note, SPN/09/29, 22 December, International Monetary Fund, Washington, DC.

Boorman, J. and A. Icard (2012), 'Palais Royal initiative – reform of the international monetary system: a cooperative approach for the 21th century', in

J. Boorman and A. Icard (eds), *Reform of the International Monetary System: The Palais Royal Initiative*, India: SAGE Publications, pp. 7–25.

Cohen, B.J. (2009), 'The future of reserve currencies', *Finance and Development*, **46**(3), September, 26–9.

Credit Suisse (2014), *Global Wealth Report*, Zurich: Credit Suisse, available at https://www.credit-suisse.com, accessed 14 October 2014.

Duncan, R. (2012), *The New Depression: The Breakdown of the Paper Money Economy*, Singapore: John Wiley & Sons.

Fields, D. and M. Vernengo (2011), 'Hegemonic currencies during the crisis: the dollar vs the euro in a Cartalist perspective', Levy Economics Institute of Bard College Working Paper 666, April.

Gilman, M. (2012), 'Can a BRICS monetary arrangement resist the G7 wall of money?', in M. Larionova and J. Kirto (eds), *BRICS, New Delhi: Stability, Security and Prosperity*, Toronto: Newsdesk Media/BRICS Research Group Higher School of Economics and University of Toronto, March, pp. 52–3.

Goda, T. and P. Lysandrou (2014), 'The contribution of wealth concentration to the subprime crisis: a quantitative estimation', *Cambridge Journal of Economics*, **38**(2), 301–27.

Greenspan, A. (2005), 'Stability and economic growth: the role of the central bank', Remarks by Chairman Alan Greenspan before the Bank of Mexico's 80th Anniversary International Conference (videoconference), 14 November, available at http://www.banxico.docx, accessed 15 July 2006.

G20 (2011), *Communique from the Meeting of Finance Ministers and Central Bank Governors*, Paris, 18–19 February, available at http://www.g20.org/Documents2011/02/COMMUNIQUE-G20_MGM_18-19_February_2011, accessed 13 May 2011.

IMF (2011), *World Economic Outlook: Tension from the Two-speed Recovery*, Washington, DC: International Monetary Fund.

IMF 2015, *Press Release*, No. 15/540, Washington, DC, International Monetary Fund, 30 November.

International Labour Organization (2011), *Statement by Mr. Juan Somavia, Director General of ILO, at the opening of the 100th International Labour Conference: Presentation of the Report of the Director General*, available at http://www.ilo.org/ilo/, accessed 1 June 2011.

Lane, P.R. and G.M. Milesi-Ferretti (2005), 'A global perspective on external position', National Bureau of Economic Research Working Paper No. 11589, September.

Magalhaes Prates, D. and M.A. Macedo Cintra (2010), 'The emerging market economies in the face of the global financial crisis', in S. Dullien, D.J. Kotte, A. Márquez and J. Priewe (eds), *The Financial and Economic Crisis of 2008–2009 and Developing Countries*, New York and Geneva: UNCTAD-Hochschule für Technik und Wirtschaft Berlin, pp. 53–72.

Mayer, J. (2010), 'The financialization of commodity markets and commodity price volatility', in S. Dullien, D.J. Kotte, A. Márquez and J. Priewe (eds), *The Financial and Economic Crisis of 2008–2009 and Developing Countries*, New York and Geneva: UNCTAD-Hochschule für Technik und Wirtschaft Berlin, pp. 73–97.

Nassif, A., C. Feijó and E. Araújo (2011), 'The long-term "optimal" real exchange rate and the currency overvaluation trend in open emerging economies: the case of Brazil', Discussion Paper 2011/620, UNCTAD, Geneva.

Piketty, T. (2014), *Capital in the Twenty-first Century*, Cambridge, MA: The Belknap Press of Harvard University Press.

Reuters (2014), 'Mayores economías, amenazadas por deflación', *El País*, available at http://elpais.com/, accessed 3 November 2014.

Salama, P. (1999), *Riqueza y pobreza en América Latina: la Fragilidad de las nuevas políticas económicas*, Mexico: Universidad de Guadalajara-Fondo de Cultura Económica.

Stiglitz, J. (2010), 'No time for a trade war', available at http://www.project-syndicate.org/commentary/no-time-for-a-trade-war, accessed 6 April 2010.

Stiglitz, J. (2012), *The Price of Inequality: How Today's Divided Society Endangers Our Future*, New York: W.W. Norton & Co.

Stiglitz, J. (2014a), 'Reconstructing macroeconomic theory to manage economic policy', NBER Working Paper 20517, October, Cambridge, MA.

Stiglitz, J. (2014b), 'Broadening our thinking on vulnerability', in UNDP (ed.), *Sustaining Human Progress: Reducing Vulnerabilities and Building Resilience*, New York: United Nations Development Programme, p. 84.

The Oakland Institute (2014), *Down on the Farm, Wall Street: America's New Farmer*, available at http://www.oaklandinstitute,org/, accessed 23 October 2014.

The World Bank (2011), *China Quarterly Update*, Washington, DC: The World Bank.

UNCTAD (2012), *World Economic Situation and Prospects 2012*, New York and Geneva: United Nations Conference on Trade and Development.

UNDP (2014), *Human Development Report, 2014; Sustaining Human Progress: Reducing Vulnerabilities and Building Resilience*, New York: United Nations Development Programme.

US Department of State (2009), *Closing Remarks for US–China Strategic and Economic Dialogue*, available at http://www.state.gov/, accessed 23 August 2009.

8. Financialization, crisis and economic policy

Hassan Bougrine and Louis-Philippe Rochon

8.1 INTRODUCTION

The recent history of capitalism indicates that the system is riddled with numerous crises, both financial and real (Reinhart and Rogoff, 2009a), some of which were so serious that they threatened its very foundations and brought it to near collapse. Perhaps the best known of these is the Great Depression of the 1930s, which has thus far become a benchmark for gauging the seriousness and severity of subsequent crises. Indeed, since the end of the Second World War, there have been at least 18 such crises in industrialized countries alone (Kaminsky and Reinhart, 1999; Caprio et al., 2005; Reinhart and Rogoff, 2008), and a great many others in the developing world (Duttagupta and Cashin, 2011). However, the most serious crisis by far in the post-Depression era is the latest one, which broke out in 2007–2008 and has been dubbed the Great Recession or still, the Lesser Depression.

Depending on the severity of the crisis in each case, economic performance has typically slowed down, with growth of real gross domestic product (GDP) sometimes becoming negative and unemployment reaching unprecedented levels. In some studies, the average duration of the downturn for output has been estimated to be around two years, and about five years for unemployment (Reinhart and Rogoff, 2009b). The economic and social costs of these crises are obviously high but particularly severe for the more vulnerable segments of the society.

In spite of the widely held belief that crises are only random and transitory and the claim that these play a corrective role when they occur, there is now strong empirical evidence pointing to the structural nature of crises. Moreover, this new evidence indicates that the causes of these crises are imbedded in the institutions of the capitalist system itself (Bellofiore and Halevi, 2010–2011; Crotty, 2012; Gatti et al., 2012). Also, while it is true that some crises are shorter than others, the fact remains that real and financial crises tend to recur at some regular intervals and their effects on some sectors of the economy linger for a long time, thereby making them 'protracted affairs' (Reinhart and Rogoff, 2009b). Scholars who have studied the long-term evolutionary tendencies of capitalism came to the conclusion that the recent history of the major industrialized countries was marked by a series of successive (long) waves of upswing and downswing, each lasting two to three decades. Hence, the last wave would have run from the 1940s to the 1970s for the upswing, and from the 1970s to the 2000s for the downswing (O'Hara, 2006).

Now, whether the current crisis that began in 2007 will mark the end of the downswing or prolong it depends on a number of factors. Among these, and certainly the most important of which is the type of policies governments choose to put in place in order to instigate a positive change and stimulate the economy. However, given the almost universal obsession with fiscal austerity measures, it is quite certain that the crisis will worsen, particularly in the Eurozone, which will then affect the rest of the world through trade and financial linkages. Therefore, it is very likely that the current downturn will last for a few more years, until a policy reversal becomes possible (perhaps when the mandate of present policymakers comes to an end or sooner if the present governments are brought down by popular revolts).

There are now a considerable number of studies, of various theoretical backgrounds, attempting to explain the causes and consequences of the recent crisis. Because the crisis first appeared in the US subprime market, the general view among mainstream economists is that this was a banking crisis, which quickly spread to the rest of the financial sector and then – as time went on – to the real side of the economy via the traditional mechanisms.

The main argument in these studies is that bankers, or rather some 'rogue loan officers', either because they were too greedy or nonchalant, extended loans to people who did not have the necessary creditworthiness usually required (ability to pay back). Other economists blamed the whole thing on the lack (or the lax implementation) of strict regulations in the financial sector and speculated that an effective regulatory system would ease the consequences of such crises in the future (Hoshi, 2011). Regardless of the precise reason, the explanation is the same: the cause of this crisis is financial in nature and is traced back to the behaviour of the banking system.

In this chapter, we argue that even the presence of the strictest regulations (the type of Dodd-Frank or the Glass-Steagall Acts, for instance) would not have averted the crisis, for the simple reason that its causes lie in the core institutions that command the functioning of the capitalist system. In other words, this was not as much a financial crisis as a crisis in the institution of capitalism. While there was certainly a financial dimension to this crisis, to argue that it was the sole cause of the crisis does not fully convey the intensity and true nature of those causes. As we argue below, the financial nature of this crisis, though an important element, was a consequence of the increased inequality in income and wealth. Together, they reinforced each other and contributed to the 2007 crisis.

The chapter is divided into three sections. In Section 8.2, we discuss the economic environment that prevailed during the last three decades prior to the crisis and show that all the warning signals were present and pointing to a coming crisis. Section 8.3 offers alternatives to current policies. Concluding remarks are given in Section 8.4.

8.2 THE CURRENT POLICYMAKING, WEALTH CONCENTRATION AND THE INSTABILITY OF FINANCIAL MARKETS

As is the case with previous crises, evidence shows that prior to crises, standard leading indicators such as output and employment usually are the first to exhibit low growth or clear downward trends. This is documented, for instance, in the study by Reinhart and Rogoff (2008, p. 343) who find that real GDP growth per capita in the USA and other industrialized countries in their sample starts to decline four years before the onset of a crisis.[1]

Gatti et al. (2012) provide an interesting explanation of the decline of real GDP growth and the rise in unemployment. Their research focuses on the structural transformations of the capitalist system and the authors argue that – just as happened in agriculture before the Great Depression – large productivity increases in manufacturing between 1980 and 2007 led to a rise in unemployment and a decline in real wages, which translated into a fall in aggregate demand.

In turn, prolonged periods of unemployment lead to a widening gap between social classes and important increases in income and wealth inequality. Under these circumstances, the problems of falling demand would be exacerbated. Evidently, this scenario could be forestalled under two conditions: first, governments could implement expansionary fiscal policies or second, the private sector could borrow to finance its spending on consumption and investment. As Seccareccia (2005) and others have shown, it was the latter solution, particularly the increase in households' indebtedness, that has temporarily sustained growth during the 25 years or so prior to the crisis. In other words, the fragility of the capitalist system was masked by consumers sustaining consumption through increased borrowing and debt.

Increased inequality has had other effects as well, since the other side of the inequality issue is the considerable wealth that has been accumulated by some individuals and financial institutions. This is where we contend the financial component to this crisis arises, since this wealth needs to be recycled and reinvested in order for it to grow – it cannot rest idle. It is always searching for higher yields. And so new instruments that can increase its value must be created for this purpose, which contributed, for instance, to the birth of markets for asset-backed securities (ABS). In turn, banks responded to the need of financiers for new financial instruments by packaging their loans into various types of financial products, labelled collateralized debt obligations (CDOs), with different risk notations ranging from triple A to 'toxic waste'. As a result, the share of short-term securities in institutional investors' asset portfolios grew exponentially between 1980 and 2006 (see below). This further encouraged banks to find an increasing number of borrowers, particularly in the housing market, thus contributing to the inflation of housing prices and creating a bubble.

Because it is practically impossible to dissociate the monetary/financial sector from the real production sector, we argue that the current crisis has its origins in the interaction between the two sectors. Our argument can be summarized in three intertwined steps: (a) prolonged fiscal austerity measures created the conditions for unequal distribution of wealth and its concentration; (b) in their search for higher yield, holders of the accumulated wealth need new financial instruments in which to 'invest' their funds – the banking system responded by creating a market for ABS, including CDOs of the subprime grade; and (c) when the borrowers were unable to meet their payments, largely as a result of continued austerity measures, the CDOs became toxic and the bubble burst. This then created fear and panic among 'investors' who rushed to dump the toxic waste in an attempt to protect the value of their wealth.

8.2.1   The Monetary Circuit and Crises

Our summarized description of the events that precede a crisis is quite consistent with the views espoused by the proponents of the monetary circuit. As we argue here, the origins of a crisis can indeed be provided by the circuit approach.

In the standard, albeit simplified, description of the functioning of monetary production economies, the source and origin of money is found in the banking sector, including the central bank. To carry out their activities, firms, households and the state must first obtain the necessary financing, which is advanced to them in the form of credit (loans) by the banks, including the central bank. These loans are deposited in the receiving agents' bank accounts, thus giving them the purchasing power necessary to begin spending.

During this first phase of the circuit, money flows from banks to households in the form of loans and salaries and to firms in the form of loans. If we consider firms as a sector, it is easy to see that money flows from firms to households in the form of wages. Acting as entrepreneurs, firms set their production plans and use the loans to hire labour. When the production process is finished and goods and services are made available, households then spend their income by consuming and acquiring these products (as well as paying their dues to the state). At this point, the reflux phase begins (see Graziani, 2003). The funds captured by firms through the sale of these traditional commodities allow firms to realize their profits and to reimburse, at least partly, the debt they have previously incurred towards the banks.

The above discussion is a very basic description of the monetary circuit. But it does offer us an idea over the potential source of crisis since a potential source of problems arises precisely when households' saving rate is positive and they express a certain preference for liquidity. In this case a portion of the amount they initially received would remain with them as bank deposits. As a result, firms will remain indebted towards the banks. So in order to capture as much as possible households' financial savings, firms as a sector must compete with the banks by encouraging households to give them their savings rather than keeping them as deposits. This is achieved by offering, on financial markets, high-yield securities. Under these circumstances, firms would obviously have to pay interest on the remainder of their debt to the banks and interest on the securities, which they have issued. As shown by Graziani (2003, p. 116), this situation would be beneficial to firms so long as households do indeed choose to increase the share of their wealth held in corporate securities. Of course, if households choose to hoard part of their savings, firms will be unable to recapture the totality of their outlays.

It is this constant need for liquidity and dependence on external finance that force entrepreneurs (assumed to be the owners of firms) to gradually relinquish an increasing portion of the firm's total assets to outside financiers. Regardless of the bargaining strategies that financiers and entrepreneurs might develop during the course of their interactions (see Rajan, 2012), the important point is that, in the end, financiers might have the final say because they can always jeopardize the firm's activities by refusing to extend finance. This necessarily places entrepreneurs (the industrial capitalists) at a disadvantage and, at the same time, explains the increasing power gained by financiers over the decades since the rise of industrial capitalism, what many now refer to as financialization, which carries two very important components.

First, as discussed above, there is this apparent hold by the financiers over material production, coupled with the introduction of various financial innovations. Second, there is also the more recent but quite successful inclusion of the middle- and lower-income classes into the borrowing chain, which in turn resulted in two important phenomena: increased household indebtedness and asset price inflation, such as in the case of the subprime market.

Our central contention is that these two components of financialization represent the most dramatic changes in the institutional structure of modern capitalism and, as we shall see, they bear in them the seeds of crises because each one has its own intrinsic limitations. In what follows, we shall focus on the limitations and problems posed by each of these developments and show their role in generating crises. In addition, we note that even though these inner contradictions tend to manifest themselves in separate areas and sectors of the economy, in reality they are intertwined at the source and exacerbated by the fact that wealth has become increasingly concentrated in the hands of a tiny minority.

8.2.2 Finance and Financial Innovations

In the era of what can now be considered the classical entrepreneurial capitalist system, the emergence of financial markets and their *raison d'être* was to offer firms producing goods and services the opportunity to raise funds to finance their long-term investments. In terms of the monetary circuit, there is no new injection of liquidity but only a transfer of savings from the bank accounts of some private agents who have succeeded in accumulating wealth. This is true even when these agents are commercial banks because in this case banks would be using their earned profits to acquire corporate bonds and/or shares and cannot create money for this purpose for obvious reasons. In the primary market, firms issue debt (bonds) and equity securities (shares) and sell them to investors who are looking to earn a higher return on their financial wealth (higher than the interest on bank deposits). Investors could easily monitor firms' performance and decide on the composition of their portfolios based on their assessment of risk and return. Profitable firms attracted investors searching for a higher yield but particularly equity investors who were eager to realize a capital gain, which meant that – at this stage of classical capitalism – finance was still linked to the real production side of the economy.

Over time, important changes were progressively introduced to the workings of financial markets. The most dramatic developments occurred only during the last 50 years or so. Indeed, the 1970s and 1980s marked the beginning of a new era in financial trading with the growth of the so-called leveraged buyouts in which the buyer (usually an institutional investor) acquires a company essentially by using that company's assets as collateral to borrow funds (either from a bank or by issuing bonds). This is in sharp contrast with previous practices in which the classical investor collateralized only his own assets or actually parted with his own money in exchange for ownership of the company or shares of it. In the new model, since very little capital needs to be committed by the so-called investor, this opened the door wide for wild bets and speculation,[2] particularly when the targeted company could be re-sold even prior to completing the initial takeover transaction.

This type of speculation is well known and has been widely practised, perhaps for centuries, for example, in urban land ownership. In this sense, it is no surprise that it has spread to financial markets. But in this specific situation, the traded commodities (shares) are still in a way 'real' in the sense that they correspond to parts of, or entire, *existing* companies. Their value might be inflated due to the use of various schemes but that is another matter.

The serious trouble in financial markets arose, however, when traders started dealing in derivatives like ABS, including CDOs and CDOs squared, which are, to put it bluntly, nothing more than fictitious assets. Because of this, it is impossible to know neither their quality nor their value, or even how to price them. This represents the first major transgression of a basic law of capitalism – the *law of exchange* by which the commodities on the marketplace must exhibit transparent information about their characteristics so as to facilitate the interaction of their supply and demand.

In most jurisdictions, the law of exchange has now been codified under contract law, which governs the exchange of property. As observed by Prasch (2010), all our important transactions (for example, purchase of automobiles, home mortgages and so on) take the form of long-term relational contracts precisely because the characteristics of the property being exchanged are not readily verifiable, that is, they cannot be 'inspected' on the 'spot'. These contracts are *relational and non-tradable*. They are designed to overcome problems of asymmetric information and to offer the parties involved in the transaction some credible guarantees and ensure a certain transparency regarding the characteristics of the commodity being exchanged. In this way, the buyer can form an idea about the commodity in question and even make an estimate of its value. The buyer is also relatively 'covered' if, for example, the automobile breaks down while it is still under warranty.

By contrast, in financial markets these relational contracts are transformed into tradable commodities that also serve as a reason and become a basis for the creation of new financial products: the ABS.[3] Financial

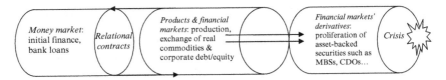

Note: MBSs – mortgage-backed securities.

Figure 8.1   *Financialization: the transformation of relational contracts into tradable commodities*

commodities of the ABS type are extremely opaque, thereby making it difficult not only to price them[4] but, more importantly, know what they actually are. Financial commodities in the form of derivatives such as CDOs, CDOs squared and cubed are indeed wealth created out of thin air! It must be emphasized here that as the commodity, which is the central element in the exchange relation, becomes ever more obscure and abstract, all the other parameters of the market (for example, risk, return) gradually lose their familiar meaning and become erratic. In this situation, it becomes difficult to value assets or trust the volatile market valuations (Foley, 2010). The logical consequence of this destabilizing force is the emergence of a wedge, a separation between the supply of and the demand for securities, followed first by a breakdown of trust in 'market forces', then a need to exit the market and finally a panic characterized by mass selling. At this point, the crisis arises. It is true that the presence of additional triggers such as the increase in interest rates by the Fed (June 2004 and after) played a role in speeding up the process leading to the crisis but the collapse was already coming (see also Wray, 2011). Schematically, the scenario looks like Figure 8.1.

Focusing closely on the financing aspect of relational contracts, Wray (2011) argues that even when banks are not initially involved, that is, even when relational contracts arise separately in the products market, they still make their way to financial markets when the IOUs sanctioning these relationships are presented to the bank, which accepts them and issues its own IOUs to finance its position.[5] Hence, according to Wray (2011, p. 13), 'This is the essence of financialization – or pyramiding – layers of debt that represent commitments of prospective future income flows . . . Yet, when the crisis hits, the shadow financial institutions find they cannot refinance positions – in other words, they cannot reissue liabilities to cover their positions in assets.'

The marketing and sale of securities are typically handled by non-bank financial intermediaries (brokers, financial advisers, different types of

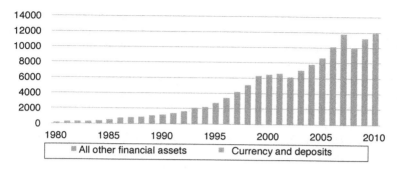

Source: OECD database, http://www.data.oecd.org, accessed 29 January 2016.

Figure 8.2 Financial assets of institutional investors in the USA (in billions $)

Funds and so on) who are now managing various types of collective invest-ment schemes on behalf of institutional investors. The growth of these financial institutions since the 1980s has been impressive.[6] In the USA, for example, data indicate that their financial assets, which are essentially securities, grew by nearly 8000 per cent between 1980 and 2007, reaching almost US$12 trillion, that is, about 84 per cent of GDP (Figure 8.2). A similar trend is observed in other major industrialized countries. How can we explain this explosive growth in financial markets?

As already mentioned, the source of the supply of these securities resides primarily with the banking sector, which packages the various relational contracts (mortgages, corporate debt and so on) into securities and offers them for sale to the so-called 'investors' on financial markets. These pack-ages or portfolios are then organized into different tranches with varying degrees of risk ranging from the safest (super senior tranche) to the most junior tranche or toxic waste.[7] The phenomenal growth of financial assets documented in Figure 8.2 indicates that the demand for these securities has been extremely high. Such high demand can only be justified in two cases: (1) if the return is relatively high compared to the risk involved; (2) if the investors have accumulated large amounts of liquidity that need to be recy-cled. With the benefit of hindsight, it is now clear that both of these factors prevailed during most of the last two decades of the twentieth century (Credit Suisse, 2011), which explains the euphoria that preceded the crisis.

In the first case, this was a period of speculative bubbles and the return was almost always 'a sure thing' in part due to the rise of *credit default swaps* (CDS), which allowed the buyers of these securities to insure themselves against the risk of default. In fact, even without buying anything, speculators could simply place a bet against the possibility of default of certain securities (such as bonds issued by the government of Greece) and purchase CDS. Speculators would pay, for example, a monthly fee to the insurer in exchange for a payment in the case that their bet materializes. On the other hand, the need for recycling the accumulated wealth, and the quest for a higher yield, is imperative for its growth and expansion; otherwise it must necessarily be withdrawn from circulation.[8] There is therefore a disproportionate pressure coming from the demand side of the market for financial securities, particularly when we consider the historic low returns on government bonds.[9] But having now discovered that a higher supply of these securities hinges on the expansion of relational contracts, the suppliers, namely, the banks, rationally responded by pushing for the increase of the number of these contracts, which was done by including additional borrowers, even of the NINJA (no income, no job, no assets) type; hence the emergence of the subprime loans. This leads us to examine the second aspect of financialization.

8.2.3   Increased Household Indebtedness and the Demand for Securities

The imperative need for recycling the accumulated wealth is the driving force behind the rise in demand for financial securities in general and ABS in particular. However, since the supply of this type of securities proved to be, at least initially, somewhat inelastic, the logic of the system led to the ingenious invention of the imaginary 'sovereign consumer' or the 'enterprising consumer' whose decisions, such as wanting to expand the stock of his assets, must now be regarded as an entrepreneurial activity that warrants all the financing needs (Foucault, 2008; Bougrine and Vihanto, 2010; Payne, 2011). Consequently, banks are called upon to meet the consumers/households' borrowing needs by extending credit for consumption purposes or mortgages for house purchases.[10] Obviously, these consumers/households are the not the High Net Worth Individuals (HNWIs) but rather the great majority of middle-class and poor families who willingly accepted their subordinate inclusion into financial markets because they believed in the illusion of making important capital gains. This explains the rising levels of households' indebtedness observed in many industrialized economies since the 1980s.

Looking at the same process from a different angle, Bellofiore (2011) has labelled this transformation in capitalism as 'the real subsumption of labour to finance' under the umbrella of what he called 'pension funds capitalism' (or what Minsky (1996) called 'money manager capitalism'). Moreover, bank credit was not the only means by which consumers/households were successfully included into financial markets. Their savings and pension contributions were also channelled through pension funds. Indeed, as Bellofiore and Halevi (2010–2011, pp. 7–8) have argued,

A system of compulsory savings became formalized with wage earners' pension contributions deposited in private funds. With the crisis of the golden age and the ensuing curtailment of the social role of the public sector, a growing proportion of the legislated employee/employer contributions to social security was compulsorily directed toward these funds, which therefore came to absorb a great deal of household savings.

They add, 'The placement ("investment") of these sums in securities, shares, and other kinds of investments created a commonality of interests between the managers of financial institutions and those of productive firms. The latter were co-opted to the strategies of the first group directly through salaries linked to stock options and economically by increasingly partaking in the objectives of maximizing dividends and share values.'

In conclusion, if the subsumption of labour to capital can be described as a situation in which the entrepreneur-capitalist succeeds in asserting his domination by establishing a set of contracts with independent workers who are now 'bound only by the need to make contracted deliveries at the stipulated time' (Rajan, 2012, p. 6), the subsumption of labour to finance would be quite simply a situation in which money managers succeed in developing clever ways to get hold of those contracts and transform them into new financial products – thus ensuring at the same time that workers' income receipts are diverted back to financial institutions in the form of debt payments, potentially serving as income streams for the holders of these assets. On this account, financialization *is* the exploitation of the poor.

8.3 TOWARDS A RADICAL CHANGE IN ECONOMIC POLICY

Given our diagnosis of the crises, we propose that economic policy should be focused on achieving two main goals: (1) full employment and (2) making finance at the service of the economy. Our justification is quite obvious: while the so-called investors in financial markets may buy CDS and other types of insurance, the real issue is whether the loans will be paid back. This in turns hinges on whether people are employed. Employment in turn depends on how the real economy is performing so in the end, it is clear that the source of the problem is real not financial. The 2007 crisis was first and foremost a crisis deeply rooted in aggregate demand failures, with an important financial element. It is clear that policies that need to be adopted must have an eye on repairing the problems with aggregate demand, and another on regulating the financial sector.

The objective of full employment implies that the government must abandon austerity policies and stand ready to finance nation-wide programmes offering jobs to all those who cannot find employment in the private sector. Job creation and long-term employment ensure that the working class will have a steady income and would ease the pressure on the need for household debt. Such a policy will contribute to reducing income inequalities, although on its own it is not sufficient. This is where the 'traditional measures' of tax and transfers will play a complementary but important role. Transfers in the form of unemployment benefits, welfare payments and so on have long been recognized as automatic stabilizers because they strengthen aggregate demand and dampen the effects of a downturn. But in the neoliberal era, it is the indirect transfers on social programmes such as health and education that have been cut severely, and it is here that we must seek a policy reversal if we are serious about regenerating economic growth. The tax component of the traditional measures is no less important but it should have teeth. That is, in addition to progressive taxation on incomes we should also have taxes on all forms of wealth.

Since the national or federal government does not rely on the proceeds from these taxes to finance its spending, it can still collect them, but through various accounting procedures it can make them accrue to local and regional governments whose role of a Robin Hood cannot be contested. Government actions seeking to reduce inequalities and achieve full employment imply an increase in government debt but that is exactly what is needed. In other words, we must substitute public debt for private debt since, as heterodox economists are well aware, only government debt is sustainable (see Bougrine, 2004). This is what we mean by abandoning austerity policies. On this point, there is now considerable research confirming the deflationary bias of austerity (see Sawyer, 2015) and, in fact, even the International Monetary Fund (IMF) is nowadays critical of austerity measures, arguing that attempts to reduce fiscal deficits have slowed growth and contributed to larger budget deficits (see IMF, World Economic Outlook, 2012).

On the financial side, we maintain that regulations are important but they must be considered as part of a greater strategy. As we have argued elsewhere (Bougrine and Seccareccia, 2013), some specific regulations are urgent. These include the need to prohibit securitization and the sale of debt (relational contracts), ban practices like originate and distribute and separate commercial banking from investment banking. The purpose of these regulations is to maintain some integrity of the financial system by preventing excessive speculative behaviour and reducing or eliminating fraudulent financial practices.

However, a more effective change in policy is for the government to regain or ascertain its sovereignty in issues of money and finance. Reversing austerity policies and increasing public debt and deficits is only one aspect

Financialization, crisis and economic policy 155

of such sovereignty. The other aspect is to decree that finance should be an instrument to promote growth in the real economy and increase the welfare of the whole society. The charter for commercial banks should be rewritten to acknowledge the social responsibility of private banks and to redefine their mandate. And since leadership is by example, the government must set the standard by providing such services through its own banks. Experience from the post-war era shows that prior to their privatization, public banks have played an effective role towards this objective in several industrialized countries (see Bougrine and Seccareccia, 2013).

8.4 CONCLUSION

In this chapter, we have offered an analysis of crises consistent with the teachings of the monetary circuit. Our analysis focused on two important aspects of financialization, namely, the growing importance of finance's influence over material production and the accompanying introduction of various financial innovations, on the one hand, and the successful inclusion of the middle- and lower-income classes into the borrowing chain, on the other. It is in this sense that financialization has resulted in an increase of households' indebtedness and gave a greater possibility to financiers to increase their wealth independently of the real production economy. We argued that household debt is not sustainable in the long run, particularly when we know that austerity policies lead to more unemployment. As for the second aspect, and in order to remedy the increasing separation between finance and real production, we proposed a set of policies, including a return to social and public banking.

NOTES

1. Demirguc-Kunt and Detragiache (1998) studied the period 1980–1994 and showed that a decline in the real GDP growth, a deterioration in the terms of trade and a rise in the real short-term rate of interest tend to hurt banks by increasing the share of non-performing loans and by affecting banks' balance sheets adversely.
2. Speculation is nothing new to financial markets. It has actually appeared earlier on and immediately with the emergence of secondary markets for assets. In Marxian terms, the commoditization of financial assets truncates the circuit M-C-M' by bypassing the C stage and exchanging M for M', a sheer speculation.
3. In this regard, Bellofiore and Halevi (2011, p.15) wrote that 'With the onset of stagnation in the 1970s the political and economic response gravitated towards the transformation of debt into a source of financial rents and of support to effective demand through household indebtedness. In this context, throughout the 1980s and 1990s the required institutional space was created by abolishing the safeguard provisions of the Roosevelt era and by changing pensions' financial flows from funds tied to specific entitlements

into funds available for financial markets in which benefits came to depend upon market capitalization'.

4. According to Das (2006, p. 126), 'The lack of transparency lies at the heart of derivative profitability. You deny the client access to up-to-date prices, use complicated structures that are hard for them to price, and sometimes just rely on their self-delusion'.
5. Wray (2011, p. 14) writes, 'Certainly, economic activity needs finance, but this is not necessarily through loans but rather through "acceptation" – accepting liabilities. And financial institutions need to finance their positions in the assets they hold by issuing liabilities, but these are not necessarily deposits. Nor are banks the only type of financial institutions capable of financing economic activity. Much of the financing activity takes place off the balance sheets of banks'.
6. This section draws on Bougrine (2012).
7. These are also known as 'structured products' whereby the senior tranche, usually with higher credit ratings (AAA – A), pays a relatively lower interest rate but it is the first to be paid out of the cash flows of the portfolio in case of a default, followed by the mezzanine tranche and then the most junior tranche (also called equity tranche, the first loss piece or toxic waste), which is unsecured but offers a higher risk-return profile.
8. As Marx (1887) put it, 'The restless never-ending process of profit-making alone is what [the capitalist] aims at. This boundless greed after riches, this passionate chase after exchange-value, is common to the capitalist and the miser; but while the miser is merely a capitalist gone mad, the capitalist is a rational miser. The never-ending augmentation of exchange-value, which the miser strives after, by seeking to save his money from circulation, is attained by the more acute capitalist, by constantly throwing it afresh into circulation'. Available at http://www.marxists.org/archive/marx/works/1867-c1/ch04.htm, accessed 29 January 2016.
9. *The Credit Suisse Global Investment Returns Yearbook* (2011, p. 5) reports that in 'the USA, over the period from the start of 1980 to the end of 2010, the annualized real (inflation adjusted) return on government bonds was 6.0%, broadly matching the 6.3% long-term performance of equities. Over the preceding 80 years, US government bonds had provided an annualized real return of only 0.2%. Similarly, for the UK, from 1980 to 2010 the annualized real return on government bonds was 6.3%. Over the preceding 80 years, UK government bonds had provided an annualized real return of just −0.5%'.
10. Wray (2009, p. 817) explains how the promotion of the idea of an 'ownership society' in recent decades served the interests of money managers and how it has led to higher inequality in the USA. In a sharp and eloquent criticism of the ideology behind this policy, he wrote, 'It is ironic that the 30-year mortgage brought to us by New Deal government guarantees – making home ownership possible for working Americans for the first time – morphed into a speculation-fuelling, debt-pushing casino that buried homeowners in a mountain of liabilities. Creditors emerge as owners of the foreclosed houses and with claims on debtors, who will be subject to a form of perpetual debt bondage . . . Many "home owners" merely occupy, manage and improve homes really owned by the *true* owner class – those with lots of wealth, particularly financial wealth' (emphasis in original).

REFERENCES

Bellofiore, R. (2011), 'Crisis theory and the Great Recession: a personal journey from Marx to Minsky', *Research in Political Economy*, **27**, 81–120.
Bellofiore, R. and J. Halevi (2010–2011), '"Could be raining": the European crisis after the Great Recession', *International Journal of Political Economy*, **39**(4), Winter, 5–30.

Bellofiore, R. and J. Halevi (2011), 'A Minsky moment? The subprime crisis and the "new" capitalism', in C. Gnos and L.-P. Rochon (eds), *Credit, Money and Macroeconomic Policy: A Post-Keynesian Approach*, Cheltenham, UK and Northampton, MA, USA: Edward Elgar, pp. 13–32.

Bougrine, H. (2004), 'Public debt and private wealth', in L. Randall Wray and M. Forstater (eds), *Contemporary Post-Keynesian Analysis*, Cheltenham, UK and Northampton, MA, USA: Edward Elgar, pp. 24–43.

Bougrine, H. (2012), 'Fiscal austerity, the Great Recession and the rise of new dictatorships', *Review of Keynesian Economics*, Inaugural Issue, **0**(1), 109–25.

Bougrine, H. and M. Seccareccia (2013), 'Re-thinking banking institutions in contemporary economies: are there alternatives to the status quo?', in L.-P. Rochon and M. Seccareccia (eds), *Monetary Economies of Production: Banking and Financial Circuits and the Role of the State*, Cheltenham, UK and Northampton, MA, USA: Edward Elgar, pp. 134–59.

Bougrine, H. and M. Vihanto (2010), 'The doctrine of consumer sovereignty and the real world', in H. Bougrine, I. Parker and M. Seccareccia (eds), *Microeconomic Analysis: Competing Views*, Toronto: Emond Montgomery Publications, pp. 92–101.

Caprio, G., D. Klingebiel, L. Laeven and G. Noguera (2005), 'Banking Crisis Database,' in P. Honohan and L. Laeven (eds), *Systemic Financial Crises*, Cambridge: Cambridge University Press, pp. 341–60.

Credit Suisse (2011), *The Credit Suisse Global Investment Returns Yearbook*, Credit Suisse, available at http://www.credit-suisse.com, accessed 29 January 2016.

Crotty, J. (2012), 'The great austerity war: what caused the US deficit crisis and who should pay to fix it?', *Cambridge Journal of Economics*, **36**, 79–104.

Das, S. (2006), *Traders, Guns and Money: Knowns and Unknowns in the Dazzling World of Derivatives*, New York: Prentice Hall.

Demirguc-Kunt, A. and E. Detragiache (1998), 'The determinants of banking crises in developed and developing countries', IMF Staff Paper, **45**(1), International Monetary Fund, Washington, DC.

Duttagupta, R. and P. Cashin (2011), 'Anatomy of banking crises in developing and emerging market countries', *Journal of International Money and Finance*, **30**(2), 354–76.

Foley, D. F. (2010), 'Lineages of crisis economics from the 1930s: Keynes, Hayek, and Schumpeter', *Eastern Economic Journal*, **36**, 413–22.

Foucault, M. (2008), *The Birth of Biopolitics*, Houndsmills: Palgrave Macmillan.

Gatti, D.D., M. Gallegati, B.C. Greenwald, A. Russo and J.E. Stiglitz (2012), 'Sectoral imbalances and long run crises', in F. Allen, M. Aoki, J.-P. Fitoussi, N. Kiyotaki, R. Gordon and J.E. Stiglitz (eds), *The Global Macro Economy and Finance*, Houndmills: Palgrave Macmillan, pp. 61–97.

Graziani, A. (2003), *The Monetary Theory of Production*, Cambridge: Cambridge University Press.

Hoshi, T. (2011), 'Financial regulation: lessons from the recent financial crises', *Journal of Economic Literature*, **49**(1), 120–28.

IMF, World Economic Outlook (2012), *Coping with High Debt and Sluggish Growth*, available at http://www.imf.org/external/pubs/ft/weo/2012/02/pdf/text. pdf, accessed 29 January 2016.

Kaminsky, G.L. and C.M. Reinhart (1999), 'The twin crises: the causes of banking and balance of payments problems', *American Economic Review*, **89**(3), 473–500.

Marx, K. (1887), *Capital*, Vol. 1, Moscow: Progress Publishers, available at http://

www.marxists.org/archive/marx/works/1867-c1/ch04.htm, accessed 29 January 2016.

Minsky, H. (1996), 'Uncertainty and the institutional structure of capitalist economies', Levy Economics Institute Working Paper No. 155, Annandale-on-Hudson, NY.

O'Hara, P.A. (2006), *Growth and Development in the Global Political Economy: Social Structures of Accumulation and Modes of Regulation*, New York: Routledge.

Payne, C. (2011), *The Consumer, Credit and Neoliberalism: Governing the Modern Economy*, London: Routledge.

Prasch, R.E. (2010), 'Markets, states, and exchange: an introduction to economics', in H. Bougrine and M. Seccareccia (eds), *Macroeconomic Analysis: Competing Views*, Toronto: Emond Montgomery Publications, pp. 22–32.

Rajan, R.G. (2012), 'The corporation in finance', NBER Working Paper No. 17760, available at http://www.nber.org/papers/w17760, accessed 29 January 2016.

Reinhart, C.M. and K.S. Rogoff (2008), 'Is the 2007 US sub-prime financial crisis so different? An international historical comparison', *American Economic Review: Papers & Proceedings*, **98**(2), 339–44.

Reinhart, C.M. and K.S. Rogoff (2009a), *This Time is Different: Eight Centuries of Financial Folly*, Princeton, NJ: Princeton University Press.

Reinhart, C.M. and K.S. Rogoff (2009b), 'The aftermath of financial crises', NBER Working Paper No. 14656, available at http://www.nber.org/papers/w14656, accessed 29 January 2016.

Sawyer, M. (2015), 'Can prosperity return to the Economic and Monetary Union?', *Review of Keynesian Economics*, **3**(4), 457–70.

Seccareccia, M. (2005), 'Growing household indebtedness and the plummeting saving rate in Canada: an explanatory note', *Economic and Labour Relations Review*, **16**(1), 133–51.

Wray, R. (2009), 'The rise and fall of money manager capitalism: a Minskian approach', *Cambridge Journal of Economics*, **33**(4), 807–28.

Wray, R. (2011), 'Is there room for bulls, bears, and states in the circuit?', Levy Economics Institute of Bard College Working Paper No. 700, available at http://www.levyinstitute.org/pubs/wp_700.pdf, accessed 29 January 2016.

PART III

Disequilibria in the Mexican economy: the export growth model, economic stagnation and labor precarization

9. The limits of the export-led growth model: the Mexican experience

Etelberto Ortiz

9.1 INTRODUCTION

The prolonged stagnation of the Mexican economy has been subject to extensive academic debate and has been analyzed from a variety of perspectives (Moreno-Brid and Ros, 2010; Huerta, 2014; Levy, 2014; Ortiz, 2014). The focus of discussion in this research is on the limitations of what we shall call failed export-led growth models, to the extent that they have not managed to maintain an even balance of payments or a balance of trade. The aim is to understand the factors that have hindered the attainment of these objectives in the Mexican economy and to analyze their impact on economic growth in Mexico.

This chapter analyzes the most significant consequences of the growth model adopted in Mexico after the first foreign debt crisis. The starting point is in 1983, when manufactured exports moved into place as the drivers of economic growth. It was hoped that there would at first be a gradual and then a more rapid process of economic openness in the sectors associated with manufacturing exports, in which these would become 'growth leaders', as described in other papers by the author (see Ortiz, 2007, pp. 51–5, 2014, p. 148). The results of the model should have been evaluated via the impact of manufactured exports on the rest of the economy when the manufacturing sector took on its role as a 'driver of growth'. The globalization discourse idealizes the effects of economic openness and the benefits of manufactured exports, with particular stress on increased and better paid jobs, and generally on the improvement of the 'quality' of employment. The debate over the characteristics of free trade versus autocracy was highly ideological in the 1970s and 1980s, even though the Mexican economy was not subject to autocracy, and the transition to trade openness took place without a safety net for trade, production or society.

Discussion over the success factors for an export-led growth model was very limited and it never became a relevant issue, and consequently the economic policies to drive this process were not foreseen. The issue continues to be important despite the passage of time, and it needs to be reformulated once again and this time some solutions need to be found.

From a theoretical perspective, there is no integrated vision that contains all the elements necessary to understand the factors that slowed down the growth of export-oriented economies, or to explain the failure to balance their external current accounts. One set of factors is emphasized by the supply side[1] theories while another is emphasized by the demand side,[2] without providing an overall analytical framework. This means that we are drawn toward more open approximations that include both perspectives, which recognize both aspects of supply and demand, with a clear place for financial processes in the analysis of growth. Taking into consideration mainstream, structuralist (Taylor, 2004) and post-Keynesian (Davidson, 1994; Lavoie, 2014; Kregel, 2015) theories, the issue may be unraveled in the context of an open economy by an analysis that uses five essential conditions, which are key to guaranteeing a rate of growth that is sustainable in the long term.

First, there should be a surplus in the balance of trade in the manufacturing sector, and in the long term this should guarantee a stable balance of trade. In other words, the balance of trade should neither be in deficit nor in surplus. It should be noted that there may be a surplus in the balance of trade in the transitional period, but this must be temporary for the model to be stable in the long term.

Second, it is vital that the coefficients of the inter-sectoral linkages of the manufacturing export sectors should be greater than one and with a rising trend (Ortiz, 2014, pp. 146–7).[3] This condition ensures that the export sector effectively becomes an efficient 'driver of growth' for the economy as a whole.

Third, productivity should be growing at a positive rate with an upward trend. This guarantees a sustained increase in the profitability of investment and makes it possible to raise real salaries. This condition is important to maintain the competitiveness of the economy and to ensure the distribution of the benefits of growth. It is also an important condition to expand effective demand and the pace of growth of production and capital.

Fourth, in line with Thirlwall's rule, the coefficient of income elasticity of imports should be less than one so as not to create a bottleneck to economic growth (Thirlwall, 2002). If this rule is not obeyed, there will not be sufficient export capacity to satisfy the needs of importing. In other words, the export model should be accompanied by an industrialization process that replaces imports with domestic production. This condition is necessary to avoid stoppages in growth through external bottlenecks (Ortiz, 2014, p. 147).

Fifth, the process of growth should be accompanied by flows of liquidity that are both timely, in terms of quantities and availability when needed, and low cost, that is, internal and external financing at suitable interest rates directed toward productive activities and not toward processes linked to speculation. In addition, the resources available should be capable of financing the foreign private deficit and the public deficit. There are two critical points in this process: the first is in the process of transition when there can be a shortage of foreign exchange to cover the current account deficit and the second comes about once the model has stabilized, and it should guarantee a sufficient flow of capital so as not to put pressure on exchange rate stability. This condition calls for a monetary policy in line with a long-term growth process, quite apart from the objective of achieving price stability at any cost (Levy, 2012; Ortiz, 2012).

This chapter is divided into four sections. Section 9.2 first analyzes the behavior of the key growth variables to achieve sustained long-term growth. Section 9.3 discusses the financing of structural economic deficits, which is one of the central problems for the Mexican economy. Section 9.4 reviews the Mexican economy's limits to growth, emphasizing the main failings of economic policy. Finally, Section 9.5 sets out the main research conclusions.

9.2 PROGRESS OF THE MEXICAN ECONOMY: KEY SECTORS FOR SUSTAINED ECONOMIC GROWTH

One of the distinctive features of the Mexican economy is that it has not grown satisfactorily in the past 30 years. In the neoliberal period from 1983 to 2014, the average annual rate of growth was 2.4 percent compared to 6.3 percent during the so-called stabilization period from 1954 to 1970, rising to 6.6 percent if the period of accelerated growth from 1979 to 1982 is included. Furthermore, the long-term growth rate[4] has fallen significantly in recent decades: 5.6 percent from 1950 to 1960, 6.5 percent from 1960 to 1970, 6.6 percent from 1970 to 1982, −0.7 percent from 1983 to 1987, 3.1 percent from 1988 to 2003 and 2.4 percent from 2004 to 2014.[5] It can be claimed on the basis of these figures that the Mexican economy is in a process of chronic stagnation, which began with the structural reforms of the 1980s and 1990s, and furthermore that this dynamic has produced adverse effects in the critical sectors of the economy.

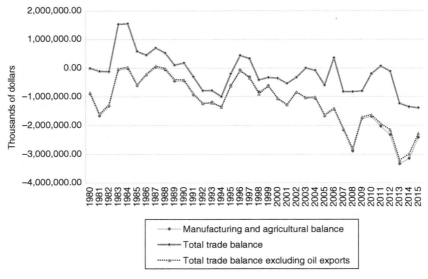

Source: Prepared by the author based on Bank of Mexico data, available at http://
www.banxico.org.mx/SieInternet/consultarDirectorioInternetAction.do?accion=consultar
Cuadro&idCuadro=CE132&sector=1&locale=es, accessed 22 March 2015.

Figure 9.1   *Mexico total trade balance, manufacturing and agriculture
trade balance, and total trade balance excluding oil exports,
1980–2015 (thousands of dollars, 1983 = 100)*

9.2.1   Analysis of the Balance of Trade: Where the Disequilibria Lie and How They Have Been Resolved

On the basis of manufacturing and agricultural exports, we could venture
that the reforms of the 1980s were a success, to the extent that these
exports rose from 5 percent of gross domestic product (GDP) in the 1980s
to 25 percent in the five years from 2010 to 2014. Nevertheless, the trade
balances of the various segments within the export sector tell another
story. Surpluses were fleeting while deficits became the norm (Figure 9.1).

Specifically, in the period of transition to the neoliberal model from 1983
to 1988 there was a surplus in the balance of trade, while the manufacturing
and agricultural sectors were in deficit, which nevertheless was unimportant
since the gap was closed by the balance of trade of the petroleum sector. The
latter became a source for making up the net excess of exports. Having said
that, the relatively balanced behavior of the petroleum sector in this period
is explained by the undervaluation of the exchange rate that restricted

imports, and by the effects of realigning the relative price structure (Ortiz, 2007, pp. 70–76) that succeeded in increasing the effective protection rates of the Mexican economy. This effect did not last long, however, except for a few years after the 1994 crisis, since trade deficits once again predominated in the 1990s and 2000s, at a time of exchange rate overvaluation (Figure 9.1).

The most harmful effect of the external disequilibria of this period was the manner in which a trade surplus was achieved during the period of transition: through the devil's mineral gift to Mexico, enabling the mass extraction and export of petroleum and extractive resources generally.

Two very significant critical factors need to be added to the above. The net gap between the trade deficit without petroleum exports and the total trade balance have grown in periods in which the price of petrol has increased significantly from 2001 to 2008 and when it fell between 2009 and 2013. Then, particularly from 2000 onwards, the Bank of Mexico followed a rigid price control policy to limit economic growth. Over recent years the growing increases in the current account deficit have resulted from this combination of factors, which according to Bank of Mexico data reached 24,983 million dollars in 2014, amounting to 8586 million dollars in the first quarter of 2015.[6] This can be largely be explained by Bank of Mexico exchange rate policies whose objective was to guarantee an overvalued exchange rate, presumably with the objective of keeping inflationary pressures under control. The periods when the gap between the total balance of trade and the balance of trade without petroleum exports was closed coincides with exchange rate adjustments arising from times of crisis, which were accompanied by negative production growth rates.

9.2.2 Inter-sectoral Linkages in Manufacturing: A Process that Runs Counter to Expectations

The model of economic growth led by manufactured exports is simply expressed by way of two elements: exports as a driver of growth, and the linkages between the export manufacturing sector and the rest of the economy. This latter is measured by the coefficients of the linkages, specifically through the total and/or backward linkages.

The linkage data for 'significant' and export leading sectors of the economy that serve as 'drivers of growth' indicate that they have weakened since the period of export-led growth (Table 9.1). This trend has continued despite programs whose purpose was to promote subcontracting, such as intensive phases of simple *maquiladoras* with cheap labor. The behavior of these indicators shows that the Mexican economy remains divided between sectors bound to the international economy and sectors tied to the internal market. This division has provoked a reduction in the growth capacity of

166 The financialization response to economic disequilibria

Table 9.1   *Total linkage coefficients of significant sectors and leading exporters of the Mexican economy*

	1950	1960	1970	1980	1990	1995	2003
Agriculture	1.788	1.717	1.919	1.634	1.562	1.556	1.54
Glass			1.906	1.849	1.625	1.489	1.42
Beer			1.134	1.1	1.062	1.051	1.06
Cars		1.178	1.12	1.122	1.037	1.016	1.023
Electronics			1.328	1.286	1.044	1.015	1.01
Autoparts			2.232	2.172	1.443	1.283	1.25
Petrochemicals			3.279	2.936	2.663	2.607	1.87
72 branches average	2.308	1.691	1.803	1.1745	1.627	1.609	1.53

Source: Prepared by the author based on input–output matrices from 1950–2003. Bank of Mexico for 1950–1960 and INEGI for 1970 onwards. Methodology based on Ortiz (1990), which relies on direct and indirect weighting coefficients of the Leontieff matrix, with the gross value of production.

the economy with the reappearance of the weaknesses from the industrialization by import substitution period, specifically, the disconnection between the dynamic sectors and the 'native' sectors that produce for the internal market. Furthermore, the industries that appear to be closer to Fajnzylber and Martínez's (1976) definition of an 'endogenous core', such as the chemical, automotive and glass industries, do not have their own technological bases, with the implications this has for models where the exports of the manufacturing sector should drive spending.

The result is that the greatest concentration of the export industry is to be found in the insertion of productive nuclei via the *maquiladora* industry, which are extraneous to the dynamics of the Mexican economy. By joining the world economy Mexico has undergone a division in its own economy. On the one hand, there is a sector that is fully integrated at an international level with moderate rates of productivity growth but hardly integrated at all at a local level; while, on the other hand, there is an industrial and services sector whose rates of growth are meager, have no knock-on effects and barely respond to stimuli that could help to increase productivity.

What factors explain the behavior of the total linkage coefficients? In successful cases of industrialization in South-east Asia and the southern cone of Latin America over the past 30 years, including countries such as South Korea, Malaysia, China, Singapore and Brazil, we find that the state has had a strong impact on growth via industrial policies aimed at creating strong links between local industry and the leading productive sectors and by promoting the use of local industrial and technological capabilities (Amsden, 2004). In contrast to these regions, Mexico has retained an outdated perspective on comparative advantages sustained by cheap labor and abundant natural resources. The net effect has been that the export sectors, which were intended to be the drivers of national growth, do not have any knock-on effects on the rest of the economy, which is why no mechanisms for boosting the growth of demand and productivity are designed. As pointed out in Ortiz (2007), the possibility of stimulating the competitive capacity of the economy as a whole is eliminated if one of the most important mechanisms for the implementation of a new economic model is kept in check.

9.2.3   Labor Productivity: A Positive Rate of Growth?

Despite the enormous importance of productivity to the success of the manufacturing export model and the great quantity of research and discussion on the subject, it may be stated that labor productivity has at best stagnated. The labor productivity growth coefficient, which is estimated on the difference between the rate of growth of production minus the rate of growth of employment, showed a tendency to stagnate between 1922 and 2012. A critical point was reached in 1970 when there was a downward trend, which stabilized from 1986, remaining more or less constant until 2012 (Figure 9.2).[7]

There was a slight upturn in the rate of growth of productivity from 2008 to 2013, which is hard to interpret because employment data are very ambiguous and inexact (Hernández Laos, 2005a, 2005b; Ortiz, 2007). From a government perspective, there is an effort to present an image of increasing employment, even if it is very precarious, which would indicate that productivity has remained practically unaltered. We may suppose that the indices related to this figure have been inflated in order to show an increase in productivity.

When we look at other productivity figures derived from sectoral accounts, a very different story emerges. This indicator shows a less homogeneous development. There are sectors with high rates of productivity growth, which include leading industrial sectors such as the automotive sector, auto parts, electronics, electrical equipment, glass, cement and petrochemicals, while others clearly show stagnation over the last 25 years (Table 9.2).

The question that arises is why there has been so little success in increasing the rates of productivity. From the author's point of view, the government authorities are seriously confused over the meaning of the term, which is evident from the package of structural reforms put through by the

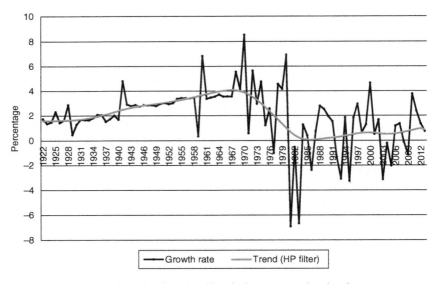

Source: Prepared by the author based on historical accounts and national accounts,
INEGI 1970 to 2013.

*Figure 9.2   Growth rate of work productivity and trend (Hodrick–Prescott
filter) in Mexico, 1922–2013*

Table 9.2   Rates of growth in labor productivity in Mexico, 1950–2011

	1950–1960	1960–1970	1970–1982	2000–2006	2006–2011	1988–2011
Total	2.9	2.88	2.28	1.69	1.22	0.705
Primary sector	2.48	2.46	1.46	3.02	2.24	1.26
Industrial	2.6	−1.6	2.92	2.92	1.22	1.49
Industry leaders	2.7	−1.4	3.79	5.9	4.2	2.4
Industry non-leaders	2.5	−1.7	3.19	2.45	2.93	1.27
Manufactures			1.01	1.24	2.35	0.83
Non-tradable	2.8	1.53	1.97	1.99	0.95	0.72

Source: Prepared by the author based on production accounts. National account system
for 1970 to 2011 and historical accounts for 1950 to 1970, INEGI.

current administration under Peña Nieto. This has come about from an
erroneous proposition that states that productivity, and hence profitability,
will increase if wages and welfare benefits are reduced, dismissal costs are
lowered and the terms of employment are made more precarious.

The first clarification to be made is that productivity should not be confused with wages, and it should be stressed that even the most primitive version of neoclassical economics does not commit this error. In reality, productivity is the result of a set of factors that are above all related to corporate management, training, market conditions as a whole and to internal technological innovation. The situation has become critical in Mexico because the authorities claim that competitiveness rests on making jobs less stable and impoverishing the terms and conditions of employment. The result is, on the one hand, a drop in real salaries, which hinders growth and the creation of 'quality' jobs, and, on the other, low levels of productivity, which lead to a lowering of the country's relative capacity to compete.

9.2.4 Income Elasticity of Imports

At the start of a discussion on the income elasticity of imports it should be warned that there are challenges to making the calculation since there are many factors external to its basic behavior, such as changes to monetary policy. In view of the above, the information is presented in the form of long-term averages, accounting for cycles, or periods in which there were critical changes in Mexican economic policy (Table 9.3).

The figures show that on average over the long term, economic agents have become more disposed to consume imported goods. A 1 percent increase in economic growth presages an increase in imports of 2 percent to 3 percent or over. This behavior severely constricts the overall growth of the economy.

It is evident that this aspect complements the arguments from the previous discussion on the balance of trade, since it is also evident from the imports that create the trade deficit. However, this is a highly controversial

Table 9.3 Import income elasticities, Mexico, 1960.01–2014.02

	GDP growth rate	Imports growth rate	Import income elasticities
1961.01–1971.01	6.64	5.6	0.76
1970.01–1982.04	6.48	12.45	2.22
1983.01–1987.04	−0.45	145.2	−18.07
1988.01–2000.04	3.45	11	2.83
2000.01–2014.02	2.32	5.04	3.76

Source: Author's calculation based on data of the balance of payments and national accounts. Bank of Mexico for 1960 to 2014 and INEGI for 1970 to 2014.

topic for two reasons. First, the Bank of Mexico's position is dogmatic when it sets monetary policy, declaring that the exchange rate depends on market fluctuations, and hence that its position on monetary policy is neutral, and that the variations do not impact on the 'real' or productive sectors. The evidence against this is overwhelming but remains unrecognized by the central bank, since it considers itself to be a passive agent in responding to the vicissitudes of the market.

The second source of controversy has its origins in the curious interpretation of the Marshall-Lerner condition,[8] which suits the authorities when arguing that devaluation generates positive effects. They state that the exchange rate should not be used to stimulate competition,[9] but exchange rate overvaluation is nevertheless used, although not publicly acknowledged, as the means of maintaining price stability. Under these circumstances the exchange rate, instead of being a price that allows for the timely maintenance of purchasing power, guaranteeing the pricing structure, becomes a genuinely decisive factor that fulfills other functions. The result of the central bank's exchange rate policies is to bring about public or private indebtedness that sooner or later becomes unsustainable, consequently leading to severe exchange rate crises, like the one that occurred at the end of 2014 and which continues in 2015.

9.2.5   Financing Production: Transitional Periods and the Operation of the Model

A reasonably accepted viewpoint, which the World Bank also holds, is that the transitional period from import substitution models to models led by manufacturing exports requires abundant financing. This is because an economy with an external deficit requires additional flows to balance the external sector and generate economic growth.

One of the basic rules for these periods is that external financing must be accessed flexibly and at reasonable cost, which obviously cannot be dependent on a country's credit history or its monetary policy framework. When monetary policy dictates strict inflation targets, as has been discussed, the exchange rate acts as an anchor in the long term, with the inconvenience of becoming rigid and ultimately creating a trap. When exchange rate overvaluation occurs, it precipitates a situation demanding the continuous financing of current account deficits. Both circumstances necessarily lead to complicated terms of financing in that they entail interest rates that are higher than the market.

History also shows that when financial crises recur, they are more closely associated with excessive debt than with periods of inflation (Reinhart and Rogoff, 2008; Reynard, 2012). Thus, since the 1990s, when this monetary policy model was in full swing, crises have led to severe adjustments to the level of economic activity, with relatively lower impacts on inflation, or at least ones that are lower than usual.

When exchange rate overvaluation is accompanied by a current account deficit, there is a double impact on the terms of financing. On the one hand, they cause foreign debt to grow and, on the other, they impact on the terms of internal financing, increasing uncertainty and bringing systemic risk. The banking system responds by increasing levels of leveraging and restricts the credit that it could feed into the economy. The following data illustrate this point. From 1980 to 1998, just before the foreign takeover of the banks came into general effect, the coverage rate (provisions for bad debt divided by non-performing loans[10]), was below 200 points, except for the period from the second quarter of 1987 to the second quarter of 1990. From 1999, however, there was an upward trend reaching a maximum rate of 687.7 points in the fourth quarter of 2005. After this date the rate fluctuated between 400 and 600 points. In the first quarter of 2014 it stood at 557.09 points.

It is notable how coverage increased dramatically after the foreign takeover of the banks and how this was accompanied by significant increases in the level of leveraging. This combination led to increased instability in the banking system without increasing total credit, which indicates that the creation of direct financing was practically nil. Curiously, this situation equates to what McKinnon (1973) paradoxically called a 'repressed' financial system, which today we might call constrained or, in other words, one that is incapable of providing financing.

9.3 FINANCING ECONOMIES WITH STRUCTURAL DEFICITS: TO CLOSE THE EXTERNAL GAP OR TO GROW

One of the central features of export-led Latin American countries with unsuccessful models is growing current account deficits with high trade deficits. Mexico is no exception, as seen in the previous section. This raises a question over what to do about the growing demands of financing the deficits under conditions of low investment and reduced income.

The answer reveals a paradox about the management of flows and assets, which can only be understood through the circuit theory. An economy like Mexico's is typified by the variety of challenges thrown up by the cycle. On the one hand, it has an income-debt cycle that is a critical component in the overall make-up of the economic cycle, and it is endogenous by nature. On the other, its assets are small and its economy is open to the global market cycle, which is a great source of vulnerability to the variations in the world economy as a whole or to those of its principal trading partners such as the United States. This combination frequently makes domestic impacts greater than those coming from abroad, or more negative when the principal commercial partner is undergoing a process of growth. This restriction arises from the accumulation of private debt, arising from trade disequilibria, which increases imports disproportionately and creates trade deficits.

The approach develops from the association formed between the trade deficit generated by manufactured imports and services and the behavior of the trade deficit as a whole. This relationship creates a perverse symbiosis between the model of growth for production with a financial bottleneck resulting from precarious cycles of expansion that are increasingly shorter and shallower.

A misunderstanding is added to this. Private deficits came about as a result of a mistaken monetary policy, which consists of using the stabilizing effect of the exchange rate as the principal anti-inflationary measure. This rapidly leads to growing trade deficits that end in public borrowing. This dynamic is not a temporary situation, or a random shock of the type so popular with orthodox macroeconomics, instead it is a permanent pattern that becomes a long-term condition.

Experience shows that it is typical for countries facing current account deficits to build up processes of private debt with drops in the rate of investment. From our point of view, the linkages that create the cycle lead to processes heading for crisis through the contraction of investment and economic activity, accompanied by higher levels of debt. It could indicate the presence of a type of mixed cycle with an endogenous component referring to the cost of capital that appears on both sides of the balance sheet (assets and liabilities), accompanied by a component coming from abroad that sets a relationship parameter between the productive and financial spheres, and which is expressed through the exchange rate. The disequilibrium in foreign trade therefore shows up a deficit that is brought about by the overvaluation of the exchange rate, in other words, the current price of the currencies used by domestic capital are converted at a rate that is higher than could be obtained by exchange at the market rate, in the absence of central bank intervention. An alternative way to state this is that domestic capitalists seek to place their investments outside the national economy, by the flight of capital or deposits in foreign banks within Mexico. This transfer process may occur because the government or the central bank should borrow abroad to fund the flights of capital. Three relevant indicators are explained below.

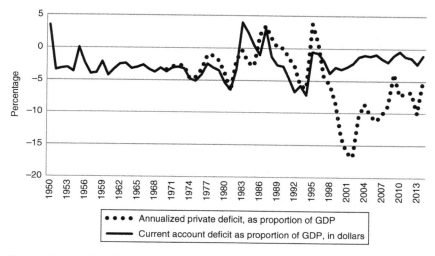

Source: Prepared by the author based on balance of payment data and real exchange rate published by the Bank of Mexico, 1950 to 2014.

Figure 9.3   *The weight of Mexican private debt in external debt and current account deficit (as a percentage of GDP), 1950–2014*

First, an overvalued exchange rate implies an opportunity cost, which is estimated by the difference between the value of imports at the current rate and an equilibrium exchange rate based on the real exchange rate. This difference has been called the 'private deficit', which is estimated as a fraction of GDP for the corresponding quarter (Figure 9.3).

Second, the negative impact of monetary policy on the expectations for investment is presented as an approximation of the resources that the capitalists withdraw from the investment process to cover themselves against growing uncertainty. According to Keynes (1937), this estimate is measured through the 'preference for liquidity', which is calculated through the extent of Mexicans' deposits in foreign banks as a percentage of GDP (Figure 9.3).

Third, the previously mentioned income elasticity of imports is considered to be a measure of the importance of external restriction on the economic cycle. According to Thirlwall's model (2011), external restriction is the principal limitation to foreign growth.

The gap between the private deficit and the current account deficit between the first quarter of 1998 and the second quarter of 2014 is explained by the petroleum surpluses resulting from increased volume and price. The history of the gap would indicate the presence of 'Dutch disease' to the extent that the nominal value of the imports and what their value would be at the equilibrium rate grew very much more than the current account deficit. This difference is attributed to the delay in adjusting the exchange rate. It should also be pointed out that in the Mexican economy, this behavior is brought on by the capital market whenever the gap between the domestic interest rate and the rest of the world widens. This set of factors activates very large deficits that do not respond to adjustments to the exchange rate, which fluctuates considerably in response to the world economy.

This is a determining factor in the explanation of the stagnation of the economy, in that the perception of the dominant productive and financial agents reflects the unfavorable business environment, which is translated into uncertainty leading to liquid deposits in dollars abroad (Figure 9.4). The rate of conversion of assets into dollars in the trade and development bank rose from 7 percent in the first quarter of 2007 to over 22 percent in the second quarter of 2014.

The description of these structural features makes it possible to outline in the following some of the means of identifying the country's hindrances to growth.

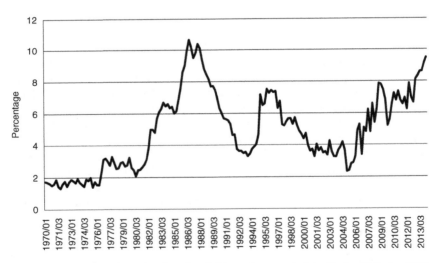

Source: Prepared by the author based on balance of payments data, Bank of Mexico, 1970 to 2014.

Figure 9.4   Dollarization in Mexico: deposits in foreign banks in proportion to GDP, 1970–2014

9.4 WHY DOES THE MEXICAN ECONOMY FAIL TO GROW?

The question will be answered without entering into debate about growth models; instead follows an argument that states that the rate of accumulated investment added in each period should incorporate technological progress, increase labor productivity and stimulate increased employment, at least at the same rate that the working population increases. The presence of open economic structures should also make production destined for foreign markets compatible with imported products. Under these conditions, long-term monetary policy should seek an exchange rate that is congruent, in other words, one that equalizes exports and imports, with a balance of trade without debt for current consumption. It has not been possible to achieve these conditions to date because the structure of domestic production is uncoupled from the export structure.

If the export sector is the traction engine, uncoupling it from the other productive sectors will result in lethargic growth. To overturn a pattern such as this also requires the financing of the economy as a whole to respond to various external and internal restrictions. The emphasis has at times been on supply and at others on demand, without paying the necessary attention to the structure of the economy itself. On the other hand, it is proposed here that attention should be given to the relationship between the domestic and foreign structures, meaning that economic policy should take note of these conditions and it should seek to generate processes of accumulation and 'virtuous' expansion, ensuring that the vision for economic policy is complete and not partial.

With the benefit of the bigger picture, we may ask why there has been no political agreement to break out of the inertia. The short answer is that there has been no understanding of how the economy works as a unit. Then again, neither has there been an understanding of the various obstacles that have arisen to protect sectors whose contribution to growth is minimal. The present dominant configuration indicates that there are few winners with big advantages while the overwhelming majority has not been able to articulate their own political agenda. This leads to imaginary outputs such as the so-called structural reforms approved by Congress, which were never seriously discussed, nor were their many limitations considered.

Thus, meaningless economic opportunities are created, with growth models driven by manufacturing exports that do not acknowledge the relationship that should be built between the 'external motor' and the industrial and productive structure as a whole. In these models neither is there any analysis of the need to manage the economic process, and therefore government action has been erratic and unfocused. The prevalence of openness at all costs has led to the establishment of patterns of consumption beyond the reach of internal production, unless an endless supply of foreign currency is made available. In principle, this is funded through petroleum exports, then by the remittances of migrant workers, with the shortcoming that the former is running out and that the latter cannot last for long.

The experience of the dominant economic model over the last 30 years shows the need for the state and government to intervene in the management of the economy, in the provision of resources to finance the fiscal policy and to channel resources or to back up credit for the non-financial sector and to steer clear of policies for rescuing companies and banks.

9.5   CONCLUSIONS

Without doubt the Mexican economy has transformed and has become interlinked with the international economy, particularly with the US economy, but has not been accompanied by a transformation of the domestic economy, despite the series of structural reforms.

A divided economy has developed that has led to conditions under which it is not feasible to 'strengthen the internal market' to the extent that the internal economy responds, and will respond, to these challenges only by increasing the demand for imports. It is common for sectors inserted into the world economy to be weakly integrated with domestic economic activity, accompanied by other sectors whose performance in local markets is precarious. These sectors are not capable of taking on the role of 'drivers of growth'. Growth then becomes dependent on foreign exchange, which may be accessed through borrowing, which has left the Mexican economy in an unstable state since it will sooner or later lead to internal bottlenecks.

In this regard, it should be noted that the financial bottleneck from foreign savings cannot add dynamism to the investment expenditure. The limit on financing can be explained on the basis, first, of primary deficits and second, by exchange rate overvaluation and third, through a weak entry into international trade. Thus, it is argued that the economy runs with two primary deficits, which appear as twins, and which relate to a series of factors. The foreign deficit is structural because of the way in which the domestic productive sector operates in relation to the rest of the world, and the public deficit seems to be inherent to the government's relationship with the seats of power in Mexico. Both became apparent in the 1980s and were resolved in that decade from petroleum income, then in the 1990s by the remittances of immigrants and more recently by using income from the mining industry. Although income from manufacturing exports has grown, this has not been sufficient to cover the brutal and growing deficit of the manufacturing sector.

Erroneous monetary policies have aggravated the disequilibria: exchange rate overvaluation has led to episodes of growing debt, and the establishment of liquid reserves in dollars. The financial sector has become fragile and its capacity to provide credit has been curtailed. It is vital to rethink the design of the national economy and the state's posture toward economic intervention should change, particularly entrapment in the taxation area. In this sense, it is fundamentally important to increase tax collection, even though this clashes with the interests of important economic groups. The dependency on external resources such as petroleum should be cut because these entail a tremendous fiscal weakness and the inability to run effective productive growth and social development policies. It is stressed that 'structural reforms' can only help close the gaps in foreign financing. Thus, it is most important to establish a strong state that is fully integrated with society, which does not imply great expenditure so much as the adequate planning of social and economic processes.

Finally, economic development not only requires growth, but also a policy of income redistribution. In the 1970s a Mexican president articulated one of the dominant ideas of his day when he said that you must increase the size of the cake in order to divide it. This notion is no longer valid. The institutional conditions that have prevailed to the present need to be broken down and redefined to create new and effective possibilities for development and growth. In order to restructure social processes, these changes must, without doubt, be responsive to the demands of society. Social development in a qualitative sense is the only way to deal with the social conflicts that exist in the ambit of the economic players, which would open up the possibility of establishing long and consistent processes of accumulation. In conclusion, it should be noted that social development creates the conditions for growth, which is summarized in a statement by Castaingts (2004): 'what there is, is a complex relationship in which civil society comes into its own and incorporates elements that belong to it, such as the market and the State'.

NOTES

1. This school of thought is based on Say's Law, and on the stimulus to production through the reduction of taxes (Laffer's curve), and from reduced government regulation of the economy. This school reached its apogee in the 1970s. It set itself up to criticize Keynesian economics and its foundations were recovered elements of classical and neoclassical perspectives, which view the level of consumption or demand as secondary consequences of the decision to produce. The New Classical School (Lucas, 1977), on

the other hand, may be considered the contemporary expression of that idea because it marries the theory of Say's Law, rationalist expectations, full employment and the determination of economic variables on the supply side.
2. In this case there is a variety of theoretical perspectives that include Keynes (1936 [1964]) and the perspectives of his followers (Hicks, 1937).
3. It is proposed that a productive structure is prone to stagnation if the linkage coefficients are less than one (see Ortiz, 1992, pp. 124ff).
4. The long-term growth trajectory is analyzed using the Hodrick–Prescott filter, based on a method that breaks down the series into their trend and cyclical components.
5. References to trends in rates of production prior to 1950 were taken from the Historical Series of the Bank of Mexico; the Gross Domestic Product series for 1960–1985 were prepared by the Instituto Nacional de Estadística y Geografía (INEGI). Subsequent data were obtained from the National Accounts of the Banco de Información Económica (BIE), INEGI.
6. http://www.banxico.org.mx/SieInternet/consultarDirectorioInternetAction.do?accion= consultarCuadroAnalitico&idCuadro=CA4&sector=1&locale=es, accessed 8 April 2015.
7. The neoclassical concept of the marginal productivity of labor is disregarded since it results from a confusion between measurement on the basis of a standard distribution, in other words, a fraction of the income destined for wages and the growth of employment, which confuses the cause with the result. See Hernández Laos (2007).
8. According to the Marshall-Lerner condition, for a devaluation to lead to positive adjustments in the balance of payments, the sum of price elasticities of imports and exports must be more than one in absolute terms.
9. After December 1994, the Bank of Mexico (2009) decided that the exchange rate would be set exclusively by market forces, which goes hand in hand with the assumption that the authorities should not interfere with the normal performance of the market (Sidaoui, 2005). This is a complete change of the institution's position compared to previous periods: 'It should be pointed out that in conjunction with a foreign trade policy that rationalizes the protective structure, the exchange rate policy adopted favors an improvement in the international competitiveness of a country's production, it encourages the natural substitution of imports and thus increases the chances of generating employment. This process allows the economy to reduce its dependency on petroleum revenues and foreign credit as sources of foreign currency, since it tends to encourage a healthy expansion of non-petroleum exports. The Mexican economy will be less vulnerable to external disturbances and the country's burden of external debt will be lightened to the extent that this occurs' (Bank of Mexico, 1983, p. 41); or 'One of the principal objectives of exchange rate policy in 1983 was to discourage imports and to promote exports' (Bank of Mexico, 1984, p. 69).
10. The author's calculations based on the banking system accounts from 1980 to 2014, available from the Bank of Mexico website, http://www.banxico.org.mx/SieInternet/ consultarDirectorioInternetAction.do?accion=consultarCuadro&idCuadro=CF445& sector=19&locale=es, accessed 19 April 2015.

REFERENCES

Amsden, A. (2004), 'Import substitution in high-tech industries: Prebisch lives in Asia!', *CEPAL Review*, No. 82, 75–89.
Bank of Mexico (1983), *Informe Anual 1982*, Mexico: Banxico.
Bank of Mexico (1984), *Informe Anual 1983*, Mexico: Banxico.
Bank of Mexico (2009), *Regímenes cambiarios en México a partir de 1954*, available

at http://www.banxico.org.mx/sistema-financiero/material-educativo/basico/{51 CCA803-9DB0-9162-1CFA-B19CE71599DB}.pdf, accessed February 2015.

Castaingts, J. (2004), 'Así vamos . . . Mercado, Estado y sociedad civil', available at https://asivamosjcct.wordpress.com/2004/12/30/asi-vamos-mercado-estado-y-sociedad-civil-por-juan-castaingts-teillery/, accessed 11 May 2015.

Davidson, P. (1994), *Post Keynesian Macroeconomic Theory*, Aldershot, UK and Brookfield, VT, USA: Edward Elgar.

Fajnzylber, F. and T. Martínez (1976), *Las empresas transnacionales: expansión a nivel mundial y proyección en la industria mexicana*, Mexico: Fondo de Cultura Económica.

Hernández Laos, E. (2005a), 'La productividad en México. Origen y distribución, 1960–2002', *Economía UNAM*, **2**(5), 7–22.

Hernández Laos, E. (2005b), *Productivity Performance of the Mexican Economy*, Vienna: United Nations Industrial Development Organization (UNIDO).

Hernández Laos, E. (2007), 'La productividad multifactorial: concepto, medición y significado', *Economía: Teoría y Práctica*, **6**, 7–22, UAM, Mexico.

Hicks, J. (1937), 'Mr. Keynes and the "Classics"; a suggested interpretation', *Econometrica*, **5**(2), 147–59.

Huerta, A. (2014), 'La problemática actual y la pérdida de soberanía exigen replantear la política predominante', in E. Ortiz (ed.), *Los Falsos Caminos al Desarrollo. Las condiciones de las políticas de cambio estructural bajo el neoliberalismo: concentración y crisis*, Mexico City: UAM-Xochimilco, pp. 177–96.

Keynes, J.M. (1936), *The General Theory of Employment, Interest, and Money*, London: First Harvest, Harcout Inc. edition in 1964.

Keynes, J.M. (1937), 'Alternative theories of the rate of interest', *The Economic Journal*, **47**(83), 241–52.

Kregel, J. (2015), 'Emerging market economies and the reform of the international financial architecture: back to the future', Public Policy Brief, No. 139, Levy Economics Institute of Bard College.

Lavoie, M. (2014), *Post-Keynesian Economics: New Foundations*, Cheltenham, UK and Northampton, MA, USA: Edward Elgar.

Levy, N. (2012), 'The effect of interest rates in developing countries: can central bank monetary policy instruments modify economic growth?', in C. Gnos, L.-P. Rochon and D. Tropeano (eds), *Employment, Growth and Development: A Post-Keynesian Approach*, Cheltenham, UK and Northampton, MA, USA: Edward Elgar, pp. 221–46.

Levy, N. (2014), 'La función del sector externo en economías financiarizadas. Un análisis de la economía mexicana', in E. Ortiz (ed.), *Los Falsos Caminos al Desarrollo. Las condiciones de las políticas de cambio estructural bajo el neoliberalismo: concentración y crisis*, Mexico City: UAM-Xochimilco, pp. 197–228.

Lucas, R. (1977), 'Understanding business cycles', *Carnegie-Rochester Conference Series on Public Policy*, **5**, 7–29.

McKinnon, R. (1973), *Money and Capital in Economic Development*, Washington, DC: Brookings Institution.

Moreno-Brid, J. and J. Ros (2010), *Desarrollo y crecimiento en la economía mexicana. Una perspectiva histórica*, Mexico: Fondo de Cultura Económica.

Ortiz, E. (1990), 'Cambio estructural y coeficientes de eslabonamiento. El caso de la economía mexicana', *Economía: Teoría y Práctica*, **14**, 107–16, UAM, Mexico.

Ortiz, E. (1992), 'Cambio estructural y exportaciones manufactureras, avance para una evaluación del nuevo modelo de política', *Economía: Teoría y Práctica*, **3**, 59–72, UAM, Mexico.

Ortiz, E. (2007), *Políticas de cambio estructural en la economía mexicana. Evaluación y perspectivas para un Nuevo proyecto de nación*, Mexico City: UAM-Xochimilco.

Ortiz, E. (2012), 'Inflation targeting by the "tyrannical auctioneer": the predominance of a normative approach in monetary policy', in C. Gnos, L.-P. Rochon and D. Tropeano (eds), *Employment, Growth and Development: A Post-Keynesian Approach*, Cheltenham, UK and Northampton, MA, USA: Edward Elgar, pp. 263–85.

Ortiz, E. (2014), 'El modelo fundado en trabajo barato y extracción de recursos naturales no genera ni crecimiento ni desarrollo', in E. Ortiz (ed.), *Los Falsos Caminos al Desarrollo. Las condiciones de las políticas de cambio estructural bajo el neoliberalismo: concentración y crisis*, Mexico City: UAM-Xochimilco, pp. 135–55.

Reinhart, C. and K. Rogoff (2008), 'This time is different: a panoramic view of eight centuries of financial crises', National Bureau of Economic Research Working Paper 13882.

Reynard, S. (2012), 'Financial crises, money and inflation', Paper presented at the EABCN conference Money is Back, London, April.

Sidaoui, J. (2005), 'Central banking intervention under a floating exchange rate regime: ten years of Mexican experience', available online at *BIS Papers: Foreign Exchange Market Intervention in Emerging Markets: Motives, Techniques and Implications*, Monetary and Economic Department, No. 24, pp. 209–30, accessed 26 May 2015.

Taylor, L. (2004), *Reconstructing Macroeconomics: Structuralist Proposals and Critiques of the Mainstream*, Cambridge, MA: Harvard University Press.

Thirlwall, A.P. (2002), *The Nature of Economic Growth: An Alternative Framework for Understanding the Performance of Nations*, Cheltenham, UK and Northampton, MA, USA: Edward Elgar.

Thirlwall, A.P. (2011), 'The balance of payments constraint as an explanation of international growth rate differences', *PSL Quarterly Review*, **64**(259), 429–38.

10. The Mexican economy in 2014: between crisis, free trade, social devastation and labor precarization

Alejandro Álvarez and Sandra Martínez

10.1 INTRODUCTION

This chapter provides an account of the two most serious problems created for workers by the prolonged application of neoliberal formulas in public policies related to wage labor and to the already precarious institutions of the welfare state: the social devastation (seen through income inequality and deteriorating welfare institutions) and job precarization (through labor market reforms and deregulation that neither solve the unemployment problem nor provide decent work for young people). In what follows, we try to show the link these have with the policies of trade liberalization and deregulation, which are two of the constants of neoliberal public policy in the Mexican economy today.

To discuss and analyze what has happened, we have divided this chapter into six sections. In Section 10.2, we present an account of the 2008–2009 crisis and its wider impact, including its global implications and issues that were left unresolved, despite the fact that a swift exit from the crisis was officially decreed in the USA on the basis of the end of recession according to the National Bureau of Economic Research (NBER). We hold that the weak growth, the continuing high level of overall unemployment, especially among young people, are the issues of greatest concern. In Section 10.3, in order to understand the unfolding and continuation of the 2008–2009 crisis, we attempt to clarify and reconstruct the characteristics of its different stages in order to show the fragility of the recovery and why in fact the crisis has not truly been overcome. Section 10.4 reviews the pillars of what may be analytically identified as a crucial part of the Obama administration's global strategy in 2013–2014. These comprise backing a segmented multi-regional integration that deepens the free trade programs by means of various legal and political instruments: the Trans-Pacific Partnership (TPP), the Trans-Atlantic Trade and Investment Partnership (TTIP) and the Trade in Services Agreement (TISA), which in truth raise questions about the administration's concern with the increase in minimum wages and employment problems.

The final three sections focus on Mexico and the arrival of Enrique Peña Nieto to power. In Section 10.5 we seek to demonstrate the agenda and sequence of what has been identified as a 'second generation of neoliberal reforms'. Based on their content and the way in which they were approved, we argue that these have been deeply delegitimizing reforms because they involve a historical shift in the basic reference points of the relationship between the state and the economy, the state and society and relations between wage labor and capital. Here, we argue that increasing inequality in income distribution and the deepening of the already serious problems of employment, particularly affecting young people and those with a higher level of education, are the most pressing problems facing Mexican society. We also engage in a discussion of the clash that is going to occur, between a political initiative seeking legitimacy with a more dynamic wage policy, and the hard reality that unemployment's deepest causes are not addressed nor effective redistributive policies really offered. In Section 10.6, we examine the role played by the two preferred neoliberal pincers to reduce Mexico's room for maneuvering and increase its subordination: deregulation and segmented integration of labor markets between the USA, Mexico and Central America, though here we focus only on Mexico. Finally, Section 10.7 presents the conclusions, arguing that without truly legitimizing political actions, the authoritarian tendencies and exclusionary policies will prevail. To this end, we discuss the balance of the reforms in terms of their political and social implications, which we believe are key to determining the future conditions of performance of the Mexican economy.

10.2   THE 2008–2009 CRISIS: IMPLICATIONS AND UNRESOLVED GLOBAL PROBLEMS

The crisis of 2008–2009 has been recognized as the most serious since the 1929 depression, with several features drawing attention: first, the dominance of the financial and banking aspect; second, the importance of public debt; and third, the increasing concentration of wealth, the persistence of high unemployment even in the midst of recovery and sustained implementation of neoliberal policies as a supposed recipe for resolving the crisis, despite growing evidence that they have the opposite effect.

When the US economy returned to growth, after applying a Troubled Asset Relief Program (TARP) and a substantial Economic Stimulus

Program that mostly involved tax breaks and subsidies to the energy sector, it was decreed that the recession had officially ended in 2009. However, several elements soon made themselves felt in the global economy to indicate that it was a fragile, limited and asymmetric recovery, with high unemployment (202 million in 2013, according to ILO, 2014) and low wages and growth.

In the United States most notably, but also in other developed countries and even in emerging economies, there are indications that the concentration of wealth intensified, since the indicators of inequality have worsened, especially the growing significance of the concentration of the wealth in the hands of a small percentage of the population. There has also been a fall in consumption, among other things, due to the excessive debt burden of households and consumers, as well as the prevalence of high unemployment and the falling purchasing power of real wages. There are data showing that a strong process of partial deleveraging of debt occurred, but that, nevertheless, financial, banking, mortgage and productive problems remain.

The crisis of 2008–2009 also represented a crisis for neoliberal globalization (as evidenced by significant falls in trade and industrial gross domestic product (GDP), rising unemployment, falling global demand and a halt in growth (WTO, 2013). Perhaps most significantly, the crisis was a turning point that brought into clearer focus the changing trends in global economic power. By this we refer especially to the rise of the so-called BRICS (the emerging economies of Brazil, Russia, India, China and South Africa), a remarkable increase in South–South trade, and the growing weight of developing countries in total world exports (WTO, 2013).

One issue of great importance is that, despite its relative weakness, the USA retains its role as the global manager of the crisis, meaning it continues to drive market outlets for all the troubled economies; but also that it decided to gain ground by the establishment of new and expanded free trade agreements; following the tradition of being the global hegemon, it has set itself the task of imposing them, by deepening neoliberal reforms in its own economy and in the rest of the world, starting with Mexico. As a result, it is hardly surprising that the recovery is vanishing, as the perpetuation of the trend toward stagnation is conducive to the continued imposition of the neoliberal policies of austerity on the working population. Tendentiously, before the entry into force of the North American Free Trade Agreement (NAFTA), a trend could be observed whereby the US economy sought to correct some of its imbalances using the Mexican economy. And above all, in addition to the prevalence of neoliberal policies in both countries, there is also a marked trend toward synchronization of

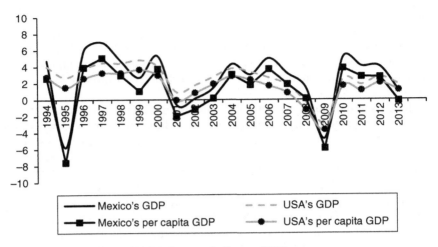

Source: World Bank, World Development Indicators (2013).

Figure 10.1 *Total and per capita gross domestic product, Mexico and the United States, 1994–2014*

economic cycles. The per capita GDP in the USA and Mexico continue to shadow the growth of total GDP, save when it falls, the per capita figure falls more in both countries. When the total GDP grows, the per capita figure grows less. This characteristic and the synchrony may be observed in Figure 10.1.

Another important thing to emphasize is that the problems with the recovery are global, at least in the case of unemployment and its greater impact on young people. This can be seen in Table 10.1, which shows youth unemployment and total unemployment. We may observe that for each country, the figure of youth unemployment is above the figure of total unemployment. The six selected countries totaled nearly 33 million unemployed in 2012.

10.3 THE 2008–2009 CRISIS: ITS STAGES AND THE FRAGILITY OF THE RECOVERY

Although it is clear that we must view the crisis as a continuum, it is also clear that it can be divided into stages, as both countries face problems and the key issues causing it to continue – to the extent that it is recognized as the most serious crisis that has occurred since 1929 – have changed.

Table 10.1 Total unemployment* and youth unemployment** in selected countries, 1994–2012

	USA		MEXICO		CANADA		SPAIN		FRANCE		BRAZIL	
	TOTAL	YOUNG	TOTAL	YOUNG	TOTAL	YOUNG	TOTAL	YOUNG	TOTAL	YOUNG	TOTAL	YOUNG
1994	6.2	12.8	4.2	7	10.4	15.9	24.3	44.1	12.6	28.3	6	11.4
1995	5.7	12.4	6.9	11.2	9.5	14.8	23.1	41.7	11.8	26.6	6	11.4
1996	5.5	12.3	5.2	9.1	9.6	15.4	22.5	41.5	12.4	27.1	6.8	12.6
1997	5.1	11.6	4.1	7.2	9.1	16.2	21	38.7	12.6	28.5	7.7	14.4
1998	4.6	10.7	3.6	6.3	8.3	15.1	19	35.3	12.1	25.9	8.9	17.2
1999	4.3	10.2	2.5	4	7.6	14.1	16	29.4	12	26.2	9.6	18.2
2000	4.1	9.6	2.6	5	6.8	12.7	14.2	26.3	10.2	20.5	9.5	18
2001	4.8	10.8	2.5	4.8	7.2	12.9	10.6	21.3	8.6	18	9.3	17.8
2002	5.9	12.3	2.9	5.8	7.7	13.7	11.5	22.9	8.7	19	9.1	18
2003	6.1	12.7	3	6.1	7.6	13.7	11.5	23.4	8.6	17.5	9.7	19
2004	5.6	12.1	3.7	7.5	7.2	13.4	11.1	22.7	9.2	20	8.9	18
2005	5.2	11.5	3.5	6.6	6.7	12.4	9.3	20.3	8.9	20.4	9.3	19.3
2006	4.7	10.7	3.2	6.1	6.3	11.7	8.6	18.5	8.8	21.4	8.4	17.7
2007	4.7	10.8	3.4	6.6	6	11.2	8.4	18.8	8	18.9	8.1	16.7
2008	5.9	13.1	3.5	7	6.1	11.6	11.5	25.5	7.4	18.4	7.1	15.4
2009	9.3	17.8	5.2	10	8.3	15.2	18.1	38.5	9.1	23	8.3	17.7
2010	9.7	18.7	5.2	9.4	8	14.8	20.2	42.4	9.3	22.7	7.9	17.2
2011	9	17.5	5.3	9.8	7.4	14.2	21.8	47.3	9.2	21.9	6.7	15.2
2012	8.1	16.5	4.9	9.4	7.2	14.3	25.2	54.3	9.9	23.7	6.9	15.5
2013	7.4	15.8	4.9	9.4	7.1	13.8	26.6	57.3	10.4	23.7	5.9	13.6

Note: * Total unemployment refers to the total active population (on percentage);
** total youth unemployment refers to the total active population between 15 to 24 years old (in percentage).

Source: World Bank, World Development Indicators (2013), last updated 22 July 2014.

A first stage was between 2008–2009, coinciding with the outbreak of the financial crisis in the USA but with a global impact, because the effects, focusing on the economic axis of the Atlantic, spread from the USA to Europe with extraordinary speed, forcing central banks to coordinate actions to address it. This collapse of the financial bubble was followed by a synchronized global recession, dominated by bank bailouts to cover 'toxic assets' and fiscal stimulus packages to stem the recessionary decline. This is also the stage in which unemployment was generalized (reaching a peak of 150 million people worldwide).

The second stage occurred in 2010–2011 and was characterized by a markedly uneven recovery, limited in scope and fragile in its sustainability. Many economies continue to bear unsustainable debts, speculation is out of control and public management of the problems of the private financial system ends up placing public finances in crisis. The persistence of a high level of unemployment is also notable (then accounting for 8 percent of the labor force in the USA).

A third phase took place between 2011–2012, officially a period in which the crisis had been declared over, but in reality marked by the outbreak of a sovereign debt crisis in Europe, which many commentators have blamed on an inadequate institutional architecture (specifically because the European Central Bank sets monetary policy whereas fiscal policy is decided by the member countries of the European Monetary Union). This stage can be recognized by major shocks to the euro, by the further spread of austerity policies supposedly intended to address the underlying crisis and the commitment to deepening of the fiscal pact, which, as mentioned, is believed to be part of a poor institutional design. By this stage unemployment was affecting more young people (with rates above 25 percent).

The fourth stage occurs between 2012–2014 and is characterized by the emergence of new and worrying phenomena: first, although there is a relative recovery of growth and employment in the USA, the prospect of a deepening economic slowdown in China becomes apparent, together with the problematic virtual stagnation of the European Monetary Union. As if that were not enough, it is evident that global unemployment remains high and that a dangerous lethargy persists in global growth, because only the USA is growing, and even there growth is meager. By now the imbalances in public finances continue to present themselves, but to this we must add greater private financial vulnerability, compounded by increasing monetary rivalry, such that the central concern that determines this whole stage is simple: where is the recovery?

10.4 THE GLOBAL STRATEGY OF BARACK OBAMA IN 2013–2014: SEGMENTED INTEGRATION IN THE WORLD ECONOMY BY MEANS OF MAJOR FREE TRADE AGREEMENTS – TPP, TISA AND TTIP

As a leader of the global player and hegemon in the world economy, the Obama administration in the USA made explicit its strategy for change through trade agreements and institutional arrangements that seek to consolidate the progress made by the USA in the global economy in some cases, and in others seek to regain ground lost to competitors. Let us examine the content and reality of the projects being promoted. The TPP is a proposal that demonstrates the intention of 'locking in' previous agreements, such as NAFTA, with a number of more or less explicit commercial objectives, which in practice involve segmenting Latin America (since it aims to deepen the integration of Mexico, Colombia, Chile and Peru), with the practical result that it would capture the most important markets and relatively exclude Brazil, which is the major player in Latin America. As for the aim of the TPP on the other side of the Pacific, this is to segment the Asia-Pacific economies, in an attempt to isolate the growing regional and global influence of China.

The little that is known about the TPP suggests that it intends to go further than NAFTA, because among other priorities the USA aims to consolidate existing trade agreements, while also developing what it calls 'quality rules' to harmonize regulations around financial services, investment, health and safety standards, intellectual property rights (patents, copyrights), mechanisms for resolving disputes between investors and governments and attracting a critical mass of new partners, although negotiations did not immediately include the most important partner of all, China. In addition, it aims to extend these rules to the entire Asia-Pacific region and beyond (Petri et al., 2014, chapters 1, 2, 6). The secrecy and the fact that the USA has placed additional requirements on new entrants to the TPP (for example, they cannot renegotiate what has already been agreed among the original members, even though the overall negotiation has not been completed) suggest there is a clear intention of segmenting the global economy. Since, as we have said, the goal is to impose a greater liberalization of public services (especially in the education and health sectors), while attempting to hinder the return of privatized services to the public domain (as has been the case with failed privatizations in Latin America), we can say that the negotiation of the TPP is a kind of regionalized tool to achieve regional and global results.

In other spheres, which have so far only been released in a partial fashion, it is known that the TPP aims to legalize in the most overwhelming manner intellectual property rights (making them valid in longer periods); that it seeks to include the sensitive issue of government procurement; that it attempts to reinforce legal mechanisms to protect investment; that it seeks to impose restrictions on national environmental regulations; and to actively promote energy liberalization, which has been one of the cornerstones of Obama's economic stimulus strategy within the USA and in relation to Mexico (Alvarez, 2014b).

There are many open problems, because there is little information about the TPP in the press and among scholars the bulk of the issues discussed is virtually unknown, on top of which the participants have imposed a long period of silence before disclosing what is being negotiated. However, it is known to contain much more than just trade rules.

The other two agreements, the TISA and TTIP, pursue the same strategy as the TPP, but are negotiated separately, even as they include the most sensitive issues and sectors: services, investment, intellectual property and logistics, both with devastating impacts on public sector workers, which form a significant proportion of the best organized workers in the developed world, and the most numerous in developing countries (Gould, 2014; Sinclair and Mertins-Kirkwood, 2014).

On the negotiation of a transatlantic agreement, we believe that the USA is forcing a transatlantic agreement with Europe in order to erode the economic power and the stability of the European Monetary Union. An expert trade analyst has recently published the findings of his quantitative research: formally, the TTIP will stimulate economic growth in Europe and the USA as well as integration between the two, but the projections of the European Commission itself, which backs the project, indicate that that will happen at the expense of intra-European trade, partly reversing the progress of the regional integration process in Europe (Capaldo, 2014).

For all these reasons, it is worth also analyzing the other economic strategies deployed domestically, to understand whether Barack Obama's project is really to fight or reinforce inequality in income: in his State of the Union Address for 2013, Obama placed a special political emphasis on acknowledging that in the USA, the richest 10 percent increase their wealth rapidly, while the poorest 10 percent suffer stagnation of their income. However, the international experience accumulated in the past three decades shows that through the initiative of the great trade agreements, TPP, TTIP and TISA, millions of jobs will be at risk in the USA. For this reason, it is worth asking: will there be enough job creation for high school leavers, as promised by Obama, using robot technology? And if we consider hard data, we see that unemployment hits the younger generation and those with a higher level of studies in both the USA and Mexico, as well as other countries.

In his State of the Union Address for 2014, Obama expressed his intention to continue with energy deregulation in oil and gas. More power at the cost of more pollution? Is the government, once again, contributing to the formation of a new financial bubble, this time with the US energy sector and the financing and support for companies deploying the controversial method of fracking? There is much evidence to confirm the existence of a financial bubble linked to energy companies engaged in fracking. The Address also proposed market mechanisms to combat climate change, except that this initiative does not stand up to too much analysis, because the first question to answer is: why was this path chosen, rather than ratifying the Kyoto Protocol, which was a global proposal?

In this Address, Obama also made clear what his key domestic strategy against inequality would be in the next period of his administration: he proposed increasing the federal minimum wage from $7.25 to $10 per hour. But this has no great significance if we consider that 21 states had wage rates higher than the federal minimum when the announcement was made. Another important issue was his declared intention to improve education: yet, once again, when the proposals are examined they give rise to many questions. Does all education improve with better tax credits, more grants and better loans, albeit now with a law to lower fees in private schools, so they can receive federal subsidies (President's State of the Union Address, 2014)? Instead, this seems to be another way of further promoting the privatization of education.

10.5 MEXICO: THE ADMINISTRATION OF PEÑA NIETO AND THE SECOND GENERATION NEOLIBERAL REFORMS (LABOR, EDUCATION, ENERGY, FISCAL, FINANCIAL AND POLITICAL)

After a crisis as serious as that of 2008–2009, labor–capital relations prove crucial to redefining relations between state and society in Mexico. This is why the Peña Nieto administration established the corporate political device known as the 'Pact for Mexico', in order to introduce structural reforms as part of a grand majority national political agreement although, strictly speaking, it was a pact between the party leaderships, who agreed to commit to the legislative agenda of Peña Nieto.

The labor and education reforms of 2012–2013 were two great pincers used against industrial and public employees (mostly teachers). The reforms came on the back of increasing income inequality, which has been exacerbated by the burden of the so-called 'educated unemployment'. These reforms were designed to create job insecurity, break with bilateralism in contractual negotiations, reduce social benefits, progress toward part-time hiring, generalize the principle of outsourcing and impose new rules on the hiring and firing of workers in the private and public sectors.

What we can say is that what has been imposed in Mexico is part of a widespread change that is being implemented for the regional labor market (in North America), the results of which are visible in the form of the loss of well-paid jobs, a fall in new contracts, an increase in low-paying jobs without social protection, mainly in services, while also criminalizing migrants. The result: growing inequality, as can be seen in Figure 10.2. In 2010 the concentration of income in Mexico remains high despite the reduction observed in the proportion of income corresponding to the best paid 10 percent of the population, since at the other end of the scale no significant increase is reported.

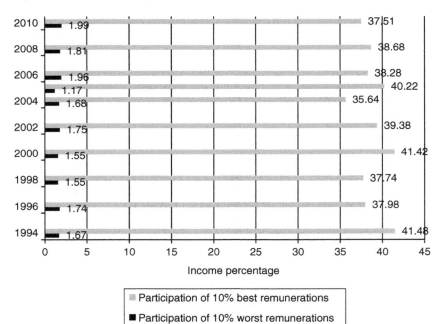

Source: World Bank, World Development Indicators (2013).

Figure 10.2   Participation in total income of the highest and lowest 10 percent remuneration in Mexico, 1994–2010

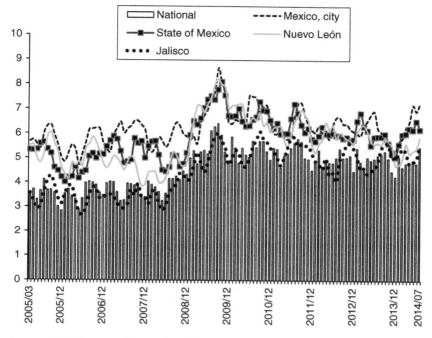

Source: INEGI, occupational and employment data (2014).

Figure 10.3 *Mexico's unemployment rate in terms of economically active population, 2005–2014*

This panorama of persistent inequality cannot be properly understood without taking into account the complex problem of unemployment. Despite the methodology used to measure unemployment in Mexico, very high rates can be detected. The data shown in Figure 10.3 correspond to the most industrialized states in the country and all have higher rates of unemployment than the national average. In the case of the Federal District, the unemployment rate, as well as being the highest, presents a growth trend that shows no sign of changing course.

10.6   TWO KEY NEOLIBERAL PINCERS: DEREGULATION AND INTEGRATION

We contend that the 2008–2009 crisis has functioned as a touchstone for reimposing austerity policies in both the USA and Mexico, but this time the strategy is directed at public employees, industrial workers and migrants. For this reason, we believe that the deregulation of labor markets has been a cornerstone and that its complement in the Mexico–USA relationship can be seen in the design of a migration policy that seeks to further segment the labor market in the USA, using Mexican and Central American workers to fill low-paid positions and thereby push all wages down, while controlling the flow of migrants with militarized and much stronger border controls, which now begin at Mexico's border with Guatemala.

The explanation of this strategy, in the case of public employees, lies in the undermining of their high rate of unionization (which stands at over 35 percent in the USA, while in the private sector it is just under 8 percent). It is a strategy that seeks to replace public employees by the intensive use of information technologies in education, while reassigning budgets to facilitate privatization. And this does not only affect education but also the health sector, by the procedure of cheapening social security (which is now touted as 'universal', but in reality has been degraded because it is being stripped of the coverage it used to provide).

This labor strategy also targets industrial workers, because it imposes profound changes on contractual benefits that impose wage cuts, clearing the way for further deployment of labor-saving technological changes, to the extent that a generalization of robotics in many productive segments is on the cards.

Finally, we hold that this is a dual strategy of both containment and attraction: the former is directed against unqualified migrants from Central America and Mexico, because for them the border fences rise, immigration checkpoints are set up, raids are carried out in the cities, mass deportations take place, anti-immigrant laws multiply and the growing militarization of borders is justified, in addition to the assertion of the need to generalize the teaching of English at all levels of the education system. All this, complex and contradictory as it is, in the knowledge that in 33 US states, Mexican immigrants now represent between 10 and 35 percent of the workforce.

At the same time, a subtle shift may be noted that seeks to attract more educated Mexican workers, who bear the bulk of unemployment in the country: thus, we see grants being promoted for students to go and stay in the USA, based on the well-documented experience that has been occurring for some time now, a combination of legal and illegal means (they go as students and when the visa or grant runs out, they stay on as undocumented immigrants).

It must be said that in Mexico labor reform happened with very little protest from the unions because they did not perceive it as an immediate danger for their benefits. However, the education, fiscal and energy reforms gave rise to serious crises of credibility and legitimacy (some polls indicated almost 70 percent national disagreement in the latter case), although education has been the one that has caused the most intense and prolonged social movements (especially by teachers, who are the heart of Mexican public sector workers). The issue became so heated that the government tried to stop the protests through the use of public force, with police repression above all in the Metropolitan Area of Mexico City. This deepened the crisis of legitimacy, which won temporarily by prohibiting sit-in demonstrations in the city's main plaza, but this was a Pyrrhic victory because they failed to convince the teachers, and nor have they managed to implement the reform, strictly speaking.

As is well known, the Metropolitan Area of Mexico City is the economic and political epicenter of the country, and this means that today it is also the test zone for supposed unilateral wage increases, which have been promoted since mid 2014 by the city government, supported by the PRI (Institutional Revolutionary Party) and the PRD (Party of the Democratic Revolution), in exchange for not questioning the president or his neoliberal reforms, but also to test out a new legitimacy. The problem is that the dynamics of the wage increases have not been supported by any significant business group, so that low wages continue to function as an 'anti-inflationary anchor' and a 'comparative advantage' of the country, without energizing the domestic market.

The credibility crisis became a new reference point due to an important political fact: that the PRD and Morena parties presented 2 million and 2.8 million signatures, respectively, for a consultation on revoking the energy reform, to be voted on the midterm elections of 2015. But, surprisingly, it seemed like all the political forces were in the business of collecting signatures, because soon after the PAN (National Action Party) presented 2.5 million signatures 'to support the wage increase' (which was never part of its action plan). Soon after, the PRI delivered 5.2 million signatures, 'to support the reduction of proportional representation in Congress' (it is worth recalling that this proposal was presented as part of its political reform to build a 'new governance', taking advantage of the anti-Congress and anti-party discontent with Peña Nieto's structural reforms). The political intent of the bipartisan (PRI–PAN) strategic alliance was clear: to convert the serious democratic task of collecting signatures throughout the country by the PRD and Morena into a deliberate farce – since no one ever saw the PRI or the PAN collecting signatures – but their actions suggested the same about the other initiatives.

Finally, to top things off, the strategic initiative to gather signatures against the energy reform left the national stage because on 26 September 2014 there was an attack by the municipal police of the city of Iguala, with the controversial participation by an organized crime group and the army, on students from the Ayotzinapa Rural Normal School, which left six dead (among whom were players on a football team), dozens injured and 43 missing students. This opened the most serious humanitarian, security, credibility and legitimacy crisis in living memory in the history of the country, one that is still being pursued intensively today (Alvarez, 2014a, pp. 15–29). This meant the issue of the signatures for a consultation on revoking the energy reform took second place, but the spread of political and social conflict throughout the country rebounded by questioning the strategy of combating drugs traffickers by way of militarization, an issue that evolved until it raised challenges to the midterm elections of 2015 and the whole administration of Peña Nieto. The credibility crisis was sealed with a deepening crisis of legitimacy.

10.7 CONCLUSION

Neoliberal reforms in Mexico are increasingly being questioned, while the resources of legitimization are increasingly precarious, as they fail to deal with serious problems of unemployment, serious deterioration in real wages and lack a comprehensive social policy or increasing democratization. This means what people perceive is the growing trend toward authoritarianism, which seeks to impose reforms by force.

There is no doubt that a policy of minimum wage increases like that in the Federal District is a positive move, but without policies for sustained employment growth and expansion in spending on education, health and social security, it may be possible to increase consumption for those who receive increases, but not to improve the living standards of workers and their families. And in the fight against inequality, political mechanisms need to be designed to draw the oligarchy out of their six entrenched ideological redoubts: 'neoliberal reforms are needed to grow', 'teachers are responsible for the disaster that is now public education', 'unemployment does not matter, if fiscally responsible entrepreneurs are promoted', 'no higher taxes', 'wage increases are inflationary, so productivity must increase first' and the idea that 'government monopolies are inefficient by nature'. Mexico is thus at a crossroads, because today an economic crisis and a political crisis are converging, in a context of social devastation fed by the implementation of neoliberal structural reforms.

REFERENCES

Alvarez, A. (2014a), 'Notas para el análisis de la coyuntura actual. Política, Economía y Perspectivas de la Lucha Social en México', Coalición Trinacional en Defensa de la Educación Pública – ATSEP-FAMA, No. 2, Ayotzinapa, Mexico, November, 15–29.

Alvarez, A. (2014b), 'Economic integration and energy in Mexico, before and after NAFTA', *International Journal of Political Economy*, **43**(2), Summer, 82–99.

Capaldo, J. (2014), 'The Trans-Atlantic Trade and Investment Partnership: European disintegration, unemployment and instability', GDAE Working Paper No. 14-03, October.

Gould, E. (2014), *TISA – Trade in Services Agreement, the Really Good Friends of Transnational Corporations Agreement*, Special Report, September, Montreal: Public Services International.

ILO (International Labour Organization) (2014), *Global Employment Trends, 2014, Risks of a Jobless Recovery*, Geneva: ILO, figure 4, 'Global Unemployment trends and projections 2003–2018', p. 17.

INEGI (Instituto Nacional de Estadística Geografía e Informática) (2014), *Estadística de Ocupación y Empleo*, Mexico: INEGI.

Petri, P., M.G. Plummer and F. Shai (2014), *The Trans-Pacific Partnership and Asia Pacific Integration: A Quantitative Assessment*, Washington, DC: The Peterson Institute for International Economics.

President's State of the Union Address (2014), http//:www.whitehouse.gov/sotu, cited in A. Alvarez (2014), 'Obama y su mensaje a la Nación: la realidad detrás de la retórica', in *Momento Económico*, UNAM, Mexico: IIEc.

Sinclair, S. and H. Mertins-Kirkwood (2014), *El TISA frente a los Servicios Públicos*, Canada, Internacional de Servicios Públicos, available at http://www.world-psi.org, accessed January 2016.

World Bank (2013), *Global Development Indicators*, Washington, DC: World Bank.

WTO (World Trade Organization) (2013), *World Trade Report 2013: Factors Shaping the Future of World Trade*, available at http://www.wto.org, accessed January 2016.

11. The accumulation mode of production in Mexico and the economic structure of the manufacturing industry

Luis Kato

11.1 INTRODUCTION

The pattern of accumulation in the Mexican manufacturing sector is distinguished by being composed of companies of a variety of sizes, with accentuated disparities in the relation of capital assets per worker, as well as in production techniques, and due to serving different types and structures of markets.[1]

As a result of this diversity, this chapter discusses the relationship between stagnation of productivity of the workforce[2] and the dominant pattern of accumulation in the Mexican context, which is characterized by the presence of large companies in the manufacturing sector that are linked through global commodity chains and seek to maximize the rate of profit on the basis of regional competitive advantages. In addition, it argues that there are a large number of micro, small and medium enterprises, which are linked to a regional and national context that is subject to multinational competition processes, without there being a productive coordination between these companies and major corporations. This system generates a stagnation that limits the dominant pattern of accumulation and guarantees the increasing rate of capital accumulation with growth rates of gross domestic product (GDP) that are not commensurate with the increase in the economically active population. In this sense, the financialization of large Mexican companies[3] determines and reproduces the slow growth of the economy by creating imbalances at the macroeconomic level that reinforce stagnation and the removal of production and employment linkages in the national economy.

This chapter is divided into three sections. In Section 11.2 the most important characteristics of the industrial establishments operating in

Mexico are analyzed, and the financial strategies imposed by the Mexican state to adapt the model of accumulation to the dynamics of an open economy guided by financial capital are described. The pattern of accumulation of the industrial establishments in relation to the decentralization strategies of the subsidiaries of transnational corporations is also examined, together with the behavior of both the rate of profit and the capital/labor relationship for different strata of the firms that comprise the manufacturing industry, on the basis of existing census data. Section 11.3 assesses the role of the financialization of large Mexican companies and its impact on the pattern of accumulation of the manufacturing sector. This takes into account the financing generated by the international market, speculation in derivatives and the mergers and sales that took place following the crisis of 2008. Section 11.4 presents the conclusions of the research.

11.2 THE PATTERN OF ACCUMULATION OF THE MANUFACTURING INDUSTRY IN MEXICO

The definition of micro, small and medium enterprises – MSMEs – includes a wide range of industrial and commercial entities with highly variable efficiency and competitiveness ratings.[4] Significantly, in the last three decades, companies comprising the group of MSMEs have been essential to generating employment (EU-LAC, CEPAL, 2015). In the Mexican economy, INEGI (2013) reports that there are 3,724,019 family businesses that account for 98.35 percent of all companies; of these, 1,858,550 are focused on commerce, 1,367,287 on services and 436,851 belong to the manufacturing industry.

For its part, the large companies operating in developing countries do so in association with multinationals or subsidiaries of large international conglomerates. The economic and technological characteristics of this type of company mean they have the capacity to segment the market and specialize in the processes of production, marketing or financing. This enables them to free themselves from the ups and downs of the national economy, and even expand their production by taking advantage of the most dynamic segments of the national market.

Consequently, and from a holistic perspective, the lack of coordination of the Mexican industrial structure is the result of a dual pattern of industrial growth characterized by the intra-sectoral heterogeneity of the industry, where large manufacturing companies maximize profits on the basis of their regional competitive advantages and commodity chains in globalized markets. These factors are absent in the case of MSMEs because they are confined to operating in a local and regional environment, which has little dynamism in technological, productive, commercial and financial terms.

This condition is reinforced insofar as the integration of large companies to the international market has increased their foreign exchange transactions, but also due to their need for external financing. In this context, the development of financial instruments for hedging risk ready to implement in the capital markets transformed the modes of company financing; to the extent that instead of using current operations to provide financial coverage for companies, these were used to speculate. Derivatives were created on the basis of variations in exchange rates, prices of raw materials, interest rates and so on. The financial instruments used by large Mexican companies for this purpose have been swaps, exchange rate and interest rate futures, as well as options.

It is in this context that the Mexican government launched the process of financialization, which dates back to the 1970s, 'when it made available secondary reserve lines to address the exchange rate instability of the period. The resources in these secondary lines were foreign loans that made up the first set of investments received by Mexico as a financialized economy, as they were placed in the main business of this kind of economy, which is debt, with the expectation they would increase in value through the simple rise in financial indicators, and they were foreign because of the then insufficient development of the nation's financial system' (Rodríguez, 2012, p. 146). In the 1980s, economic policy was used to encourage financialization, and by guaranteeing leveraged buyouts, financial valorization mechanisms were inserted in the national economy relating to domestic exchange rate and monetary policy. This laid the foundations of what would later become the permanent expansion of value and profit through the business opportunity that debt was becoming.

In the 1990s, with the opening up of the Mexican economy, the deregulation and liberalization of the financial system, and entry into foreign ownership of banks, the government established the yields of domestic financial instruments in line with the international market, with the aim of attracting greater financial investment in the domestic market, although this did not necessarily imply greater financing for the MSME sector.

Thus, economic deregulation and financial globalization altered the behavior of the main components of expenditure, particularly productive investment, which had a very low share of GDP (about 18 percent from 1980 to the time of writing; see Levy, 2007). So while the financial markets grew and corporations financialized themselves via the sale of large quantities of financial assets, the rest of the industrial establishments in the manufacturing industry faced credit rationing, which prevented them from expanding their operations. This, in part, explains the joint fall in productivity and employment, which has generated a shortfall in demand, and the strengthening of a strategy to maximize shareholder value, associated with corporate policies aimed at reducing labor costs and rationalizing the structure of assets.

Thus, since the early 1980s the behavior of corporate management based on 'maximizing' shareholder value, through indiscriminate administration of excess cash flows, has led to structural changes in employment, which may be summarized in the 'rationalization' of costs (closure of factories), the 'commodification' of senior management positions (high mobility of managers and executives between companies, on the basis of dividends) and the 'globalization' of the workforce (outsourcing of jobs to countries with lower wages). These very changes have contributed to the generation of successive economic crises followed by slow recovery, accompanied by permanent loss of jobs.

11.2.1 The Pattern of Accumulation of the Manufacturing Industry

One of the peculiarities of Mexican manufacturing is that it underwent a process that led to the formation of complex chains of production of goods and services, which are fragmented geographically and functionally integrated under the control of transnational capital, which productively and financially respond to the interests of the global market. Technological innovations deployed in dynamic segments of the economy cannot spread to less advanced manufacturing sectors due to the weak level of coordination with the MSMEs. These types of companies, in addition to being located in less productive sectors of the economy, seek to survive on the basis of overexploitation of the labor force as a way to maintain their profitability. Thus, the cumulative effects of the weak coordination of this sector lead to a progressive dismantling of the endogenous production systems of national economies, which are converted on the basis of the needs for restructuring of the production process and for accumulation of transnational corporations.

Meanwhile, the transnational corporations that establish themselves in underdeveloped economies generate a linkage with global markets that gives them operational independence from their parent companies. This same decentralization allows them to maximize their profits not only as a result of the national and regional conditions in which they operate (regardless of whether they channel their output to the domestic or foreign markets) but by establishing profitability at the core of its competitiveness (Guadalupe and Wulf, 2010; Unidad Ecológica Salvadoreña (UNES) OXFAM, 2010).

As a matter of fact, multinational companies have a greater need to decentralize themselves from their foreign subsidiaries because their local administrators possess higher levels of information. This involves the implementation of mechanisms of industrial localization, based on the vertical transfer of the competitive capacity of the supply chains of the multinationals, which are adapted in consideration of two objectives. Glaeser and Kerr (2008) identify the first of these as optimizing the infrastructure of multinational supply chains according to the competitive advantages of the countries where the various links of these chains are located. This is based, on the one hand, on the tendency to transform special and varied products in order to respond to an increasingly diversified demand and, on the other, on substituting such products and reducing their life cycles. This process involves limiting the time and costs needed to obtain inputs, produce and distribute the new products.

Another important element of this process is that the size of large companies means they can respond immediately to changes in demand through flexible production, improved product quality, just-in-time processes, integration of operational functions and solutions to benchmarking problems.

In the product market, competition from transnational corporations leads to the disappearance of local companies, which weakens or even cancels out the innovations at the level of goods made by local businesses. Moreover, the transnationals expand by taking advantage of local markets. That is, transnational control over productive innovation is a key incentive to decentralization processes. This is explained by the fact that more competitive environments increase reaction time in response to an increased sensitivity of profitability in relation to the relative cost and quality differences between companies. In Latin America, the proliferation of bilateral agreements between countries that incorporated the principles of the North American Free Trade Agreement did not lead to a disruption of traditional patterns of production and supply of local markets, but rather an overlap of local and international market structures, without hindering the advance of trade agreements, whose dynamic established, in practice, the new direction of integration.

What enabled independent dynamic growth among local and international markets was, firstly, the existence of poorly integrated industrial structures, comprising reduced productive hubs of capital goods, with growing subsectors producing consumer durables that were increasingly dependent on imported inputs and components and, secondly, the existence of a sector comprising a large number of micro enterprises that cover very small markets in geographical area. In this context, the overexploitation of labor causes a decline in the competitiveness of all economic activities generated because of the limits to expanding profitability without increasing the rate of investment.

In this scenario, foreign companies maintain high rates of turnover of capital into their countries and regions of origin, using various mechanisms. Prominent among these are interest and service payments for external financing, sending profits to the parent company, the payment of royalties, patents and technical support, the imposition of surcharges on intra-firm relations or simply the displacement of capital to regions where the macroeconomic conditions are more secure and attractive. This process ensures that their capital inflows are higher than the investments initially made, thereby generating a significant process of appropriation of capital and foreign currency by transnational corporations (Heijs, 2006).

The heterogeneity between local and transnational companies has triggered a deindustrialization process in developing countries (that is, a reduction of activities in the manufacturing sector) because investments are made only in sectors where profit rates are guaranteed to match those on the global market. As a result, profit rates are defined by the great international monopolies and oligopolies. This, as well as increasing specialization in manufacturing, lead to a strangling of job creation, as these can only grow to the limit set by the level of specialization in the manufacturing sector, which is imposed by the world market and unrelated to the needs and characteristics of the economically active population in the countries where they operate. In that sense, the financialization of transnational companies operating in Mexico has helped to increase the structural polarization of Mexican industry (Kato, 2008).

The clearest evidence of industrial polarization may be observed in the fact that while large companies are efficiently coordinated with the dynamics of international markets, micro and small enterprises are limited to operating almost exclusively in local and regional markets, and mid-size companies tend to concentrate their production on the domestic market. The Industrial Census 2009 (INEGI, 2009) shows that in the case of MSMEs, the contrast between large enterprises and medium enterprises is startling, with less than 1 percent of MSMEs selling goods on foreign markets, and of this 1 percent, one-tenth of these companies account for 80 percent of all foreign sales. The pattern of accumulation for the different strata of firms in the manufacturing sector is explained based on census information (INEGI, 1982, 1985, 1986, 1999, 2003, 2009), allowing us to estimate both the rate of profit and the capital/labor ratio (Figures 11.1 and 11.2).

The behavior of the profit rate of all strata that make up the manufacturing industry until 1976 followed the same downward trend. During the recession period of 1983–1987 the downward trend in the rate of profit was reversed only by large industry through trade liberalization and wage restraints. It is argued that the measures implemented after the

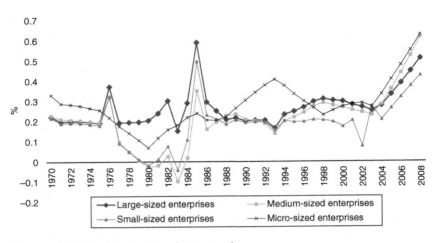

Source: Author's calculations based on census data.

Figure 11.1   Profit rate by size of establishment in the Mexican economy

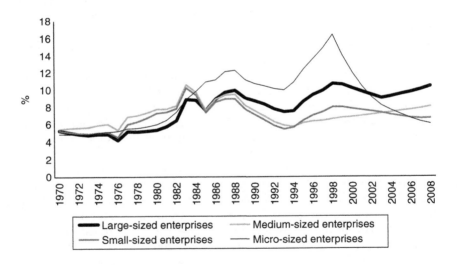

Source: Author's calculations based on census data.

Figure 11.2   Working capital ratio by size of enterprises in the Mexican economy

1982 devaluation crisis (less state involvement in the productive sector of the economy, trade liberalization and concentration of the manufacturing industry) helped reverse this downward trend in the rate of profit. It is clearly observed that since 1988 the effects on the recovery of the profit rate have been differentiated for the different strata of industry players.

Between 1994 and 1998 micro and small businesses presented significant growth in the capital/labor relation. With trade liberalization this business sector showed a decrease of production costs as a result of the indiscriminate entry of intermediate inputs and capital goods. This continued until 1998 when the increased penetration of foreign products in the domestic market and the aftermath of the devaluation of the peso prevented further reductions to costs by importing cheaper raw materials. The inelasticity of these companies with regard to reducing wage costs, as a result of their technological features, and because most of the capital is invested in working capital, indicates that in this sector the possibility of maintaining profitability rests almost exclusively on reducing wage costs. This would explain the significant reduction in the capital/labor ratio between 1998 and 2008 and the recovery of profit rates in the same period. That is, they recovered their profit rate through a process of accelerated decapitalization.

The MSME Observatory Survey 2002 (Secretaría de Economía/ Comisión Intersecretarial de Política Industrial, 2003) indicates that in the manufacturing industry 73.1 percent of small- and medium-sized companies make their sales in the domestic market. The sales structure of this group of companies by type of customer may be broken down as follows: 25 percent goes directly to the public; 22 percent to wholesalers; 19.4 percent is sold to other industrial companies; and 19.1 percent is channeled to retail businesses. Consequently, increasing foreign competition, the contraction of the domestic market and the concentration of income have a direct impact on these companies' ability to maintain their market.

The capital/labor ratio for mid-size companies presents the following trends: between 1970 and 1986 this relationship tended to grow; whereas between 1987 and 1994 it decreased, beginning to grow again in 1994.

In large companies, the growth of employment is associated with productivity performance, presenting a direct relationship between the two variables. The increase (decrease) is similar to the capital/labor ratio, which is an indication that these companies are able to establish processes of growth of labor productivity based on adjusting their relative prices (prices of inputs and final goods) to a pattern of management of the workforce based on the production of relative surplus value. This phenomenon can be explained by two reasons. The first is the ability of these companies to transfer the increased costs to their end products when there is a greater reliance on domestic production chains and, second, when the production chains are dismantled, they increased imports of intermediate and capital goods in order to establish highly efficient and competitive productive linkages. This allowed them to increase their participation in the domestic market and support their sales of products on the international market.

Finally, it should be noted that the large companies did not propose any strategy to promote the integration of their productive chains with the domestic market, thereby hindering the growth of the productivity of the labor force in the sectors that could potentially be integrated, such as the automotive, cement, food processing and secondary petrochemicals industries, to mention only a few.

11.3   FINANCIALIZATION IN THE PATTERN OF ACCUMULATION OF THE MEXICAN MANUFACTURING INDUSTRY

The major multinational companies, owned by national or foreign capital, inserted themselves into the logic of financialization. Its principal characteristic is the preponderance of the financial factor in determining the competitive strategies of integration into world markets. In the case of Mexico, the process of financialization of large companies is related to the development of financial and business strategies, oriented in the first instance toward financing the expansion of companies and providing coverage of its operations and, secondly, to increase corporate profits through speculation and borrowing in the financial markets through the increased use of derivative financial instruments.

According to Morales (2009, p. 118),

> The main users of financial instruments are import and export companies. The former normally settle their operations in US dollars, and have the following alternatives: a) buy the instruments at the moment they contract the obligation to pay in dollars; b) buy them shortly before making the payment; or c) buy a futures contract on dollars on Mexder or any other futures market, with the advantage that you only have to pay out a small percentage of the total value of the transaction, and set the exchange rate at which you will buy. For the exporter who receives foreign currency there is a risk that when this is converted to local currency, the parity has fallen and thus he incurs losses. Credit users also use these instruments to guarantee the levels of interest rates to be paid for the credits and the price of foreign currency (in the case of credits obtained abroad).

It became evident during the great economic crisis of 2008 that the group of large national companies operating on the international markets had developed financial leveraging strategies that combined various derivative financial instruments: for hedging of commodity prices; for obtaining liquidity using exchange rate and interest rate hedging; and finally, for speculation. As a result of the crisis, it became apparent that due to their speculative practices these companies were facing financial problems. For hedging contracts with financial derivatives denominated in dollars and in euros the companies most affected were Maseca Group (Gruma), Cementos Mexicanos (Cemex), Vitro and Fomento Economico Mexicano (FEMSA), which based their internationalization processes both on high levels of leverage and on a preference for liquidity that remained well above productive investment.

Another business strategy they used was to accelerate mergers among their subsidiaries. This allowed them to focus their corporate nucleus on their core businesses. In this sense, the result of financialization was somewhat different because in the middle of the crisis they could maintain control over various assets abroad. This meant that in a single operation, they had revenue streams to finance the expansion of their markets without having to allocate new resources to productive investment (Morales, 2009). These practices were followed by Autlan, Bimbo, Grupo Modelo (Gmodelo), Herdez, MoH, Grupo La Moderna (Gmodern), Comercial Mexicana (Comerci), United Bottling Group (Geupec), Grupo Industrial Saltillo SA (Gissa), Gruma, Industrias CH (Ich), Maseca, Mexichem, Peñoles San Luis, Simec, Vasconi and Vitro.

The companies that used derivative financial instruments to hedge interest rates and currencies include Bimbo, Gmodelo, Herdez, Gmodern, Autlan, Geupec and Mexichem. Although these instruments were acquired with a very low initial investment, variations in exchange rates and interest rates prior to the outbreak of the 2008 crisis exposed these companies to leverage that was beyond their ability to pay.

Another group consists of companies that used financial derivatives to manage the risks of the costs of financing, which include Gmodern and Geupec. These companies used derivatives to set the maximum level of financing costs, that is, they purchased derivative instruments to reduce their exposure to risks of fluctuations in the prices of various assets.

The financial performance of these companies shows that before the 2008 crisis speculation with derivative financial instruments was based on the assumption that the price of the dollar would remain at levels below those that would allow the futures contracts acquired to be sold. As a result of exchange rate adjustments, Mexican companies ended with losses in excess of 2.5 billion dollars, with Cemex, Alfa and Bachoco – and above all Comerci – the most affected (Ramírez et al., 2008). Meanwhile, companies that raided their cash reserves to make a profit on the currency markets, betting on the price of the euro and the dollar, included Cemex, America Movil, Femsa, Telefonos de Mexico (Telmex), Elektra and Bimbo.

All major Mexican companies saw a rapid growth of their dollar liabilities due to the loss in value of the Mexican peso, which suffered a 32 percent depreciation in 2008. In addition, their short-term foreign currency debt grew by an average of 23 percent, according to Banamex Accival data (Martinez, 2008).

To alleviate the debt crisis of these companies the Mexican government used resources from the state development bank, which allocated 50 billion pesos (3.9 billion dollars) in equity guarantees to refinance the short-term trading operations of large Mexican companies experiencing financial problems and thus relieve some of their liquidity problems (Centro de Estudios de las Finanzas Públicas, 2008).

In addition, as a result of the crisis and the financial problems of debt and liquidity experienced by large Mexican companies, some of them were bought by large foreign multinationals. Of particular note due to the volume of transactions are the following: the assets of Cervecería Cuauhtemoc, part of the Femsa conglomerate, were acquired by Heineken, in exchange for a 20 percent stake in the multinational brewer, in a transaction valued at more than 7.3 billion dollars; Belgian beer giant Anheuser-Busch InBev took control of the Mexican group Modelo, in a transaction estimated at 20.1 billion dollars (15.4 billion euros), at a price of 9.15 dollars (7.02 euros) per share; and the paint manufacturer Comex signed a contract of sale with the company PPG Industries in a transaction valued at approximately 2.3 billion dollars. Finally, Iusacell was acquired by US telecoms giant AT&T in a deal worth 2.5 billion dollars, including taking on Iusacell's debt.

All of this allows us to affirm that with financialization, debt is no longer a factor in domestic economic growth because the financial funds are concentrated in speculative circuits with the expectation of making money with borrowed money, which means that such investments do not have a direct positive impact on productive investment. This explains why in the past decade the financial assets of large enterprises, as a percentage of property, plant and equipment, experienced a net increase from 20 to over 40 percent (Powell, 2013). At the same time there has been a process of concentration in the Mexican manufacturing industry that tends to emphasize the polarization between different companies.

Hence, if large companies in Mexico, according to economic censuses, account for more than 80 percent of gross capital assets of Mexican manufacturing, and other industrial companies limit their scale of operations due to the dynamics of low domestic growth, the consequence is that the productivity of the industry as a whole depends on the performance of

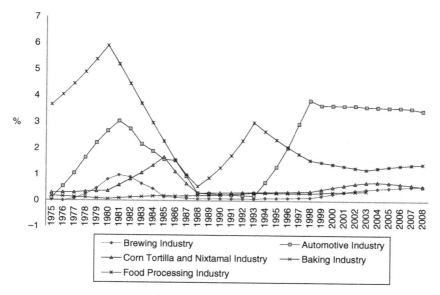

Source: Author's calculations based on census data.

Figure 11.3   Profit rate for industrial sectors in the Mexican economy

the big companies, which are now fully integrated into global production chains and multinational financing. This situation is reinforced by the unprecedented levels of profitability in sectors dominated by large companies operating in Mexico, and which in some cases not only exceed those experienced during the period of stabilized development but were also able to reverse the trend of the falling rate of profit in the domestic market (Figure 11.3).

From the above, it is clear that the recovery of the profit rate between 1994 and 2008 was based on the decline in real wages, the specialization in the market, the sale of branded products, integration of inputs and capital goods organized on the basis of international standardization and marketing models, and the acquisition and accumulation of skills through strategies of vertical specialization of the value chain, such as outsourcing and offshoring.

This behavior has generated three phenomena. Firstly, the basis of financialization is an accelerated process of profit accumulation, which has enabled the internationalization of Mexican corporations. Secondly, the pattern of accumulation for large companies has been successful and the scale of capital accumulation oriented toward the world market has allowed them to become independent of the behavior of the national economy. Thirdly, their links with foreign markets depend on management of the exchange rate and price stability to enable them to operate in a context of relative prices commensurate with their projected accumulation requirements.

Thus, the phenomenon of financialization in the Mexican manufacturing industry has deepened the stagnation of the micro and small businesses versus a sector of large firms that are functionally articulated with the speculative dynamics of international financial markets. This not only demonstrates the failure of the current finance-based pattern of accumulation but will make it much more difficult to overcome the economic stagnation in the country rapidly and in accordance with the population's need for employment.

11.4　CONCLUSIONS

The liberalization of the Mexican economy strengthened the dual pattern of growth in manufacturing, where there is differential growth of the industries making up each of its divisions. At the same time, the growth differentials among the various nuclei of capital that make up the manufacturing industry led to a contraction of the domestic market and a process of deindustrialization that cannot be countered by those companies whose space of reproduction is oriented toward the domestic market.

Under these conditions, the financialization of the 1990s has accentuated the structural polarization in Mexican industry because while the MSME operations were limited to the domestic market, the process of articulation of large Mexican companies with global production chains boosted their links with international markets. The problem for large Mexican companies is that they sought to integrate into international value chains by way of speculative financing and market concentration.

With the 2008 crisis, large companies that had greater exposure to risk and suffered significant losses had to choose to sell their assets to large foreign corporations. This was despite the efforts of the Mexican government to help them compensate their losses with funds from the state development bank.

Given the trend observed between the 1980s and the succession of crises experienced until 2008, and the increasingly slow recovery, we may say that financialization in major Mexican companies not only further increased the heterogeneity of the industry but represented an obstacle to growth. Despite the strong increases in productivity in leading sectors, most other productive activities were characterized by unemployment and informality, which taken together represents low growth in productivity.

Finally, financialization caused the domestic economy and industry to enter a permanent state of stagnation, and generated a greater reliance on foreign capital in the domestic manufacturing industry, with little chance of recovery for employment and productivity as a whole.

NOTES

1. 'Pattern of accumulation refers to the articulation of a certain operation of *economic variables*, linked to a defined *economic structure*, a particular *form of state* and the *struggles between the existing social blocks*' (Basualdo, 2007, p. 6, emphases in original).
2. The social productivity of labor refers to the social structures that capitalists use to exploit collective labor, emphasizing the investment rate, the capital/labor ratio, integration of productive chains, scientific and technological research and development, the level of use of installed capacity, government laws and regulations, the characteristics of the machinery and equipment, the wages rate, the length of the working day, systems of labor organization and unions.
3. A process whereby companies formed with domestic capital that have an oligopolistic, productive and financial structure gain access to the international capital market to increase their borrowing capacity and economic power. This empowered them to obtain financing they allocated to expanding into the international market and speculate with financial assets, with the intention of maintaining their conditions of profitability.
4. The criteria for classifying micro, small and medium enterprises are different in each country; traditionally, the number of workers has been used as a criterion to stratify companies by size, and complementary criteria include total annual sales, income and/or fixed assets. In the case of Mexico, the 2014 census defined micro enterprises as economic units hiring up to 10 employees; small enterprises 11 to 50; medium enterprises 51 to 250; and large enterprises 251 and over.

REFERENCES

Basualdo, E. (2007), 'Concepto de patrón o régimen de acumulación y conformación estructural de la economía', Maestría en Economía Política Argentina Área de Economía y Tecnología de la FLACSO, Document No. 1, March.

Centro de Estudios de las Finanzas Públicas. Cámara de Diputados (2008), *Programas Crediticos para las Empresas nacionales a través de la Banca de Desarrollo*, available at http://www.cefp.gob.mx/intr/edocumentos/pdf/cefp/2008/cefp0822008.pdf, accessed 29 August 2015.

EU-LAC, CEPAL (2015), *Espacios de diálogo y cooperación productiva: el rol de las pymes*, Fundación Unión Europea-América Latina y el Caribe, available at http://repositorio.cepal.org/bitstream/handle/11362/38233/espaciosdedialogo_es.pdf?sequence=1, accessed 3 August 2015.

Glaeser, E.L. and W.R. Kerr (2008), 'Local industrial conditions and entrepreneurship: how much of the spatial distribution can we explain?', NBER Working Paper Series, No. 14407.

Guadalupe, M. and J. Wulf (2010), 'The flattening firm and product market competition: the effect of trade liberalization on corporate hierarchies', *American Economic Journal: Applied Economics*, **2**, October, 105–27.

Heijs, J. (2006), 'El papel de las empresas extranjeras en el desarrollo tecnológico de las economías nacionales. Los intangibles de la internacionalización empresarial', Información Comercial Española, No. 830, May–June.

INEGI (1985), Censo Industrial 1985, Mexico, available at http://www.inegi.org.mx/.

INEGI (1986), Censo Industrial 1986, Mexico, available at http://www.inegi.org.mx/.

INEGI (1999), Censo Industrial 1999, Mexico, available at http://www.inegi.org.mx/.

INEGI (2003), Censo Industrial 2003, Mexico, available at http://www.inegi.org.mx/.

INEGI (2009), Censo Industrial 2009, Mexico, available at http://www.inegi.org.mx/est/contenidos/espanol/proyectos/censos/ce2009.

INEGI (2013), Censo Industrial 2013, Mexico, available at http://www.inegi.org.mx/.

Kato, L. (2008), 'Industria Manufacturera y economía Globalizada', *Trayectorias*, **X**(27), 65–81.

Levy, N. (2007), 'El Comportamiento de la inversión: Revaloración de Factores micro y macroeconómicos en mercados globalizados en la economía mexicana', in G. Vargas Sánchez (ed.), *Microeconomía Heterodoxa, Lecturas del primer seminario de micro heterodoxa*, Mexico: Castdel, pp. 110–33.

Martinez, J.M. (2008), 'El rescate a las empresas, una bendición', *CNN Expansión*, **22**, October, available at http://www.cnnexpansion.com/negocios/2008/10/22/aval-de-nafin-2018bendicion2019-para-empresas, accessed 4 September 2015.

Morales, J.A. (2009), 'Análisis de los instrumentos financieros derivados en la Bolsa Mexicana de Valores: reducción de riesgos financieros de las empresas y especulación', *Economía Informa*, 361, November–December.

Powell, J. (2013), 'El sub-financiamiento y la Financiarización en México: paradoja mexicana o una parábola de economías con ingreso medio?', in N. Levy and T. López (eds), *Financiarización y modelo de acumulación. Aportes desde los países en desarrollo*, Mexico City: UNAM, pp. 261–90.

Ramírez, Z., G. Vázquez and A. Bello (2008), 'El casino de los derivados', *CNN Expansión*, 23 November, http://www.cnnexpansion.com/expansion/2008/11/12/doble-o-nada, accessed 1 September 2015.

Rodríguez, V. (2012), 'La política económica mexicana de los ochenta reinterpretada bajo la hipótesis de la Financiarizacion', *Problemas del Desarrollo*, **169**(43), April–June, 145–81.

Secretaría de Economía/Comisión Intersecretarial de Política Industrial (2003), *Observatorio PyME, Primer reporte de resultados 2002*, Mexico.

Unidad Ecológica Salvadoreña (UNES) OXFAM (2010), *Estrategias de Acumulación de Capital de las empresas transnacionales en Centroamérica*, San Salvador: UNES OXFAM.

PART IV

Disequilibria in Mexico: the financial and fiscal trap

12. Economic growth and financial development in Mexico: from a virtuous circle of a bidirectional causality to a financial subordination

Teresa López and Eufemia Basilio

12.1 INTRODUCTION

The historical background of the discussion on the relationship between the financial system and economic growth dates back to the work of Bagehot (1873 [1999]) and Hicks (1969). They argued that the financial system had played a key role in the industrialization of Great Britain, because it facilitated the channeling of large amounts of capital for the creation of major infrastructure projects. Meanwhile, Schumpeter (1911 [2004]) noted that when banks work well they stimulate technological innovation, because they have the information required to locate and finance the best investment projects. He also argued that such projects frequently lead to innovations in production processes and create new products.

A contrary view is that of Joan Robinson (1952), who claimed that company development precedes the development of finance, because the former is the basis for economic growth. According to this economist, economic development stimulates the development of the financial system, because the demand for financing stimulates the creation of new instruments and mechanisms of financing, while the financial system automatically responds to that demand.

The controversy about the causal relationship between the development of the financial system and economic growth did not end with the development and modernization of this system; on the contrary, this and the subsequent deregulation of financial systems in the United States, Great Britain and Canada in the early years of the 1970s paved the way for the revival of the old debate about the aforementioned relationship.

Under the new institutional framework characterized by financial deregulation in the industrialized economies, and which would initiate the process of integration of local financial systems, liquidity increased dramatically worldwide. These conditions encouraged the governments of developing countries in general, and Latin America in particular, to undertake reforms in the early 1980s to deregulate their economies, in particular with regard to the liberalization of the external sector and the financial system. These countries included Argentina, Brazil, Chile, Colombia and Mexico, which became the main destination of flows of short-term capital from industrialized countries to developing and emerging economies.

The massive influx of foreign capital was manifested in an increase in indicators of financial depth, such as the M4/GDP ratio (FitzGerald, 2006), which is generally considered an indicator of financial development. However, this indicator and others, such as the increase in the credit portfolio/total assets relationship, was not reflected in increased funding for productive activities in developing economies. By contrast, the opening up of the capital account as a means of financial integration into international financial markets not only led to a contraction of lending to productive activities, but also became one of the main sources of financial instability due to asymmetries in the size and structure of their financial systems compared with those of developed countries. Thus, credit expansion generated financial instability in general, and fragility in the banking market in particular, which led to the exchange rate and banking crises of Mexico (1994–1995) and Brazil (1999).

In the case of Mexico, the entry of large amounts of short-term capital between 1989 and 1994, attracted by the financial reforms and the sale of public enterprises and banks, deepened structural distortions in the functioning of domestic financial channels, such as a poorly developed private securities market and high dollarization of liabilities (Studart, 2003). To this was added the oligopoly power of banks in the credit market, which before financial deregulation was characterized by the financing of private partnerships, granting short-term loans, maintaining high amounts of government securities and excluding low- and middle-income sectors from savings circuits.

The aim of this chapter is to analyze the evolution of the relationship between financial development and economic growth in Mexico for the period 1990–2013. This analysis is placed within the context of financial deregulation and the formal adoption in 2001 of the macroeconomic model of inflation targeting. The hypothesis guiding the analysis argues that during the period that the Mexican financial system was regulated by mechanisms controlling interest rates and selective credit policies, the relationship between the financial system and economic growth formed an interdependent relationship that gave rise to a virtuous circle. This circle was broken by deregulation and financial liberalization, since the commercial banks in their quest to increase profit margins favored granting short-term credit to sectors whose sensitivity to changes in interest rates is low, such as consumer credit, and to a lesser extent, the mortgage sector.

The exchange rate and financial crisis of 1994–1995 was the result of these practices and the financialization of the resources of commercial banks, as this increased their investments in synthetic instruments (derivatives, swaps and so on) and government bonds.

The chapter is divided into three sections. Section 12.2 first presents the empirical results of recent research on the relationship between financial development and economic growth in the case of Mexico. Section 12.3 analyzes the relationship between the development of the banking system and economic growth in Mexico, by constructing a number of statistical reasons of financial depth and carrying out a Granger causality test. In addition, the behavior of gross fixed capital formation (GFCF) and the structure of bank credit is assessed, in order to understand the weakening of the intermediation function of commercial banks. Finally, Section 12.4 sets out the principal conclusions.

12.2 FINANCIAL DEVELOPMENT AND ECONOMIC GROWTH IN MEXICO: A REVIEW OF RECENT LITERATURE

Research by Venegas-Martinez et al. (2009) on the relationship between financial development, financial repression and economic growth in Mexico for the period 1961–2007 yields results that lead these authors to the following conclusions. (1) Financial development had a positive impact on growth; however, this was small, that is, a weak unidirectional causal relationship between the first and the second is observed. (2) In the long term financial repression caused a negative effect on economic growth. (3) Financial repression has a negative effect on financial development. According to the results of this research, the magnitude of the effect of financial repression on financial development is inversely proportional, but no short-term effect could be identified between financial development, financial repression and economic growth (measured by gross domestic product (GDP)). In other words, neither financial repression nor financial development affected the short-term dynamics of GDP; similarly, financial repression had no impact on financial development in the short term.

These results differ from those of other investigations in the case of Mexico, which used the Time Series methodology, such as the work of Bandiera et al. (2000), who performed an analysis for Chile, Ghana,

Indonesia, Korea, Malaysia, Mexico, Turkey and Zimbabwe for the period 1970–1994, and whose results show a non-significant positive impact of interest rates on private savings and that financial repression positively influenced financial development, particularly in the increase in private savings. According to these authors, the explanation of the negative impact of financial development on private savings lies in low incomes and the existence of imperfect financial markets.

The study by Arestis and Demetriades (1999) sought to evaluate the effects and the causal link between the institutional conditions, financial policies and economic growth for a representative sample of industrialized and developing countries for the period 1949–1992; in the case of Mexico, the existence of a bidirectional causality between financial development and economic growth was identified.[1]

The study by Rodríguez and López (2009) to assess the causal relationship between financial development and economic growth in Mexico for the period 1990–2004 yielded results that reinforced the previous investigations, identifying the presence of a positive bidirectional causal relationship, although it is unclear what the transmission mechanisms of the positive effects of the financial system to economic activity are.

Finally, research by De la Cruz and Alcántara (2011), using the Vector Autoregressive (VAR) and Error Correction (VEC) techniques for the case of Mexico, assessed the existence of a causal link between bank credit and the main sectors of economic activity and if this is a long-term relationship, for the period 1995–2010. The results lead the authors to present three conclusions.

First, the only credit that impacts the economy is that allocated to consumption and services. While the results do not refute that lending by commercial banks has a positive impact on economic activity, the authors point out that the positive and long-term relationship between credit and economic growth is only sustained by consumer credit. This argument is demonstrated with the existence of a bidirectional causality between the Global Indicator of Economic Activity (IGAE)[2] and consumer credit for the years 1993–2010. According to the authors, this ratio is an indicator of the penetration of banking into consumption, which has been recorded since the early 1990s.

Second, it was found that the growth of consumer credit generated a credit bubble prior to the 2009 crisis. In this regard, the authors argue that the increase in consumer credit in conditions of low economic growth is one factor that underlies financial instability. Hence, they indicate the need to establish mechanisms to regulate the banking system.

Third, there is limited interaction between the real sector of the economy and the financial system due to two factors: (a) the banking credit granted to the productive sectors registered a downward trend compared with consumer credit and (b) the yield of economic activity has been modest and weak.

This research shows that the positive effect of consumer credit on domestic demand – and to a lesser extent mortgage lending induced by federal government policy to stimulate economic growth by constructing social housing – is an unsustainable relationship in the long run, because this type of credit by itself does not generate large-scale multiplier effects required to reactivate economic activity at the macroeconomic level.

Consequently, to the extent that consumer credit increases at a faster rate than the growth in income and employment, this private banking strategy will become a source of financial instability.

Just as in the case of empirical research on the international level, research into the relationship between financial development and economic growth in the case of Mexico is not conclusive. This raises, first, the need for a more disaggregated econometric analysis and, second, to incorporate other variables to measure both financial development and the impact of banking credit on economic growth.

12.2.1 The Relationship Between Financial Development and Economic Growth: A Bidirectional and Historical Relationship

In the absence of strong and sufficient empirical evidence that allows us to accept that financial development has a unidirectional and positive effect on economic growth, we can argue that development of the financial system per se does not guarantee economic growth, and nor does it ensure that savings in the economy are converted into financing of investment.

Considering the low level of growth registered by the Mexican economy since 1996, resulting from the application of a pro-cyclical fiscal policy, which is part of the regime of inflation targeting to keep inflation low by shrinking domestic demand, we can argue that economic growth depends on several factors and not only on the development of the financial system. Of course, one of these factors is financing from banks, but other equally important – or perhaps even more so – factors exist, such as the growth of effective demand and employment, because these factors generate positive earnings expectations, which in turn determine new investment decisions.

In accordance with the foregoing, we propose that the causal link between the financial development and growth of an economy is the result of a process that is mutually determined, that is, which is bidirectional. In this regard, we share the view of Schumpeter (1911 [2004]) who held that when banks operate 'well', that is, when credit reaches all the productive sectors, and especially the sectors driving growth and technological innovation, the financial system becomes important for economic growth. In addition, we agree with the approach of Joan Robinson (1952) who argued that development of firms precedes the development of finance, because, according to the Keynesian framework she employed, the development of firms implies economic growth, and this entails the expansion of investment. To the extent that the effective demand rises, the profits of the companies will be realized and, as a result, the reinvestment of profits will increase and internal savings, as a remainder, will rise. This will promote the development of financial systems in a manner that will depend on the structure and historical development of each country.

Historically, economic development stimulated the modernization of financial systems, as demand for financing from companies induced banks to create new instruments and funding mechanisms with the aim of generating greater liquidity and reducing the lag time between the deposits (usually short term) and credit (usually medium and long term). This interdependent relationship established a virtuous circle, that is, a process with bidirectional causality, which was strengthened with the establishment of mechanisms for monitoring and control of financial operations in general and banking in particular.

This view is implicit in the historical analysis of Chick (1993) on the evolution of banks, to understand the endogenous nature of money and the institutional and policy changes of central banks. This approach is complemented by the contributions of Toporowski (2001, 2013) on the historical character of technological innovations in the financial system, which are inherent to the development of capitalism.

The virtuous circle between financial development and economic growth is broken by the removal of regulatory and supervisory mechanisms for financial activities. For developed economies, the interdependence between financial development and economic growth lasted nearly four decades, if we consider that in 1933 the Glass-Steagall Act (Banking Act) came into force in the United States, and that the regulations contained in this Act were weakened in the early 1970s to make way for the liberalization of its financial system.[3]

In the case of developing economies, this relationship held for more than three decades, as the financial regulatory systems were generally established in the early 1940s as part of the policies adopted to boost the process of industrialization of these economies, and these were eliminated in the first years of the 1980s, in the context of the debt crisis experienced by several economies in Latin America, including Mexico.

The policies of deregulation and liberalization of national financial systems by eliminating the prudential oversight and mechanisms of control over deposit and lending rates and channeling of credit to priority economic activities, caused the bidirectional relationship that had formed between economic growth and modernization of the financial system to became a vicious circle, as the new technological innovations that marked the development of financial systems led to a reduction in funding for productive investment. In other words, the development of the financial system was separated from the financing needs of the real economy.

12.3 LIBERALIZATION AND FINANCIAL DEPTH VERSUS FINANCING ECONOMIC GROWTH IN MEXICO

This section analyzes a number of statistical and graphical indicators on the relationship between financial development and economic growth in the case of Mexico, in the context of financial deregulation and the full adoption in 2001 of the macroeconomic model of inflation targeting.

12.3.1 Monetary Stability with Low Economic Growth: A Macroeconomic View

Over the long period between 1950 and 1976, under a regulated financial system and countercyclical management of fiscal policy centered on public investment in basic infrastructure and the production of basic goods and services through public companies, the Mexican economy grew at a rate of between 4 and 7 percent, as an annual average. During the period 1958–1970, known as the 'stabilizing development', sustained growth meant that monetary stability was achieved, accompanied by low primary deficits of 2 percent as a proportion of GDP, as an annual average (López, 2010).

In a macroeconomic context marked by severe recession and financial fragility generated by the oil boom years of 1979–1982, which led to the outbreak of the debt crisis, the rhythm of stable and sustained growth was interrupted. Beginning in 1983, stabilization policies and orthodox macroeconomic adjustment were implemented to address the severe recession and inflationary pressures. In parallel, economic reforms were implemented aimed at deregulating the economy, and specifically the financial and external sectors.

Liquidity problems and restrictions on access to external financing exacerbated the recessionary and inflationary effects generated by the external debt crisis of 1982. In 1988, structural reforms accelerated under the argument that it was necessary to create the institutional and economic conditions to permit the adoption of a macroeconomic strategy based on export growth and on the dynamics of the private sector of the economy.

This meant accelerating the economic and institutional reforms that were initiated in 1983, that is, the deregulation of the financial system and liberalization of the external sector, in order to make progress with the elimination of state involvement in economic activity (Solís, 1996).

From 1983 to 2013, GDP has grown at a low and irregular rate, since the phases of expansion are very short in duration, and growth has been no more than 2 percent as an annual average, while the recessionary phases are very deep with a longer recovery time; without approaching the rate of growth recorded in the period of stabilizing development. The stability of prices and balance in public finances recorded since 2000 is the result of the containment of economic growth by way of reduced domestic demand.

12.3.2   The Vicious Circle, Financial Depth and Low Financing of Productive Activities

Various indicators have been constructed to measure the degree of financial development (M4/GDP, portfolio credit/total credit, total credit/total assets and so on). For the purposes of this chapter we have taken as a proxy measure the M4/GDP ratio in nominal terms, agreeing with the arguments of Asteriou and Price (2000) insofar as M4 is a broad measure of money and the (M4/GDP) index increases (decreases) over time if the development of the financial system accelerates (decelerates) compared to the real sector of the economy.

Figure 12.1 shows that there is no relationship between the natural logarithm (Ln) of the M4/GDP ratio and real GDP growth, and this decoupling has deepened since 2000. Since 2005, the depth and development of the financial system resumes the upward trend that began in 1990, with the exception of 1994–1995 and 2002–2004, in response to the acceleration of the deregulation process in the sector. In nominal terms, the M4/GDP ratio was 35.75 on average in 1990, and 70.45 percent in 2013. Considering this extraordinary increase, we might say that the Mexican financial system has undergone a high rate of development; however, this contrasts with the weak and uneven growth of GDP per capita and total GDP. The latter recorded sharp declines in 1995, 2001, 2009 and 2013, while the natural logarithm of GDP per capita shows an accelerated declining trend. The improvement recorded by this indicator over the years in which the growth rate of real GDP fell is a result of the combination of an increase in the population (numerator) and a drastic drop in the real growth rate of GDP (denominator). This is demonstrated by the fact that when GDP grows, the GDP per capita decreases.

In general, this latter indicator registered a downward trend over the period 1990–2013, as a result of low and irregular growth of GDP.

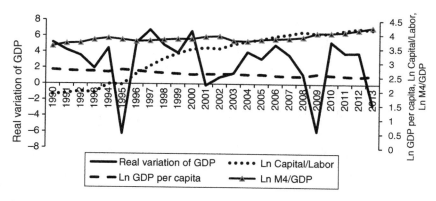

Note: M4: broad monetary aggregates.

Source: Authors' calculations using data from INEGI and the Bank of Mexico.

Figure 12.1   *Mexico: economic growth in terms of GDP and the capital and labor ratio*

As for the capital/labor ratio, estimated with the natural logarithm of the ratio of GFCF and the economically active population, it shows rapid growth during the 1994–2001 period, and following a fall in 2002, after 2003 it indicates weak growth with a tendency to stagnation (Figure 12.1).

After the currency and financial crisis of 1994–1995, the GFCF, as a share of GDP, has seen a gradual decline; in 1990, it accounted for 29 percent, while by 2000 this percentage drops to 27 percent. Over 13 years this trend has increased: from 26 percent in 2001, the percentage dropped to 21 percent in 2013. This suggests a direct and positive relationship between growth of GFCF and GDP, with a certain lag shown by the first with respect to changes in GDP, which is explained by the periods of maturation of new fixed assets incorporated into economic activity (Figure 12.2).

These data lead us to argue that, on the one hand, the contraction of GFCF as a share of GDP has been one of the determinants of the low and irregular growth of the Mexican economy and, on the other, that the greater depth or development of the financial system, as measured by the M4/GDP ratio, has led to its detachment from the real sector of the economy; that is, the Mexican banking system has ceased to fulfill the role of financing investment.

Following the exchange rate and financial crisis of 1994–1995, commercial banks increased the rationing of credit to productive activities. This reduction was due to several factors. At the microeconomic level,

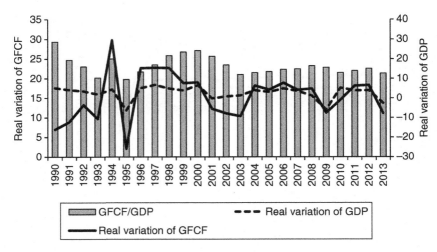

Source: Authors' calculations using data from INEGI and the Bank of Mexico.

Figure 12.2 *Mexico: economic growth in terms of GDP and gross fixed capital formation*

commercial banking reactivated its strategy of short-term profit by increasing credit to highly profitable sectors, such as consumer credit. The high moral risk of these sectors is more than offset by high interest rates and the fees charged by them, particularly credit cards. These conditions and the low elasticity of this type of credit to changes in interest rates have turned consumer credit into one of the main sources of income for commercial banking. This is despite the high levels of non-performing loans that are often recorded with this type of credit.

At the macroeconomic level, the policy of sterilized intervention in the foreign exchange market by the Bank of Mexico, intended to avoid sudden variations in the level of the monetary base, and thus to maintain a stable nominal exchange rate has contributed to the contraction of credit to productive sectors. In this sense, the issuance of government bonds has not only become an important component of the monetary policy of inflation targeting, but also become a source of high and secure profits for commercial banks, since the rate yielded by these instruments is higher than the external rate.

This, coupled with the uncertainty about the recovery of economic activity, generated largely by the practice of pro-cyclical fiscal policy and high lending rates, are two factors that inhibit the demand for credit by companies. Table 12.1 shows that credit to the private sector increased in

Table 12.1 *Mexico's commercial banking distribution of total credit,*[a] *1990–2013, percentage structure*

| Year | Total Private sector | | | | | | Other sectors[c] |
	Total	Total Private sector	Agricultural sector	Industrial sector	Services sector, other activities and consumption[b]	Housing credit	
1990	100.0	91.56	11.54	35.85	34.81	9.35	8.44
1993	100.0	96.72	9.35	30.23	35.54	21.60	3.28
1996	100.0	86.08	5.47	24.37	31.81	24.43	10.79
1999	100.0	72.25	4.06	20.20	24.69	23.30	25.83
2002	100.0	65.24	2.15	16.70	29.89	16.51	33.86
2004*	100.0	68.92	2.07	16.28	36.52	14.04	31.08
2005	100.0	73.75	1.93	15.51	41.85	14.46	26.25
2008**	100.0	85.13	1.61	18.43	48.51	16.59	14.87
2011	100.0	81.28	1.54	20.75	41.81	17.18	18.72
2013	100.0	81.69	1.77	19.94	43.69	16.30	18.31

Notes:
a. From July 1995, includes subsidiaries of foreign banks operating in Mexico. Information after December 2004 does not include data from banks in the process of liquidation or bankruptcy.
b. Until 1994, the heading 'Commerce' was used instead. In 1994, using a new methodology the heading 'Consumption' was created. In order to construct a series for 1990–2013, we include in the heading 'Services sector and other activities' the credit for Commerce for the years 1990–1993. This accounts for part of the increase in the share of total credit by the 'Services sector and other activities' for the years 1990–1993.
c. This heading includes the domestic financial sector, not including inter-bank loans; the public sector from 1994, where credit to the government includes governmental programs to support debtors, loans to public administration, defense and social security services of the federal government; ADE support programs, state and municipal governments, the government of the Federal District and public, state and decentralized bodies and corporations; it refers to the financing granted to long-term productive infrastructure projects both in Mexican and foreign currencies and includes PIDIREGAS, IPAB and FONADIN and the Fideicomiso Fondo Nacional de Infraestructura D.O.F. 7/02/2008 (previously FARAC), the external sector, including services for international and offshore financial and non-financial bodies, and inter-bank loans.
* Information after December 2004 does not include data from banks in the process of liquidation or bankruptcy.
** From March 2008 commercial banking is presented consolidated with its subsidiaries the SOFOM Regulated Entities (ER) and credit cards (Tarjetas Banamex, Santander Consumo, Ixe Tarjetas and Sociedad Financiera Inbursa), which increases the figures for consumer credit. In addition, as a result of this consolidation, the balances of credit granted to non-bank financial intermediaries are reduced.

Source: Authors' calculations using data from the Bank of Mexico.

the early 1990s; however, following the 1994–1995 banking crisis a gradual decline was recorded, until 2004. In 1990, credit to the private sector accounted for 92 percent of total credit provided by commercial banks; by 2004 this percentage had dropped to 69 percent, that is, a fall of 23 percentage points in 14 years. Although a slow recovery in credit to the private sector has been observed since 2005, it has not recovered the level of 1990, and by 2013 credit to the private sector stood at 82 percent.

The contraction of credit was more severe for the industrial and agricultural sectors – particularly for the latter – while the services and consumer sectors have maintained a high share of total bank credit. Nevertheless, lending to these sectors has also fallen; from 82 percent in 1990, it fell to 65 percent in 2013 (Table 12.1). This reduction coincides with an increase in holdings of government bonds and investments in synthetic instruments (derivatives, swaps and so on) by commercial banks.

In short, the current structure of Mexican commercial banking has the following characteristics: (1) the dominance of foreign capital and a high concentration of assets and liabilities in the four largest banks; (2) the consolidation of the dual power of the market: the oligopolistic power in the credit market that allows it to set rates above the rates of government securities and foreign lending rates, and the oligopsonistic power of the deposits market to set deposit interest rates lower than government bonds; (3) the strengthening of their rentier and speculative character, which has become a permanent source of financial instability; (4) weak financial intermediation with productive activities and high profit margins despite lowering intermediation costs; and (5) increasing dollarization of bank liabilities.

12.3.3 Empirical Evidence on the Causal Relationship Between Financial Development and Economic Growth

Table 12.2 presents the results of the Granger causality tests on the relationship between financial development and economic growth, the first measured by the M4/GDP ratio, and the second by GDP, for the period 2000–2013.[4] The result for the causal link between M4 and GDP for the period 1990–2013 shows that the x^2 statistic is significant at 5 percent, meaning that M4 cannot be considered exogenous. Since it meets the requirement for endogeneity of this variable, we can argue that it is GDP growth that determines financial development.

The result for the ratio between bank assets – which is another variable used to measure financial development – and GDP per capita, for the period 2000–2013, also shows that the causality runs from the latter to the former, because, just as in the previous case, the x^2 statistic is significant at

Table 12.2   Results of the Granger causality test

VAR Granger causality/block exogeneity Wald tests

Sample: 1990–2013

Dependent variable: M4

Excluded	Chi-sq	df	Prob.
PIB	3.944894	2	0.0139
All	3.944894	2	0.0139

Dependent variable: GDP

Excluded	Chi-sq	df	Prob.
M4	1.868464	2	0.3929
All	1.868464	2	0.3929

Sample: 2000–2013

Dependent variable: BANK LIABILITIES

Excluded	Chi-sq	df	Prob.
GDP PER CAPITA	7.186663	2	0.0275
All	7.186663	2	0.0275

Dependent variable: GDP PER CAPITA

Excluded	Chi-sq	df	Prob.
BANK LIABILITIES	0.959331	2	0.619
All	0.959331	2	0.619

VAR Granger causality/block exogeneity Wald tests

Sample: 1990–2013

Dependent variable: LOGBANK ASSETS

Excluded	Chi-sq	df	Prob.
GDP PER CAPITA	3.924716	2	0.014
All	3.924716	2	0.014

Dependent variable: GDP PER CAPITA

Excluded	Chi-sq	df	Prob.
LOGBANK ASSETS	0.154802	2	0.9255
All	0.154802	2	0.9255

Sample: 2000–2013

Dependent variable: LOGBANK CREDIT

Excluded	Chi-sq	df	Prob.
GDP PER CAPITA	5.963446	2	0.0507
All	5.963446	2	0.0507

Dependent variable: GDP PER CAPITA

Excluded	Chi-sq	df	Prob.
LOGBANK CREDIT	1.413741	2	0.4932
All	1.413741	2	0.4932

5 percent. This implies that bank assets cannot be considered exogenous and, therefore, the requirement for endogeneity of the bank assets variable is met.

The result for the relation between bank liabilities, as an indicator of financial development, and GDP, with the probability of this causality being significant at 5 percent, again shows that economic growth is what determines economic activity.

Finally, the result for the causal link between bank credit, another indicator of financial development, and GDP per capita is presented, the x^2 statistic being significant at 5 percent, as in the three previous cases, shows that the causality runs the GDP per capita to bank credit, which means that bank credit cannot be considered exogenous, and hence the requirement of endogeneity of this variable is met.

Based on these results of the Granger causality tests, we can argue that in the case of Mexico, the banking sector was no longer a major source of financing for economic growth during the years 2000–2013. Figure 12.3 shows the spread between GDP per capita and credit to the private sector, which accounts for the decoupling of the development or depth of the banking system and the financing of economic activity in Mexico.

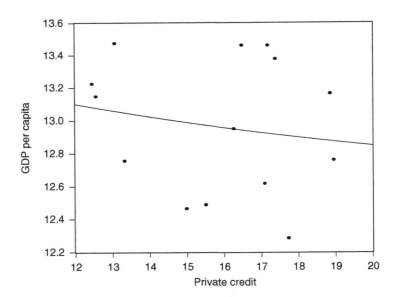

Source: Authors' own work using econometrics package Eviews 8.

Figure 12.3   Mexico: private credit and GDP per capita

Considering that this lack of coordination between the financial sphere and the real economy arises in the context of increasing foreign ownership of commercial banks, and coincides with the acceleration of the modernization process and depth of the financial system, it is clear that the development of the financial system, if we understand that to mean modernization and depth, is not in itself a guarantee of increased financing for economic growth, and nor does it ensure that savings in the economy are converted into financing for investment. Also, the expansion of consumer credit and mortgages in a context of low growth and high unemployment represents a source of financial instability, because their multiplier effects are very limited and temporary.

The pro-cyclical practice of fiscal policy under the inflation targeting regime, which in Mexico was adopted in full in 2001, has greatly contributed to the formation of a vicious circle between financial development and economic growth. On the one hand, the low and uneven economic growth justifies commercial banks rationing credit to businesses, and these in turn reducing their demand for credit due to uncertainty about future earnings. On the other, this situation warrants commercial banks expanding consumer credit and increasing their investments in government bonds and derivative instruments, which provides high yields.

These results allow us to argue that there is a bidirectional relationship between financial development and growth, and that this can be positive or negative. The latter question will depend on macroeconomic behavior, economic policy – particularly fiscal and monetary policies – and institutional factors such as the existence of a regulatory framework and oversight of financial transactions in general, and banking operations in particular.

12.4   CONCLUSIONS

The deregulation of the Mexican financial system caused a contraction of credit for productive activities and deepened the rentier and speculative character of Mexican commercial banks. The latter ceased to fulfill their historic intermediary role, that is, for the financing of productive activities and therefore economic growth.

The concentration of assets and liabilities in four major financial groups led by foreign capital is the result of the policies of deregulation and liberalization, which assumed a priori that the removal of control and oversight mechanisms would automatically lead to an increase in domestic and foreign savings, and efficient integration of the Mexican financial system into international financial markets.

A review of the literature on the relationship between financial development and economic growth both generally and in the case of Mexico produces inconclusive results suggesting that the financial system determines economic growth. In the case of Mexico, the reducing or rationing of credit to productive activities is parallel to the process of financial liberalization.

The reduction of bank credit to productive sectors, such as the industrial and agricultural sectors, in the context of weak growth caused by the macroeconomic policy of inflation targeting, establishes the vicious circle linking modernization and liberalization of the financial system and low economic growth. Low expectations about the future growth of the economy discourage new investment decisions, a situation that is heightened by high interest rates and credit rationing productive activities.

In a context of low GDP growth and employment, provision of consumer and mortgage credit is not the best strategy to induce growth in domestic demand, because their multiplier effects are weak in these conditions, and in the medium term they can become a source of financial instability, because consumer and mortgage credit grows at a faster pace than income, which will raise the ratio of non-performing loans held by commercial banks.

NOTES

1. The sample of countries comprises France, Germany, United Kingdom, Japan, United States, South Korea, India, Greece, Spain, Turkey, Mexico and Chile. In the case of Mexico, the period was 1951–1992.
2. The Global Indicator of Economic Activity (IGAE) shows the evolution of the real sector of the economy in the short term. IGAE monthly figures are available from January 1993.
3. Strong criticism of the Glass-Steagall Act, generally known as the Banking Law Act, considering it an obstacle to the adjustment of the US banking system to the development of international financial markets, eventually led to its repeal in November 1999, and the approval of the Financial Services Modernization Act, also known as the Gramm-Leach-Bliley Act.
4. It is important to note that the limited availability of data for a short period of analysis (2000–2013) did not allow us to build a vector autoregression (VAR) model, which is generally used for assessing causality between financial development and economic growth. For this reason, we used the simple Engler-Granger technique to allow us to strengthen the statistical and graphical analysis presented. The Granger causality test assumes that the relevant information for the prediction of the variables to determine, X and Y, is contained solely in the time series data on these variables. The test involves the following estimates:

$$Y_t = \sum_{i=1}^{n} \alpha_i X_{t-1} + \sum_{j=1}^{n} \beta_i Y_{t-j} + u_{1t} \tag{12.1}$$

$$X_t = \sum_{i=1}^{n} \gamma_i X_{t-1} + \sum_{j=1}^{n} \delta_i Y_{t-j} + u_{2t} \tag{12.2}$$

where it is assumed that the perturbations u_{1t} and u_{2t} are not correlated. Equation (12.1) postulates that the current value of Y is related to past values of Y, as well as with those of X. Equation (12.2) postulates a similar behavior for X. Four possible types of Granger causality are distinguished (Gujarati, 2001). (1) *Unidirectional causality from X to Y*, where the estimated coefficients on the lagged X in (12.1) are statistically different from zero when considered in a group, that is, $\Sigma\alpha_i \neq 0$ and the set of estimated coefficients on the lagged Y in (12.2) is not statistically different from zero, that is, $\Sigma\alpha_i = 0$. (2) Conversely, the *unidirectional causality of Y to X* exists if the set of coefficients of the lagged X in (12.1) are not statistically different from zero, that is, $\Sigma\alpha_i = 0$ and the set of coefficients of the lagged Y in (12.2) is statistically different from zero, that is, $\Sigma\alpha_i \neq 0$. (3) *Feedback, or bilateral causality*, is what occurs when the coefficient sets of X and Y are statistically significant, and different from zero, in both cases. (4) *Independence* exists when the sets of coefficients X and Y are not statistically significant in both cases.

REFERENCES

Arestis, P. and P. Demetriades (1999), 'Finance and growth: institutional considerations, financial policies and causality', *Zegreb International Review of Economics and Business*, **2**, 37–62.

Asteriou, D. and S. Price (2000), 'Financial development and economic growth: time series evidence for the case of UK', *Ekonomia*, **4**(2), Cyprus Economic Society and University of Cyprus, Winter, 122–41.

Bagehot, W. (1873), *Lombard Street: A Description of the Money Market*, London: Armstrong and Company. London, reprinted in 1999, New York: Wiley, available at http://www.gutenberg.org/cache/epub/4359/pg4359.html, accessed 8 July 2015.

Bandiera, O., G. Caprio, P. Honohan and F. Schiantarelli (2000), 'Does financial reform raise or reduce saving?', *Review of Economics and Statistics*, **82**(2), 239–63.

Chick, V. (1993), 'The evolution of the banking system and the theory of monetary policy', in S.F. Frowen (ed.), *Monetary Theory and Monetary Policy: New Tracks for the 1990s*, New York: Palgrave Macmillan, pp. 79–92.

De la Cruz, J.L. and J.A. Alcántara (2011), 'Crecimiento económico y el crédito bancario: Un análisis de causalidad para México', *Revista de Economía*, **XXVIII**(77), July–December, Mexico, 13–38.

FitzGerald, V. (2006), 'Models of saving, income and the macroeconomics of developing countries in the Post-Keynesian tradition', in P. Arestis, J. McCombie and R. Vickerman (eds), *Growth and Economic Development: Essays in Honour of A.P. Thirlwall*, Cheltenham, UK and Northampton, MA, USA: Edward Elgar, pp. 247–62.

Gujarati, D.N. (2001), *Econometría*, 3rd edn, Mexico: McGraw-Hill.

Hicks, J. (1969), *A Theory of Economic History*, Oxford: Clarendon Press.

López, T. (2010), 'La política fiscal y el crecimiento económico México. Crecimiento con estabilidad monetaria *versus* estancamiento con estabilidad monetaria', in G. Mántery and N. Levy (eds), *Cincuenta años de políticas financieras para el desarrollo en México (1958–2008)*, Mexico City: DGAPA-UNAM and Plaza y Valdes, pp. 75–105.

Robinson, J. (1952), 'The generalization of the general theory', in *The Rate Interest and Others Essays*, London: Macmillan, pp. 69–142.

Rodríguez, D. and F. López (2009), 'Desarrollo financiero y crecimiento económico en México', *Revista Problemas del Desarrollo*, **40**(159), Instituto de Investigaciones Económicas, UNAM, Mexico City, 39–60.

Schumpeter, J. (1911), *The Theory of Economic Development*, 10th edn reprinted in 2004, New Brunswick, NJ: Transaction Publishers.

Solís, L. (1996), *Crisis económico-financiera 1994–1995*, Mexico City: El Colegio Nacional and Fondo de Cultura Económica.

Studart, R. (2003), 'Integración financiera, inestabilidad y desempeño macro-económico en los noventa: posibles conexiones perversas', in G. Mántey and N. Levy (eds), *Financiamiento del desarrollo con mercados de dinero y capital globalizados*, Mexico City: Miguel Ángel Porrúa and ENEP-Acatlan-DGAPA, pp. 43–68.

Toporowski, J. (2001), 'El factor crítico de las finanzas en la economía del siglo XX', *Revista Momento Económico*, **113**, Instituto de Investigaciones Económicas-UNAM, Mexico, January–February, 2–15.

Toporowski, J. (2013), 'El neologismo como una innovación teórica en la economía: El caso de la financiarización', in N. Levy and T. López (eds), *Financiarización y modelo de acumulación. Aportes desde los países en desarrollo*, Facultad de Economía-UNAM, Mexico, pp. 31–46.

Venegas-Martinez, F., M. Tinoco-Zermeño and V. Torres Preciado (2009), 'Desregulación financiera, desarrollo del sistema financiero y crecimiento económico en México: Efectos de largo plazo y causalidad', *Revista Estudios Económicos*, **24**(2), July–December, Mexico, 249–83.

13. Private sector finance in the era of deregulation and economic openness: Mexico 2000–2014

Christian Domínguez and Juan Marroquín

13.1 INTRODUCTION

The performance of the Mexican economy in the first 14 years of the twenty-first century has been characterized by low economic growth, with 2.3 percent achieved between 2000 and 2014, and by relative macroeconomic stability, which has led to a situation that some economists have labeled 'stabilizing stagnation' (Suárez, 2005). This outcome is at odds with the promises given at the end of the 1980s by the promoters of deregulation and economic openness who claimed that they would make it possible to overcome Mexico's economic backwardness.

One of the main objections to the new organization of the Mexican economy is that it hinders the availability of financing to the productive sector at internationally competitive interest rates that would support capital accumulation. One of the factors that leads to this situation is that interest rates are relatively high in the domestic market, where the emphasis of monetary and fiscal policy is on the purchasing power of the currency rather than on economic growth.

The case put forward in this chapter is that deregulation and economic openness have conditioned monetary and fiscal policy to the setting of relatively high domestic interest rates in comparison to those to be found in developed countries, such as the United States of America (USA), which pushes up the cost of financing while reducing access by non-financial private sector companies, particularly those operating at a local level.

This chapter is divided into four sections. Section 13.2 discusses the principal facets of the neoliberal model, highlighting the problems arising from economic openness in certain sectors of national economies. Section 13.3 analyzes the effects of the processes of deregulation and economic openness on the organization of the Mexican economy, stressing their implications for the application of restrictive monetary and fiscal policies. Section 13.4

analyzes the characteristics of financing in the private non-financial sector in Mexico from 2000 to 2014, such as cost and distribution by type and company size. The final section gives the conclusions of the research.

13.2   THE NEOLIBERAL PROPOSITION AND ITS EFFECTS ON ECONOMIC ORGANIZATION

According to neoclassical economic theory, the market is a more efficient allocator of resources than the state, and furthermore when an economy is running below full employment, it is the adjustment of interest rates and real salaries that are used to restore the balance between savings and investment. However, this proposition was challenged, particularly as a result of the 1929 crisis, giving rise to theories pointing to the need for state intervention in the productive sector.

After the period of state intervention policies, neoliberal theorists returned to the neoclassical proposition, pointing out that developing economies in particular found themselves in this position because of inefficient state intervention, which led to price distortions in the market for goods and services, as well as in the finance market, hindering the efficient allocation of resources (McKinnon, 1974). These theorists specifically criticized state regulation that channeled finances to sectors considered to be strategic for economic development at interest rates lower than those that would have prevailed if market mechanisms were operating (McKinnon, 1974). It was also argued that the presence of trade protection measures, such as duties and tariffs on foreign trade, led to low levels of competition.

The case outlined above was the basis for a strong movement in favor of the deregulation of the financial sector, to transfer the setting of interest rates to the financial market and to increase the financing channeled to the most profitable projects.

Neoliberal theorists posited, on the one hand, that financial openness would permit the entry of foreign capital, which in addition to internal savings would supplement development financing, and, on the other, that free trade would bring in foreign competition, which would lower costs and prices, thus making the productive sector more competitive.

The neoliberal proposition was widely promoted by the developed countries, as well as by the multilateral bodies such as the World Bank and the International Monetary Fund.[1] During the 1970s and 1980s it was adopted particularly by the underdeveloped countries, as an alternative to the state-led growth strategy, which was showing signs of weakness.

Therefore, deregulation implied the dismantling of systems of financing, and economic and trade policies whose objective was to boost the domestic productive sector. In the financial sector limits on lending and deposit interest rates were eliminated, which had made, on the one hand, to channel financing from banks under conditions favorable to capital accumulation in the productive sector, and, on the other, to establish limits to the costs of deposit funding, ensuring the profitability of commercial banks (Russell, 2008). Mechanisms hindering speculative activities, such as the separation between commercial and investment banking, were abolished, as occurred in the USA with the Financial Services Modernization Act of 1999. Thus, financial institutions acquired greater freedom to determine their prices and the allocation of their financing, governed by microeconomic criteria such as profitability.

Financial openness was also promoted, boosting the stock market as the principal means of capturing external flows of capital. Many countries, notably in Latin America, had to make institutional changes to smooth the passage from a financial system based on the banking system to one centered on the stock market. In the period after liberalization in the 1990s and the 2000s, this process evolved into one of greater regional and global stock market integration, which made the international flow of capital even easier.

One of the conditions that made the above measures feasible was the amendment to the objective of monetary and fiscal policy, which changed from boosting economic activity to prioritizing price stability, assuming that this is the best way to support the economy. This is the context for the reforms that led to autonomous central banks whose principal mandate has been to keep inflation rates low, restricting governments' direct access to credit. Financing via the stock market was promoted in its stead, as it was considered not to be inflationary.

Meanwhile, laws promulgating fiscal and public borrowing responsibility sought to reduce public deficits. In other words, monetary and fiscal policy was coordinated to maintain an environment of macroeconomic stability incentivizing the movement of capital and preventing devaluation.

In spite of this, one of the problems with the new monetary and fiscal policy system is that it encourages relatively high interest rates in developing countries, in order to maintain the entry of capital. In addition, since the same policy is adopted by a number of countries, it leads to instability for capital flows (that is, of foreign savings), which were intended to finance investment in underdeveloped countries; in the majority of cases these later adhered strictly to the doctrine of no direct state intervention in the economy, and consequently there has been no insistence on establishing mechanisms to ensure that foreign capital contributes to the financing of the productive sector.

Foreign direct investment has been attracted by factors that increase its value, including the following, amongst others: lower rates of tax; lower labor costs; and the international treaties of the recipient country. In this context, competition is brought about among the various countries seeking to appropriate this investment, in a similar manner to an auction in which the foreign sector is prioritized above the internal market, and global corporations above domestic corporations.

It is therefore necessary to make it clear that at the heart of economic openness, the locus of the activities of corporations passed from a national to a global scale, creating circumstances for the reduction of salaries while favoring the worth of capital, without achieving the expected results for underdeveloped economies. In this regard, Bhaduri (2011) indicates that unless full employment is assumed in the economy, the wellbeing of the consumers can fall to the extent that international competition captures a higher share of the market and reduces the level of domestic employment; further, this latter implies an inefficient use of economic resources.

The above reference provides a succinct description of the situation resulting from neoliberal reforms in the majority of the countries where they have been applied, bankrupting domestic companies unable to face foreign competition, which is superior technologically and has access to lower financing costs.

Bhaduri (2011) warns that when this strategy is adopted simultaneously by a group of developing companies, it leads to a zero-sum game that only benefits the large corporations. Thus, they can reduce their costs and increase their profitability, at the expense of depressing the wages of the countries receiving direct foreign investment.[2]

Therefore, although this corporate strategy can create benefits at the level of the company, it has negative effects at the macroeconomic level. For example, the same author points out that corporations reduce their costs and increase their share in the market, but they also reduce the size of the market and acquisitive power, therefore, so long as they capture external markets, the size of a country's market will only expand at another's cost.

Consequently, the environment created by pro-market neoliberal reforms gives priority to international capital mobility and the earnings of global corporations, without a necessary link between this wealth and the creation of conditions propitious for a process of internal accumulation that permits the sustained economic growth of the underdeveloped nations.

Some theorists argue that this state of affairs does not imply that countries should be unaware of the benefits of international interdependence, but rather – and this is the challenge – that they should be selective in the areas of trade, investment and finances (Bhaduri, 2011).

13.3 IMPLICATIONS OF THE PROCESSES OF FINANCIAL DEREGULATION AND OPENNESS ON THE ORGANIZATION OF THE MEXICAN ECONOMY

From the 1940s Mexico had an economic model in which the state took on a directing role, and this changed in the 1970s with the first steps toward deregulation with the gradual elimination of the legal reserve on bank deposits and authorization for multiple banking in 1976 (Bank of Mexico, 1989–1992).

In addition, the stock market was boosted with the creation of new public financial instruments such as *Petrobonos* in 1977 and *Cetes* in 1978. It is important to point out that because of the role adopted by the state toward the economy, this took place by government bonds rather than private equity.

Nevertheless, the turning point in the deregulation process took place in the early 1980s, as a consequence of the breakdown of the financing mechanism based on funds from petroleum exports and syndicated bank loans. Thus, falling oil prices in the early 1980s triggered the foreign debt crisis of 1982, in an environment where US monetary policy was strengthening, and this was translated into higher interest rates.

Adepts of neoliberal theory among the governing classes sprang forth during the crisis, pushing deregulation and economic openness even further. Thus, by 1989 the legal reserve had been completely eliminated and the selective channeling of credit disappeared, as did limits on interest rates. Moreover, there was an extensive process of state enterprise privatization (for example, Telmex and the Mexican National Railways in communications) that included the re-privatization of the banks in 1991 and 1992 that had been nationalized in 1982. This gave a new boost to the stock market.

In the area of trade, Mexico signed up to the General Agreement on Tariffs and Trade (GATT) in 1987, while the North American Free Trade Agreement (NAFTA) came into force in 1994. In 1993 the new Foreign Investment Law also came into force, authorizing foreign participation in sectors of the economy that had been previously reserved for the state and local investors.

Against this backdrop, monetary and fiscal policies were aligned to achieving low rates of inflation to preserve the purchasing power of the currency. The first policy was to establish credit limits for the central bank's lending to the government,[3] and the setting of inter-bank interest rate targets, which would make it possible to influence the credit market with the objective of achieving levels of inflation within a range of

2 percent to 4 percent per year. The central bank also carried out monetary sterilization operations, notably by selling bonds to strengthen investment in government bonds.

Meanwhile, since the 1980s fiscal policy has been diverted in the quest to balance public revenue and expenditure. The Public Finance Budget and Responsibility Law of 2006 is an example of the importance of this policy. The fiscal discipline policy is justified, from the perspective of conventional economic literature, by an argument stating that public expenditure entails a risk of creating inflationary pressures that devalue the purchasing power of financial capital and repel foreign capital.[4]

The change in economic policy has been a success in terms of inflationary strategy and the performance of the export sector. Firstly, levels of inflation have fallen, from an average of 69.7 percent in the 1980s to 20.2 percent in the 1990s and to 4.9 percent in the 2000s (authors' calculations based on data from Bank of Mexico, 2015a). To a large extent, this was associated with greater exchange rate stability, particularly in the period from the third quarter of 1998 to the third quarter of 2008 in which the monthly average nominal FIX exchange rates at the date of determination oscillated around ten pesos per dollar, with an average of 10.3 pesos per dollar for the aforementioned period (authors' calculations based on data from Bank of Mexico, 2015a). An increase in volatility and exchange rate depreciation were, however, observed at the root of the 2008 crisis.

Secondly, exports grew from 40.7 billion dollars in 1990 to 397.6 billion in 2014. Since 1996 they have become the most important component of aggregate demand, to the extent that their share increased from 13.8 percent in the fourth quarter of 1993 to 26.1 percent in the fourth quarter of 2014. In spite of this, during the same period, imports increased from 41.6 billion dollars to 400 billion in 2014. The boom in the foreign sector has not therefore implied an improvement in the balance of trade, which was in deficit for the majority of the period of the study (Figure 13.1).

Due to these results, it became necessary to attract capital flows, increasing foreign debt in the form of foreign investment. On the one hand, direct foreign investment increased from an average of 8.6 billion dollars in the 1990s to a peak of 44.2 billion in 2013, with an average of 24 billion dollars a year in the 2000s (Figure 13.1). On the other, there was also an increase in foreign portfolio investment when economic liberalization began, although to a lesser degree, and it accelerated after 2009, which would indicate that the Mexican economy served as a profitable refuge for financial capital after the 2008 crisis, which had a greater impact on the US economy (Figure 13.1).

It should be pointed out that direct foreign investment was the predominant component between 1994 and 2009, except for 1995, the year of the

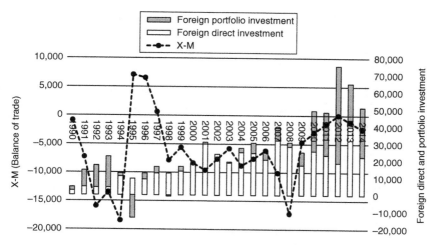

Source: Authors' calculation based on data from the Bank of Mexico.

Figure 13.1 *Balance of foreign trade and investment portfolio in Mexico, 1990–2014 (millions of dollars)*

Mexican crisis. However, not everything was related to the establishment of new companies because an important part of this was associated with the acquisition of existing assets, hence did not represent new investments. The acquisition of the commercial banks at the start of the twenty-first century was notable in this process (see Garrido, 2005).

This is demonstrated by the behavior of gross fixed capital formation (GFCF), which increased from 15.8 percent of total aggregate demand in the fourth quarter of 1993 to just 16.9 percent in the fourth quarter of 2014 with a maximum of 18.2 percent in 2007 and 2008 (authors' calculations based on data from Bank of Mexico, 2015a).

Consequently, the entry into Mexico of foreign direct investment did not significantly increase levels of employment or expand the internal market. On the contrary, in many cases it is evident that the processes of acquisition and merger by foreign corporations led to the disappearance of domestic firms and the breakdown of productive supply chains built up over the decades prior to openness. This is reflected in consumption trends, whose share as a percentage of aggregate demand fell from around 69.6 percent in the fourth quarter of 1993 to 59.1 percent in 2014 (authors' calculations based on data from Bank of Mexico, 2015a).

From the above, it may be deduced that the export boom did not have knock-on effects for the Mexican economy as there was no significant increase in the share of investment in the productive sector. The breaking of the link is explained by the high imported content of the exports, which in turn is related to the historical technological dependency of the Mexican economy.

Therefore, what at first sight would appear to be a successful strategy was not quite the case. The situation has been aggravated in recent years due to the increased emphasis on the fiscal discipline policy adopted in the USA, which affects demand for Mexican exports. To this is added the displacement effect as a result of the growth of Chinese exports in the US market. Therefore, the weakness of the economic strategy that arose from deregulation and economic openness is related to its high dependence on foreign demand (see Palley, 2012), particularly demand for imports from the US market.

Despite this stagnant economic situation, economic policy in Mexico is still focused on pro-market reforms, which is evident from the recent labor and energy reforms. While labor reform aims to reduce labor costs by favoring fixed length contracts, energy reform will allow increased private sector participation, particularly in the petroleum industry, which facilitates the entry of capital.

An area of economic policy affected by neoliberalism is access to financing in the non-financial private sector, which reinforces weakness in the process of accumulation and limits the expansion of its activities, jobs and economic growth. This is analyzed in the following section.

13.4   THE EFFECTS OF DEREGULATION AND ECONOMIC OPENNESS ON THE STATE OF FINANCING IN THE NON-FINANCIAL PRIVATE SECTOR

The economic model created by deregulation and economic openness has been a success in terms of the increase in exports, however, its results in terms of the domestic market are questionable. Specifically, this strategy has a negative impact on the availability of financing for the non-financial private sector.

The dependence on foreign capital to tackle the disequilibria in the balance of trade has led to the establishment of higher interest rates than those found in developed economies, such as the USA. Nevertheless, this leads to exchange rate over-valuation, which although making imports cheaper, creates a vicious circle where the growth of exports depends on cheap labor costs and the exchange rate over-valuation itself, which requires further interest rate increases.

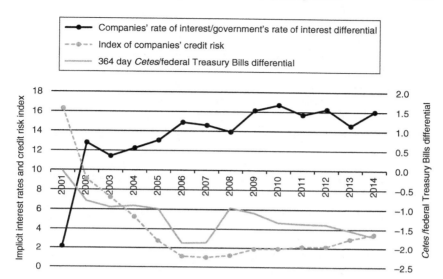

Source: Authors' calculation based on data from the National Banking and Securities Commission, Federal Reserve (2015).

Figure 13.2 *Margin between the implicit interest rate of credit to companies and credit to government in the Mexican economy (averages as percentages)*

This dynamic has a direct impact on the profitability of companies, as it reduces the competitiveness of local as opposed to imported products (Puyana and Romero, 2010, 2013; Ros, 2013). Thus, it will eventually be translated into limits on the growth of domestic productive sector companies, contributing to the stagnation of investment, employment and economic growth.

The presence of high domestic interest rates can be understood from the difference between the rates of interest on *Cetes* at 364 days and the rate of interest on US federal funds (the monthly average of Treasury Bills at one year), which despite falling were 3.25 times higher in 2014 (Figure 13.2).[5] In other words, the risk-free rate in Mexico still includes a risk premium, which is transferred to all the other domestic interest rates.

Furthermore, an analysis of the margin between the implicit rate of interest on bank loans to business and the government reveals that this is wide, despite the fact that the credit risk index has tended to fall (Figure 13.2).

This trend in implicit interest rates is a contradictory finding, since one would expect that in a banking system with a certain degree of competitiveness the combination of relative macroeconomic stability with a fall in the credit risk index would be reflected in a reduction in interest rates. This was one of the promises of the financial openness system in the early 1990s.

The low share that companies presently have in the credit portfolio of multiple banks compared to gross domestic product (GDP) is a reflection of the unsuitability of the terms of bank financing. This figure did not exceed 8 percent for the period December 2000 to December 2014 (authors' calculations based on data from Bank of Mexico, 2015a and National Banking and Securities Commission, 2015a). The Bank of Mexico's credit market survey (2015b) yields significant data on companies' sources of financing. It is noteworthy that for the period 2009 to 2014, the majority, or 82 percent, responded that they had obtained financing from their suppliers (Table 13.1). Then, much further down, the second most-quoted source of financing was from commercial banks (33.6 percent), while third place went to companies under the same corporate umbrella (24.5 percent). In fourth place were loans from foreign banks (5.2 percent), while development banks came fifth (4.8 percent). Debt issues came in last place with 2.4 percent.

The make-up of financing within the different types of companies included in the survey classification is similar. It is, however, noteworthy that in companies with less than 100 employees, or small and medium enterprises, as well as in the commercial and services sector, fewer companies resorted to financing from commercial banks, development banks or from foreign banks (Table 13.1).[6]

On the other hand, the percentage of large companies, with more than 100 employees, and productive sector companies that state that they have access to commercial bank financing increases to 37.8 percent and 35.8 percent, respectively (Table 13.1). Something similar occurs with access to other sources of financing, particularly with access to financing from foreign banks at 7 percent and 5.9 percent, respectively, and from development banks with 6.5 percent and 6 percent, respectively.

These results confirm the hypothesis that reduced access to financing has a more noticeable effect on smaller-sized companies, as well as on those unrelated to the export sector, which include companies from the services and commercial sector.

The statistics on the distribution of multiple banks' existing credit portfolio to business from the first quarter of 2009 to the third quarter of 2014 demonstrate that on average 73.6 percent of the credit portfolio was accounted for by large businesses and only 22.6 percent went to small and medium enterprises and microenterprises (authors' calculations based on data from National Banking and Securities Commission, 2015b).

Table 13.1 Mexican companies receiving financing, 2009–2014 (averages as percentages)

	From suppliers	From commercial banks	From foreign banks	From companies from the corporate group/ head office	From the development bank	Through debt issue
Total companies	82.1	33.6	5.2	24.5	4.8	2.4
Companies with up to 100 employees	81.4	27.6	2.8	18.3	2.6	0.5
Companies with more than 100 employees	82.7	37.8	7.0	28.1	6.5	3.7
Manufacturers	84.4	35.8	5.9	25.7	6.0	2.1
Service and commercial companies	83.3	32.9	5.6	25.5	4.4	2.8

Source: Authors' calculation based on the credit market situation survey of the Bank of Mexico.

The results of the credit market survey for the period from the fourth quarter of 2010 to the third quarter of 2014 confirm the effect that high interest rates have on demand for credit. An average of 46.1 percent of companies surveyed responded that interest rates were a factor in not receiving or not requesting new bank credit. It was only exceeded by the general economic situation, which was cited as the main reason by 54.4 percent of those surveyed.

Among companies with under 100 employees, the percentage citing interest rates as a factor for not seeking credit rose to 55.1 percent of the companies surveyed, while those giving the general economic situation as a reason rose to 61.9 percent.

In addition to the above, the statistics of the National Banking and Securities Commission show that larger companies were charged lower bank interest rates, to the extent that in the period 2009 to 2014, the average rate of interest charged to large companies in Mexican peso-denominated credit was 7.4 percent, with 8.7 percent for medium-sized enterprises, 11.1 percent for small companies and 12.9 percent for micro-enterprises (authors' calculation based on data from National Banking and Securities Commission, 2015b).

The statistics of the current market situation also underscore the fact that 77.4 percent of companies state the main destination of the financing they receive is for working capital and only 23.5 percent say it is for investment. Finally, 4.6 percent of those surveyed state that the financing is for 'other purposes', while 4.3 percent say it is for 'foreign trade operations'.

Thus, the economic structure deriving from the neoliberal reforms failed to reduce the cost and increase the amount of financing for the productive sector, which has a major impact on companies that do not have access to the international financial markets, which is the case for the majority of small and medium enterprises.

In the stock market the financing situation is not very different. The capitalization of the capital market rose from 30.1 percent of GDP in 1993 to 40.7 percent in 2014. However, this does not imply that the number of companies that have access to this type of financing has increased. On the contrary, the number of companies listed by the Mexican Stock Exchange fell from a peak of 209 in 1991 to just 140 companies in 2014 (Mexican Stock Exchange, 2008–2013).

Consequently, these results indicate that the resources in this market are restricted to large corporations, which unlike companies acting on a national level, also increased their level of debt on the international financial markets at interest rates below those seen in the local financial market. This is facilitated because their earnings are managed at a global level (see Álvarez and Luengo, 2011), and they can take on debt in the same currency in which they receive their income. This, however, also exposes them to an increased exchange rate risk derived from a fall in earnings from their foreign markets.

The above information demonstrates that financing on favorable terms is lacking, but it also points to the financial sector lacking confidence in the local productive sector. Otherwise, the evaluation survey of the credit market situation would not show that the majority of companies state that they are receiving financing from their suppliers and from other companies under the same corporate umbrella, whether local or foreign.

13.5 CONCLUSIONS

The performance of the Mexican economy in the last decade, and practically since the application of deregulation and economic openness processes, brings into question the functionality of the economic growth model for Mexico, whose direction comes from the foreign sector. Specifically, the private sector has not brought about the levels of investment and economic growth necessary to increase levels of employment and to improve people's lives. To a degree this is because the current economic setup gives a lower priority to national economic development compared to the stability of certain macroeconomic variables that particularly benefit the earnings of global corporations.

This is reflected by the lack of non-financial private sector financing under favorable terms, that is, at lower rates of interest, particularly to companies without access to international financial markets or, in other words, the majority of the Mexican economy. This is largely because of the role of monetary policy creating adverse conditions for the financing of the productive sector, including amongst others interest rates that are higher than those prevailing in other developed countries. The fiscal discipline policy also limits the application of public spending to tackle cyclical effects.

Under these circumstances it is important to reflect on the proposition of certain economists, in the sense of recovering the fiscal and monetary policy, when it is borne in mind that in the present environment an unused installed capacity is assumed, which would make it possible to expand production without generating inflationary pressures. Nevertheless, it should be warned that this must be articulated under an industrial policy whose purpose is to create durable economic relationships between companies operating solely within the country and those with external links, whether Mexican or foreign.

Finally, mechanisms should also be established to ensure that foreign investment contributes to the development of Mexico by means of agreements for technology transfer to domestic companies.

NOTES

1. On many occasions the processes of deregulation and fiscal discipline programs were imposed as part of the commitments, known as 'letters of intent', taken on by developing countries in exchange for financial aid from the International Monetary Fund (IMF).
2. In fact, it should be noted that since the 1970s the guiding principles of the corporations' behavior has changed from the retention and reinvestment of profits to the maximization of financial value of the company in the market. To this end they employed a strategy of reduction and redistribution (Lazonick and O'Sullivan, 2000; Stockhammer, 2004). This involves reducing the size of the company and redistributing the dividends.
3. See Bank of Mexico Law, http://www.banxico.org.mx/disposiciones/marco-juridico/ley-del-banco-mexico.html, accessed 21 March 2015.
4. Nevertheless, some economists argue that so long as the rate of growth exceeds the interest rate in real terms, the debt relationship produced tends to stabilize (Bhaduri, 2011).
5. Implicit interest rates are published by the National Banking and Securities Commission (CNBV) and are calculated by dividing revenue from monthly interest from the credit portfolio of the segment in question, multiplied by 12, divided by an average of the existing credit portfolio, which is an average of the existing portfolio values in the present and previous months for the corresponding segment.
6. The government has implemented different programs for the financing of microenterprises, but these have limited coverage (Garrido, 2011).

REFERENCES

Álvarez, I. and F. Luengo (2011), 'Financiarización, acumulación de capital y crecimiento salarial en la UE-1', *Investigación Económica*, **276**(LXX), 125–62.

Bank of Mexico (1989–1992), Annual Reports.

Bank of Mexico (2015a), *Estadísticas*, available at http://www.banxico.org.mx/estadisticas/index.html, accessed 22 January 2015.

Bank of Mexico (2015b), *Credit Market Survey*, available at http://www.banxico.org.mx/SieInternet/consultarDirectorioInternetAction.do?accion=consultarCuadro&idCuadro=CF471&sector=19&locale=en, accessed 22 January 2015.

Bhaduri, A. (2011), *Repensar la Economía Política: En busca del desarrollo económico con equidad*, Buenos Aires: Manantial.

Federal Reserve (2015), *Selected Interest Rates*, available at http://www.federalreserve.gov/releases/h15/data.htm, accessed 31 May 2015.

Garrido, C. (2005), *Desarrollo Económico y Procesos de Financiamiento Económico en México: transformaciones contemporáneas y dilemas actuales*, Mexico City: UAM-Siglo XXI.

Garrido, C. (2011), 'Nuevas políticas e instrumentos para el financiamiento de las pymes en México: Oportunidades y desafíos', in C. Ferraro (ed.), *Eliminando Barreras: El financiamiento a las pymes en América Latina*, Santiago: ECLAC, pp. 101–46.

Lazonick, W. and M. O'Sullivan (2000), 'Maximizing shareholder value: a new ideology for corporate governance', *Economy and Society*, **1**(29), 13–35.

McKinnon, R. (1974), *Dinero y Capital en el Desarrollo Económico*, Mexico City: CEMLA.

Mexican Stock Exchange (2008–2013), Annual Reports.

National Banking and Securities Commission (2015a), *Portafolio de información*, file 040-1A-R0, available at http://portafoliodeinformacion.cnbv.gob.mx/bm1/Paginas/infosituacion.aspx, accessed 21 January 2015.

National Banking and Securities Commission (2015b), *Portafolio de información*, files 040-11L-R1 and 040-11L-R2, available at http://portafoliodeinformacion.cnbv.gob.mx/bm1/Paginas/carteraempresas.aspx, accessed 21 January and 21 July 2015.

Palley, T. (2012), 'The rise and fall of export-led growth', *Investigación Económica*, **276**(LXX), 125–62.

Puyana, A. and J. Romero (2010), '"De qué sufre la economía mexicana?" falta de recursos u oportunidades de inversión', *Economía Informa*, **363**, March–June, 5–33.

Puyana, A. and J. Romero (2013), 'Baja rentabilidad de las inversiones y dualismo en la economía mexicana', in M. Levy and T. López (eds), *Financiarización y Modelo de Acumulación: Aportes desde los países en desarrollo*, Mexico City: Universidad Nacional Autónoma de México, pp. 417–48.

Ros, J. (2013), *Algunas Tesis Equivocadas Sobre el Estancamiento Económico de México*, Mexico City: El Colegio de México, Universidad Nacional Autónoma de México.

Russell, E. (2008), *New Deal Banking Reforms and Keynesian Welfare State Capitalism*, New York: Routledge.

Stockhammer, E. (2004), 'Financialization and the slowdown of accumulation', *Cambridge Journal of Economics*, **5**(28), 719–41.

Suárez, F. (2005), 'Del "estancamiento estabilizador" hacia una política activa de financiamiento del desarrollo', *Economía UNAM*, **2**(6), 43–54.

14. Pro-cyclical fiscal policy and the fiscal support of the Mexican monetary policy

Luis Á. Ortiz

14.1 INTRODUCTION

Following the currency and financial crises that hit emerging economies in the 1990s, the policy of pegging the nominal exchange rate was strongly criticized for producing systemic risks. As a result, most central banks in these emerging economies repeatedly state that they have a floating exchange rate, and that the economy's nominal peg is monetary policy, which they claim operates through interest rates and a policy of transparent and timely communication with the public. The facts indicate otherwise, however, since most central banks in such economies have kept the exchange rate pegged by managing either the fluctuations in the nominal exchange rate or the pace of the real exchange rate's appreciation (De Gregorio and Tokman, 2005; Contreras et al., 2013).

The fact that the exchange rate is the fastest channel of inflation transmission in developing and emerging economies (Ball, 2000; Hausmann and Panizza, 2003) explains why the adoption of an inflation targeting regime may force central banks to define objectives or undeclared operational bands for the nominal exchange rate, even though this introduces strong fluctuations at the level of gross domestic product (GDP) (Cukierman et al., 2004).

This chapter examines the repercussions of the sterilized intervention policy in the foreign exchange market in order to maintain monetary stability and the pro-cyclical administration of fiscal policy in order to comply with the condition of fiscal consolidation, as a requirement for the adoption and success of the inflation targeting regime in Mexico. The chapter's hypothesis is that issuing government bonds to sterilize the monetary effects caused by external capital flows on the monetary base and, in this way, maintain price stability by pegging the nominal exchange rate, represents a fiscal prop for Mexico's central bank (Banco de México). This leads us to argue that the issuing body is engaging in an antidemocratic bias, not only because as an autonomous institution it requires this fiscal support in order to meet its target of low inflation but also as it prevents the counter-cyclical exercise of fiscal policy.

The chapter is divided into four sections. Section 14.2 looks at the institutional changes in connection to the central bank's independence. Section 14.3 analyzes the operation of monetary policy with regard to inflation targets in developing and emerging economies. Section 14.4 examines the pro-cyclical effects of fiscal policy according to Mexico's inflation targeting regime. And finally, Section 14.5 presents the main conclusions.

14.2   THE INDEPENDENCE OF MEXICO'S CENTRAL BANK AND PRICE STABILITY AS A PRIORITY OBJECTIVE OF MONETARY POLICY

Up until the 1970s, most central banks operated monetary policy in conjunction with finance ministries; therefore, by law, custom or both, they were responsible not only for ensuring the stability of the domestic currency's value but also for the achievement of other objectives, such as the sustained growth of GDP and employment, financing government expenditure and the stability of the financial system. They even resolved problems related to the balance of payments. The price stability objective was one of the many objectives enshrined in central banks' organic laws, and it was not assigned any special or priority status.[1]

Some central banks handled monetary policy with a certain degree of legal independence. In practice, developing countries enjoyed less de facto autonomy than that indicated in their statute books. With the occasional exception, central banks lacked independence in choosing the instruments used, and the job of maintaining price stability was placed, at least implicitly, in the hands of the finance ministries and other government departments (Gutiérrez, 2003). As for industrialized economies with developed capital markets, such as West Germany, the United States, the United Kingdom and Japan, price stability was maintained through conservative measures taken by a treasury department of a bank with effective or de facto autonomy. This was the case of the US Federal Reserve, which was more independent in practice than in a legal sense, due to the development and depth of its capital markets. West Germany's Bundesbank, meanwhile, was an exception, since it enjoyed both legal and effective autonomy.

Although a broad consensus exists on central banks' responsibility to ensure stability of prices and the financial system, there is a debate about their role in achieving other objectives, such as economic growth and job creation. In this sense, it is argued that central banks have the responsibility and commitment to help governments achieve the objectives of economic policy without sacrificing the objective of price stability.

Some authors (Cukierman et al., 1994, 1996; Stella, 2005) argue that granting unlimited independence to central banks to operate monetary policy, that is, to choose the instruments used and to set a priority objective, such as an inflation target, must be accompanied with accountability criteria and strict transparency, given that the institution is not democratically elected. When central banks have limited or no independence, in the sense that they could only set an inflation rate, the need did not arise to examine the accountability and transparency of their operations. However, when they have almost unlimited legal and effective autonomy, it becomes necessary to review the connection between the performance of macroeconomic fundamentals and the exercise of the central bank's autonomy, as well as the effects derived from the instruments used to ensure compliance with the inflation target in the context of the choice of a nominal anchor of the economy (Padoa-Schioppa, 2003).

Choosing the inflation targeting regime has turned the objective of price stability and the central bank's independence into an incontestable binomial, since, according to the argument that the central bank's independence is required in order to stabilize prices (closing the inflation gap), no questions are asked about strong fluctuations in the GDP level (widening the GDP gap) and the high rates of unemployment that enable inflation targets to be met. Aspects of accountability and transparency therefore become relevant, since the central bank's autonomous measures can cause a trade-off between democratic accountability and the independence of the central bank when, for example, it carries out operations that lead to significant losses for the economy as a result of meeting its inflation target (Cukierman, 2006a, 2006b).

In the case of developing economies, losses are related to the sterilization policy in the foreign exchange market, which has currently become the main monetary policy instrument of inflation targets. This happens because such economies' foreign exchange markets are very small compared to those of countries with a reserve currency, also since central banks equipped with more information can make significant interventions in foreign exchange markets (Loayza and Schmidt-Hebbel, 2002; Canales-Kriljenko, 2003).

In this regard, the conventional argument is that that the effectiveness of interventions in the foreign exchange market will depend on the secrecy of central banks' operations, as one of the main reasons for such interventions is to alter the behavior of agents by pretending that the changes are the spontaneous result of market forces (Hüfner, 2004). Therefore, according to this line of reasoning, the policy of transparency and information that should be adopted by every central bank will always be biased (Aizenman and Glick, 1996; Geraats, 2002).

14.3 OPERATING THE INFLATION TARGETING REGIME IN DEVELOPING AND EMERGING ECONOMIES

Recent research (Bofinger and Wollmershäuser, 2003; Hüfner, 2004; Frenkel and Rapetti, 2009) shows that, given the hypothesis of uncovered interest rate parity not being met because the financial assets negotiated on international markets are not perfectly interchangeable substitutes, it is indeed possible to overcome the impossible trilemma[2] if there is an oversupply of currencies and the central bank sterilizes the surplus foreign currencies once it has previously fixed the target exchange rate or a band (Calvo and Reinhart, 2000, 2002).

This has been the strategy applied by the central banks in developing and emerging economies since they adopted the inflation targeting regime (Obstfeld et al., 2010; Levy-Yeyati et al., 2013). The over-accumulation of foreign reserves and sterilized intervention in the foreign exchange market enables their central banks to control simultaneously both the exchange rate and the interest rate with free movement of capital and commercial openness (Levy-Yeyati et al., 2013; Daude et al., 2014). The oversupply of foreign currencies at the nominal exchange rate previously set by the central bank is a key factor, because the central bank can purchase the oversupply of foreign currencies that generate the capital flows at the same time as controlling the interest rate by issuing government bonds. This is possible because through this second operation the central bank sterilizes the capital flows' monetary impact on the monetary base and in this way maintains the stability of the nominal exchange rate (Galati and Disyatat, 2005).

Empirical evidence (Hüfner, 2004) shows that central banks cannot directly influence modifications to the exchange rate through the interest rate because the interest rate differentials only account for a small part of exchange rate fluctuations. In the case of countries with weak currencies, the stability of their exchange rates does not depend on the liquidity of their financial markets but instead on their current account balance and external capital flows. This means that in these countries, unlike in the case of economies with a reserve currency, operations on the open market may be insufficient to ensure financial stability, and market operations may be accompanied by sterilized interventions on the foreign exchange market (Adler and Tovar, 2013).

Sterilized interventions are made by contracting or expanding the central bank's net internal credit, in line with the expansion or contraction of the monetary supply as a result of the central bank's purchase or sale of dollars. This process is divided into two stages. In the first, once the nominal exchange rate objective or band has been previously established, the central bank then buys the surplus foreign currency created by short-term capital flows. In the second stage, the issuing body places government bonds through operations on the open market in order to sterilize the monetization of the oversupply of foreign currencies. This prevents capital flows from causing sudden changes to exchange rates and therefore maintains price level stability. In other words, the inflation rate target is achieved by pegging the exchange rate.

14.4 PRO-CYCLICAL FISCAL POLICY AND FISCAL SUPPORT FOR MONETARY STABILITY IN MEXICO

In the case of Mexico, a policy of sterilized intervention in the foreign exchange market was applied regularly after the currency and financial crisis of 1994–1995, and became systemic since 2001, when the inflation targeting macroeconomic model was adopted completely (Mántey, 2010). Since that year, the Banco de México has been intervening in the foreign exchange market in order to sterilize the monetary effects generated by large short-term capital flows on the monetary base, on the one hand, and to reduce the net internal credit provided by the government to commercial banks, on the other. This measure prevents the growth of international reserves from outstripping the demand of the monetary base.

A stable monetary base allows the Banco de México to maintain its target interest rate, which will be set according to a differential of positive rates in order to attract new capital flows (Mohanty and Turner, 2006). In this way, the Banco de México can carry out operations on the open market (buying/selling government bonds) to determine the economy's liquidity level and therefore achieve monetary stability by pegging the nominal exchange rate. In turn, the high levels of accumulated foreign currencies create trust in the Mexican peso, further reinforcing this strategy's effectiveness.

The Banco de México, in common with other central banks of developing and emerging economies, bases its argument for the effectiveness of its policy of sterilized intervention in the foreign exchange market on three factors: (1) a surplus of international reserves, needed to face any speculative attack on the peso; (2) a growth of internal debt above the government-defined financial requirements, even though the implementation of the fiscal policy is limited by the principle of fiscal consolidation; and (3) a drastic reduction in the Banco de México's net internal credit, a necessary measure to counterbalance the expansive effect that short-term external capital flows have on the monetary base (Mántey, 2010).

The combination of these factors allows the Banco de México to maintain the stability of the nominal exchange rate and the price level at the same time as upholding its monetary autonomy, since it can buy the excess supply of foreign currencies on the foreign exchange market and control the interest rate, sterilizing the monetary effect of this intervention by placing bonds issued by the government or by the central bank itself on the money markets, with the resulting appreciation of the real exchange rate (Eichengreen and Hausman, 1999; Eichengreen, 2002; Bofinger and Wollmershäuser, 2003; Eichengreen et al., 2003; Aizenman and Glick, 2008, 2009).

Insofar as the surplus foreign currencies and policy of sterilized intervention on the foreign exchange market has enabled the Banco de México to meet its inflation target, the effectiveness of this strategy is reinforced, and confidence is raised in the domestic currency. However, the fiscal, quasi-fiscal and seigniorage costs related to the sterilized intervention operations on the foreign exchange market can be very high (Mántey, 2013a). These will depend on the interest payment due to the issue of government bonds and the reduction or loss of government revenue from seigniorage and in terms of the central bank's profits.

14.4.1 Overcoming the Impossible Triad, Quasi-fiscal Support and Loss of Seigniorage

If external capital flows are very high, it is highly likely that the increase in international reserves will be greater than the increase in the demand of the monetary base. In this case, the central bank will reduce net internal credit in order to prevent the monetization of the international reserve, creating more liquidity than necessary in order to maintain the target interest rate, and the extra liquidity will be sterilized through the issuing of government bonds or the regulatory requirement for commercial banks to make monetary deposits.

This is the monetary policy applied by Mexico, in particular since 2001, when the inflation target was set at 3 ± 1 percent. Faced with an increase in international reserves derived from strong inflows of capital, the Banco de México cuts net internal credit, to the point of being negative, at the same time as issuing government bonds to sterilize the surplus liquidity, with the resulting increase in internal public debt. This allows it to set its target interest rate, with a view to maintaining an attractive differential vis-à-vis external rates in order to ensure the oversupply of the foreign currency (Ortiz, 2013a, 2013b).

This shows that it is possible for a monetary policy, through the free international movement of capital, to assign independent objectives for the interest and exchange rates, but that implies a strong contraction of net internal credit provided by the central bank (Moreno, 2003). This strategy can be converted into a factor of instability for the financial system, since the contraction of net internal credit and sterilization of surplus liquidity prevents a lowering of the interest rate.

Furthermore, the setting of an interest rate as an intermediate target of monetary policy may reduce the government's revenues from seigniorage; this reduction can happen in two ways (Mántey, 2013a). The first comes about through the influence of interest rates on the short-term net capital inflow, because an increase in international reserves as a result of capital flows can cause a rise in the demand for the monetary base. However, if this surplus liquidity is sterilized to avoid foreign capital flows being monetized, then the government's residual revenue from seigniorage will be reduced compared to the revenue it would have received if the excess liquidity were not sterilized, that is, if the central bank had allowed an increase in the demand for the monetary base. In other words, the sterilization of foreign capital flows reduces the government's residual revenue from seigniorage.

The second way consists of the net internal credit that the central bank provides to the government and commercial banking institutions. In an unregulated banking system, setting a target interest rate forces the central bank to carry out operations on the open market using government bonds to maintain the target interest rate. If the net capital inflow is greater than the demand for the monetary base, the central bank must sell government bonds to reduce liquidity. If, on the contrary, the net capital inflow is lower than the demand for the monetary base, the central bank must buy public debt instruments or provide more credit to private banks or the government.

The central bank's decision to offer credit to the government or private banks will have effects on revenues from seigniorage, even when the outcome for the target interest rate is the same (Mántey, 2013a). The effect of a greater public deficit and the increased credit for the private banking sector on the economy's liquidity is similar, since the revenue generated by government expenditure will necessarily be received by private banks as liquid reserves. Therefore, in terms of setting the target interest rate it makes no difference if the central bank provides credit to the government or the private banking sector.

The situation is different in the case of revenues from seigniorage, because if the central bank provides credit to the government for an amount equivalent to the demand of the monetary base less the monetization of the international reserve, this credit forms part of its seigniorage, since the central bank does not pay interest to holders of currency that has been issued, and financing the government represents a part of the earnings of the central bank, which by law must be transferred to the government administration. And, on the contrary, when the central bank issues credit to private banks (and restricts credit to the government) at the target interest rate, the government only receives the revenue obtained by the central bank from the flow of interest payments (Mántey, 2013b, p. 69).

As a result, when a central bank decides to accumulate reserves, sterilizing its monetary effect by placing government bonds and at the same time offering credit to the commercial banking sector, the quasi-fiscal costs for the government and the financial losses for the central bank are both greater. In the former case, the quasi-fiscal costs are raised because the central bank will only set the target interest rate by issuing internal public debt at an amount equal to the total of the international reserve's monetization (which will be sterilized) and the net internal credit that has been provided to the commercial banks. In the second, the central bank's financial loss will be equal to the differential between the low interest rates earned from the international reserve and the high internal interest rates paid for the government bonds issued for sterilization.

These interest rate differentials, apart from lowering the value of the international reserve in the national currency that results from the appreciation of the national currency in volatile and uncertain conditions in the international financial markets, can trigger a currency and financial crisis that the policy of intervention in the foreign exchange market sought to prevent. This is explained by the high levels of accumulated international reserves and the development of the government bond market in national currency proving incapable of reducing the country's vulnerability to the exchange rate. To this we can add the fact that the capital flows fed into this market, boosting the accumulation of foreign currencies, are covered with foreign exchange derivatives, which will be liquidated whenever confidence is weakened (Mántey, 2014).

14.4.2 Pro-cyclical Fiscal Policy and Monetary Stability

The sharp drop in inflation between 1989 and 1991 strengthened criticism of the active fiscal policy applied during the 1958–1980 period. With the argument that the expansion of the government's deficit spending produces inflation and the crowding out of private investment, monetary policy became established as the main instrument of macroeconomic policy.

Since 1990, the management of fiscal policy was subordinated to the control over inflation, on the one hand, and to 'fiscal balancing,' on the other. In practice, this has meant cutting government spending, in particular capital expenditure, and a low primary public deficit. Such restrictions make it impossible to implement counter-cyclical fiscal measures that tend to stimulate growth by expanding internal demand.

The achievements in reducing inflation and the primary deficit between 1990 and 1994 were taken as signs of the success of the restrictive monetary policy and the consolidation of government finances. However, the currency and financial crisis at the end of 1994 exposed the high margin of appreciation of the real exchange rate produced by the policy of pegging the exchange rate. This crisis brought into focus the systemic risks as well as the fiscal and financial costs implicit in the strategy chosen by the Banco de México (oversupply of currencies and sterilized intervention in the foreign exchange market) in order to meet its low inflation target (Figure 14.1).

Between 1995 and 1996, the pro-cyclical management of fiscal policy and restrictive monetary policies were bolstered despite the economic nosedive. In 1997, fiscal measures were loosened slightly, but not enough to reactivate economic growth and job creation. Current spending climbed a little, but at the same time it was absorbed by financial bailout programs, and to a lesser extent by targeted social programs. This, combined with the low level of capital spending, explains why the total increase in government spending will not lead to positive multiplying effects in the components of

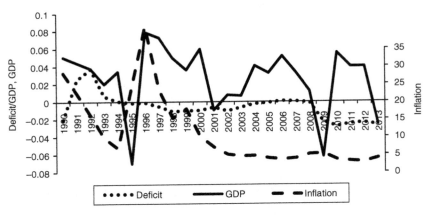

Source: Author's calculation using data from the Bank of Mexico.

Figure 14.1   Fiscal consolidation and monetary stability in Mexico

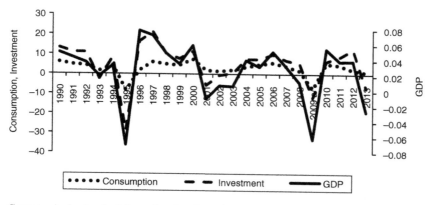

Source: Author's calculation using data from the Bank of Mexico.

Figure 14.2   Economic growth and internal demand in Mexico

private expenditure on investment and consumption or, therefore, to economic growth (Figure 14.2).

Once inflation and the primary deficit were reduced, in 2001, the Banco de México formally adopted the inflation targeting regime, thus explicitly establishing price stability as the priority objective of monetary policy, with the inflation target set at 3±1 percent. This implied that the management of fiscal policy would be subordinated to achieving the inflation target and fiscal consolidation.

In a macroeconomic context noted for a low and irregular growth of GDP and high unemployment, monetary stability is unsustainable in the long term because it is the result of – rather than the condition for – economic growth. Low levels of tax revenues, a disjointed manufacturing sector, high import coefficients and worsening living conditions for large sectors of the population reveal the economic and social costs of prioritizing the objective of monetary stability.

14.4.3   Scope for Action in Fiscal Policy: 1950–2013

In order to assess the response of fiscal policy during the 1950–2013 period, the following elasticities were calculated: fiscal balance and GDP; GDP and capital spending; and GDP and total spending. The period was divided into four stages: 1950–1976, 1977–1988, 1989–1995 and 1996–2013 in order to identify the pro- or counter-cyclical aspect of fiscal policy. The elasticities were calculated on the basis of real growth rates in tax revenue, capital spending and total spending (the sum of current and capital

Table 14.1   *Elasticities of the principal components of fiscal policy in*
            Mexico, annual averages

	1950–1976	1977–1988	1989–1995	1996–2013
Fiscal balance vis-à-vis variations in GDP	0.039	1.534	−0.1	−0.195
Tax revenues vis-à-vis variations in GDP	2.464	−0.903	0.511	1.43
GDP vis-à-vis variations in capital spending	0.024	0.05	0.045	0.015
GDP vis-à-vis variations in total spending	0.01	−0.054	−0.038	0.035

Source: Author's calculation using data from the Bank of Mexico.

spending), and of the relation between the primary deficit/surplus (fiscal balance) as a percentage of GDP. Table 14.1 shows the results.

The results for the first period between 1950 and 1976, which includes the phase of strong growth with monetary stability, known as the *stabilizing development* (1958–1970), show that the fiscal balance reacted positively to variations in GDP and less than during periods of instability and crises, such as the 1977–1988 period. This result corroborates that the low primary deficit, as a percentage of GDP, is the result of economic growth. For its part, the GDP's elasticities in reaction to fluctuations in the capital spending and total spending were positive, with capital spending having a greater impact on GDP. Finally, government revenues responded positively to variations in GDP, and more so than during the other three periods.

These results for the first stage demonstrate that active fiscal policy, in particular the constant increase in investment in basic infrastructure, helped maintain a sustained growth of GDP together with low inflation and a manageable primary deficit as a percentage of GDP.

In the second stage (1977–1988) there were various recessive and unstable effects, as a result of the 1976 peso devaluation, the over-heating of the economy caused by the oil boom (1978–1981), which was primarily financed by external debt. This situation, together with the increase in international interest rates, led to the peso's devaluation in 1982, which created the conditions that led to the external debt crisis, with the ensuing recession and financial instability. After the implementation of a macroeconomic policy of adjustment and orthodox stabilization during the *sexenio* or six-year period of government between 1983 to 1988, in order to control the inflationary pressures by lowering internal demand, the Mexican stock exchange (Bolsa Mexicana de Valores) collapsed in 1987, and immediately (in November) the peso was devalued.

The accumulative effects of these events produced strong inflationary pressures and a deep recession, even with negative rates, earning the 1980s the sobriquet as the 'lost decade.'[3] It is this macroeconomic context in which the results of the elasticities of the second stage must be understood. The fiscal balance responded positively to variations in GDP and was the highest of the four periods; in other words, the variations in GDP had strong effects on the balance of public finances (primary deficit/surplus). This is due to the fact that public investment in the oil sector and oil export revenues determined the evolution of public finances (the *petrolization* of public finances). Meanwhile, the response of public revenues to variations in GDP was lower or negative (−0.903) compared to the preceding period (2.464). One explanation for this behavior is the fact that a high proportion of public spending went on creating infrastructure for the oil sector, which has a medium- to long-term maturation process. The first stage of this process consists of looking for wells and extracting the oil, and the second involves exporting it, which is dependent on the external demand for this fossil fuel.

In regard to GDP's elasticity in response to variations in capital spending, its value was the highest of the four stages, which is understandable if we consider that the high amount of government spending on oil exploration and extraction created positive immediate multiplier effects in the construction and services sectors linked to the oil sector.[4] This result is in contrast with GDP's negative response to variations in the total spending. One possible explanation could be that the concentration of public spending in the oil sector (the *petrolization* of public spending) produced negative effects within the sector. One indicator of this is the sharp decrease in agricultural and manufacturing output (Ros, 1986).

The third stage (1989–1995) is marked by a deepening of the structural reforms in the financial and external sectors, major institutional changes, such as the granting of autonomy to the Banco de México, and the effects of the foreign exchange and financial crisis of 1994. Under a macroeconomic policy defined by a monetary policy that has prioritized price stability and a fiscal policy limited by the compliance with fiscal consolidation, the negative reaction (−0.1) of the fiscal balance to variations in GDP is understandable. The achievement of fiscal consolidation during 2000–2013 (2 percent, as a proportion of GDP, as an annual average), was more the result of the contraction in public spending than economic growth.[5] The increase in exports of manufactured goods and rising international oil prices also made a contribution. This type of fiscal balance was contrary to that registered during the 1950–1976 period, when the reaction was positive (0.039) as it was itself the result of economic growth.

The low elasticity of tax revenues in the presence of variations in GDP (0.511), lower than those observed during the 1950–1976 period (2.464), is caused by the pro-cyclical managing of fiscal policy as a macroeconomic policy to keep down inflation and balance the government's finances. The low and irregular growth of GDP caused the tax base to contract and, as a result, tax revenues fell too, given the pro-cyclical nature of this type of government income. The GDP responded positively to the variations in capital spending, although almost the same (0.045) as in the 1977–1988 period (0.05), when capital spending in the oil sector was very high; on the contrary, the GDP reacted negatively to variations in total spending. The GDP's weak reaction to changes in capital spending and its negative response to total spending are the consequence, on the one hand, of the combination of fiscal and monetary policies applied since 1993 in order to prevent inflationary increases from exerting pressure on the exchange rate and, on the other hand, the sharp contraction in capital spending that has been recorded since 1994.

The results for the last period (1996–2013) must be seen in the framework of the transition and strict adherence to the inflation rate targeting and the effects of the financial crises experienced in the second half of the 1990s (in Brazil, Russia and Southeast Asia) and of the 2008 financial crisis.

These results are very similar to those seen in the previous stage, with the increasingly restrictive monetary policies and pro-cyclical use of public spending. This explains the negative and stronger reaction of the fiscal balance (−0.195) to variations in GDP than in the previous stage (−0.1), as the GDP's contraction reduced the tax base and, therefore, the government's revenues.[6]

For its part, the taxation measures implemented to generate revenue[7] had the effect of contracting economic activity, yet it only had a minimally positive and short-term impact on tax revenues, since the negative effect on growth ended up contracting the tax base.

In terms of the GDP's response to variations in capital spending and total spending, both were positive, although the former was less (0.015) than the latter (0.035). The latter was the result of the increase in current spending, especially the spending on social projects to ameliorate the serious deterioration in the quality of life of the most vulnerable groups in society. Despite this improvement in the GDP's response to variations in government spending, the GDP's reaction to variations in capital spending was lower (0.015) than that registered between 1989 and 1995 (0.045).

14.5 CONCLUSION

The adoption of the macroeconomic model of inflation rate targeting in developing and emerging economies characterized by high levels of technological dependency and liability dollarization, such as in the case of Mexico, forces central banks to resort to sterilized interventions in the foreign exchange markets in order to maintain a stable nominal exchange rate, and in this way ensure that the inflation target is achieved.

Setting objectives that are independent from the interest rate and exchange rate, which in practice implies the prior establishment of interest rate targets (base rate) and the exchange rate, forces the Banco de México to take coordinated measures of sterilized interventions in the foreign exchange market and to establish a base interest rate that ensures the flow of capital in order to maintain a currency surplus.

This strategy to maintain monetary stability has very high quasi-fiscal and financial costs, which imply fiscal support for the Banco de México in order to manage the inflation rate targeting regime. It is questionable for an autonomous central bank to receive fiscal support from the government in order to achieve its price stability objective, which it had fixed unilaterally, while opposing the implementation of counter-cyclical fiscal measures to encourage economic growth through the expansion of internal demand.

The achievement of monetary stability objectives and fiscal consolidation in Mexico in the 2001–2013 period has been more the result of the combination of increasing exports and lower government spending than of the growth of internal demand and job creation. However, increasing exports has been insufficient to maintain a stable and sustained growth; as a result, the Mexican economy is not able to escape the perverse circle of low growth with monetary stability, which could be termed 'stabilizing stagnation'.

NOTES

1. According to Cukierman (2008), in the case of Spain and Norway, the price stability objective is absent from the respective organic laws of the central banks.
2. The impossible trilemma of monetary policy was set forth by Mundell (1963) and Fleming (1962), with the argument that with the free capital organic laws it is impossible for monetary policy to achieve both monetary and foreign exchange stability simultaneously. According to these authors, the only correct or possible foreign exchange policies are floating currencies (with monetary autonomy) or fixed exchange rate (foregoing control over inflation) because the adoption of intermediate foreign exchange regimes based on the establishment of a predefined target exchange rate or band were unsustainable because such regimes required a vast number of independent instruments.
3. GDP records irregular growth and with a clear downward trend: in 1977, it grew at a real

rate of 3.4 percent; from 1978 to 1981 (oil boom) at an average annual rate of 9 percent, before dropping to a negative rate of −0.6 percent in 1982. From that year and until 1987, the Mexican economy did not manage to recover its historical growth rates of between 4 and 5 percent. Meanwhile, the inertial forces on prices made it hard to control inflation; from a rate of 26 percent in 1977, from 1980 the inflationary spiral shot up to 98 percent in 1983 and to 113 percent in 1988.

4. The extraordinary growth of this oil sector – with an annual average real growth rate of 18 percent for the years 1979–1981 – determined the GDP's annual average real growth rate of 9 percent over the same period.

5. The primary deficit dropped sharply from −23 percent to −6 percent and −0.16, as a proportion of GDP, in 1988, 1989 and 1995, respectively, and this is reflected in the weak and irregular growth of GDP, 1.2 percent, 3.3 percent and −7.05, for the same period.

6. GDP grew between 1996 and 2000 at real rates of 6 percent, on average per year; a phase of weak growth began again from 2001 to 2003, with 2004 beginning with an irregular and diminishing recovery, which was halted in 2008 as a result of the negative effects of the international financial crisis.

7. Between 1995 and 1996 the small-scale taxpayer regime began (*Repecos*) and VAT was raised to 15 percent (with a zero rate on food and medicines). In 1999, taxation measures were approved to increase revenues, including the elimination or reduction of certain tax breaks, such as the limits placed on consolidating taxable income for business groups, the elimination of the immediate reduction of investments, the elimination of the subsidy for companies' research and development; the income tax for individuals was raised to 40 percent and for corporations to 35 percent, plus 5 percent on the distributed profits. During the administration of Vicente Fox, modifications to the income tax were authorized, and the rate for individuals reduced from 40 to 32 percent, and for corporations from 35 to 32 percent; the retention of 5 percent on distributed profits was eliminated and the immediate deduction for investments reintroduced. Under Felipe Calderón's government, the Single-Rate Business Tax (IETU) was introduced to replace the Asset Tax (IMPAC), and the Cash Deposit Tax (IDE) was also introduced. In 2009, the VAT rate was raised to 16 percent and the income tax for individuals and corporations also rose slightly.

REFERENCES

Adler, G. and C.E. Tovar (2013), 'On the effectiveness of foreign exchange intervention. Evidence from rules-based regimen changes', Mimeo, International Monetary Fund.

Aizenman, J. and R. Glick (1996), 'Transparency and the evolution of exchange rate flexibility in the aftermath of disinflation', in M.I. Blejer, Z. Eckstein and L. Leiderman (eds), *Financial Factors in Economic Stabilization and Growth*, Cambridge: Cambridge University Press, pp. 105–40.

Aizenman, J. and R. Glick (2008), 'Pegged exchange rate regimes, a trap?', *Journal of Money, Credit, and Banking*, **40**, 817–35.

Aizenman, J. and R. Glick (2009), 'Sterilization, monetary policy, and global financial integration', *Review of International Economics*, **17**(4), 777–801.

Ball, L. (2000), 'Policy rules and external shocks', NBER, Working Paper No. 7910, September.

Bofinger, P. and T. Wollmershäuser (2003), 'Managed floating as a monetary policy strategy', *Economics of Planning*, **36**(2), 81–109.

Calvo, G.A. and C.M. Reinhart (2000), 'Fixing for your life', NBER, Working Paper No. 8006, November.

Calvo, G.A. and C.M. Reinhart (2002), 'Fear of floating', *Quarterly Journal of Economics*, **117**(2), 379–408.

Canales-Kriljenko, J.I. (2003), 'Foreign exchange intervention in developing and transition economies: results of a survey', FMI, Working Paper WP/03/95, May.

Contreras, M.G., A. Pistelli and C. Sáez (2013), 'Efecto de intervenciones cambiarias recientes en economías emergentes: Notas de investigación', *Journal Economía Chilena (The Chilean Economy)*, Central Bank of Chile, **16**(1), April, 122–37.

Cukierman, A. (2006a), 'The limits of transparency', available at http://www.tau.ac.il/~alexcuk/pdf/Past%20present%20and%20Future.pdf, accessed 20 January 2015.

Cukierman, A. (2006b), 'Legal, actual, and desirable independence: a case study of the Bank of Israel', available at http://www.tau.ac.il/~alexcuk/pdf/boiactvslegl-4.pdf, accessed 17 March 2015.

Cukierman, A. (2008), 'Central bank independence and monetary policymaking institutions. Past, present and future', *European Journal of Political Economy*, **24**(4), December, 722–36.

Cukierman, A., M. Kiguel and L. Leiderman (1994), 'Some evidence on a strategic model of exchange rate bands', in L. Leiderman and A. Razin (eds), *Capital Mobility: The Impact on Consumption, Investment and Growth*, New York: Cambridge University Press, pp. 156–72.

Cukierman, A., M. Kiguel and L. Leiderman (1996), 'Transparency and the evolution of exchange rate flexibility in the aftermath of disinflation', M.I. Blejer, Z. Eckstein and L. Leiderman (eds), *Financial Factors in Economic Stabilization and Growth*, Cambridge: Cambridge University Press, Vol. 4, pp. 105–40.

Cukierman, A., Y. Spiegel and L. Leiderman (2004), 'The choice of exchange rate bands: balancing credibility and flexibility', *Journal of International Economics*, **62**(2), March, 379–408.

Daude, C., E. Levy-Yeyati and A. Nagengast (2014), 'On the effectiveness of exchange rate intervention in emerging markets', OECD, Development Centre, Working Paper No. 324.

De Gregorio, J. and A.R. Tokman (2005), 'Flexible exchange rate regime and forex intervention', BIS Papers, No. 24, *Foreign Exchange Market Intervention in Emerging Markets: Motives, Techniques and Implications*, 127–38.

Eichengreen, B. (2002), 'Can emerging markets float? Should they inflation target?', Banco Central de Brasil, Working Paper No. 36, February.

Eichengreen, B. and R. Hausman (1999), 'Exchange rates and financial fragility', NBER, Working Paper No. 7418, available at http://www.nber.org/papers/w7418, accessed 25 March 2015.

Eichengreen, B., R. Hausmann and U. Panizza (2003), 'The pain of original sin', available at http://eml.berkeley.edu/~eichengr/research/ospainaug21-03.pdf, accessed 15 April 2015.

Fleming, J.M. (1962), 'Domestic financial policies under fixed and under floating exchange rates', *IMF Staff Papers*, **9**, November, 369–79.

Frenkel, R. and M. Rapetti (2009), 'A developing country view of the current global crisis: what should not be forgotten and what should be done', *Cambridge Journal of Economics*, **33**(4), July, 685–702.

Galati, P. and G. Disyatat (2005), 'The effectiveness of foreign exchange intervention in emerging market countries', BIS Papers, No. 24, *Foreign Exchange*

Market Intervention in Emerging Markets: Motives, Techniques and Implications, 97–113.

Geraats, P. (2002), 'Central bank transparency', *The Economic Journal*, **112**, November, F532–F565.

Gutiérrez, E. (2003), 'Inflation performance and constitutional central bank independence: evidence from Latin America and the Caribbean', IMF Working Paper, March.

Hausmann, R. and U. Panizza (2003), 'On the determinants of Original Sin: an empirical investigation', *Journal of International Money and Finance*, **22**(7), 957–90.

Hüfner, F. (2004), *Foreign Exchange Intervention as a Monetary Policy Instrument: Evidence from Inflation Targeting Countries*, Centre for European Economic Research, ZEW Economic Studies, No. 23, Heidelberg: PhysicaVerlag.

Levy-Yeyati, E., F. Sturzenegger and P.A. Glüzmann (2013), 'Fear of appreciation', *Journal of Development Economics*, **101**, 233–47.

Loayza, N. and K. Schmidt-Hebbel (2002), *Monetary Policy: Rules and Transmission Mechanisms*, Santiago: Banco Central de Chile.

Mántey, G. (2010), 'El "miedo a flotar" y la intervención esterilizada en el mercado de cambios como instrumento de la política monetaria en México', in G. Mántey and T. López (eds), *Política monetaria con elevado traspaso del tipo de cambio. La experiencia mexicana con metas de inflación*, Mexico City: FES-Acatlán, DGAPA, UNAM, pp. 165–96.

Mántey, G. (2013a), 'La evolución de las deudas en México: mayor crecimiento económico o mayor especulación financiera?', in G. Mántey and T. López (eds), *La nueva macroeconomía global. Distribución del ingreso, empleo y crecimiento*, Mexico City: FES-Acatlán, DGAPA, UNAM, pp. 299–322.

Mántey, G. (2013b), 'El apoyo fiscal al banco central y la pérdida del señoreaje', *Revista Economía UNAM*, **10**(30), Universidad Nacional Autónoma de México, Mexico City, 58–74.

Mántey, G. (2014), 'Integración de México al mercado financiero global', in G. Mántey and T. López (eds), *La integración monetaria de América Latina. Una respuesta a la inestabilidad global*, Mexico City: FES-Acatlán, DGAPA, UNAM, pp. 165–200.

Mohanty, M.S. and P. Turner (2006), 'Foreign exchange reserve accumulation in emerging markets: what are the domestic implications?', *BIS Quarterly Review*, September, 39–52.

Moreno, R. (2003), 'Fiscal issues and central banking in emerging economies: an overview', BIS Papers, No. 20, *Fiscal Issues and Central Banking in Emerging Economies*, 1–9.

Mundell, R.A. (1963), 'Capital mobility and stabilization policy under fixed and flexible exchange rates', *Canadian Journal of Economics and Political Science*, **29**, November, 475–85.

Obstfeld, M., J.C. Shambaugh and A.M. Taylor (2010), 'Financial stability, the trilemma, and international reserves', *American Economic Journal: Macroeconomics*, **2**, 57–94.

Ortiz, L.Á. (2013a), 'La deuda pública interna como mecanismo de estabilización monetaria en México'; in G. Mántey and T. López (eds), *La nueva macroeconomía global. Distribución del ingreso, empleo y crecimiento*, Mexico City: FES-Acatlán, DGAPA, UNAM, pp. 209–27.

Ortiz, L.Á. (2013b), 'La financiarización de la deuda pública interna en México.

Esterilización en el mercado cambiario y estabilidad monetaria', in N. Levy and T. López (eds), *Financiarización y modelo de acumulación. Aportes desde los países en desarrollo*, Mexico City: Facultad de Economía, UNAM, pp. 201–31.

Padoa-Schioppa, T. (2003), 'Central banks and financial stability: exploring a land in between', in V. Gaspar, P. Hartmann and O. Sleijpen (eds), *The Transformation of the European Financial System*, Frankfurt: European Central Bank, pp. 270–306.

Ros, J. (1986), 'Del auge petrolero a la crisis de la deuda. Un análisis de la política económica en el periodo 1978–1985', in R. Thorp and L. Whitehead (eds), *La crisis de la deuda en América Latina*, Colombia: Editorial Siglo XXI, pp. 69–109.

Stella, P. (2005), 'Central bank financial strength, transparency and policy credibility', *IMF Staff Papers*, **52**(2), 355–65.

Index

.